Gifted Students in Regular Classrooms

Gifted Students in Regular Classrooms

BEVERLY N. PARKE

Wayne State University

ALLYN AND BACON
Boston London Sydney Toronto

Library of Congress Cataloging-in-Publication Data

Parke, Beverly N.
    Gifted students in regular classrooms.

    Bibliography: p.
    Includes index.
    1. Gifted children—Education.   2. Mainstreaming
in education.   I. Title.
LC3993.2.P36   1989   371.9'046   88–16820
ISBN 0-205-11736-8

Printed in the United States of America
10   9   8   7   6   5   4   3   92   91

Contents

Preface xi

PART ONE:
Establishing the Framework 1

1 Gifted Students: Who They Are and What They Need 3

Who Are the Gifted? Dispelling the Myths 3
Definitions of Giftedness 7
Why Educators Should Be Concerned 12
What Can Be Done? 14
Summary 15
Action Steps 15
References You Can Use 16

2 Finding Gifted and Talented Students 17

Characteristics of Gifted and Talented
    Students 18
Assessing for a Purpose 23
Model for Assessment 24
Gathering Assessment Information 28
Sample Assessment Plans 33
Developing Profiles of Ability 37
Making Placement Decisions 38
Summary 39

Action Steps   40
References You Can Use   41

3   **Planning the Programs**   42

Learning Characteristics of Gifted Students   42
Differentiating the Educational Program   43
Selecting Programming Options   44
The Role of Creativity in Programs
    for the Gifted   51
Patterns for Grouping Gifted Students in the
    Regular Classroom   51
Individualization as a Framework
    for Program Planning   57
Individualized Educational Plans (IEPs)
    for the Gifted   60
Assembling the Mosaic   60
Summary   62
Action Steps   62
References You Can Use   63

4   **Developing an Environment for Learning**   64

Shifting the Focus of Learning Toward
    Students   65
Self-Directed Learning: One Approach to Joint
    Decision Making   68
Managing Learning in a Student-
    Centered Classroom   70
Teacher's Responsibilities to Environmental
    Concerns   76
Students' Responsibilities to Environmental
    Concerns   77
Summary   78
Action Steps   78
References You Can Use   79

PART TWO:
Selecting the Programs   81

5   Adjusting the Pace of Learning   83

Program Options for Flexible Pacing   84
Assembling the Mosaic   93
Teacher's Responsibilities to Adjusting the Pace
of Learning   94
Students' Responsibilities to Adjusting the Pace
of Learning   95
Summary   95
Action Steps   96
References You Can Use   96

6   Varying the Depth of Learning   97

Program Options for Varying the Depth
of Learning   98
Assembling the Mosaic   108
Teacher's Responsibilities to Varying the Depth
of Learning   108
Students' Responsibilities to Varying the Depth
of Learning   110
Summary   110
Action Steps   111
References You Can Use   111

7   Accommodating Individual Interests   112

Program Options for Accommodating
Individual Interests   113
Assembling the Mosaic   121
Teacher's Responsibilities to Accommodating
Individual Interests   123
Students' Responsibilities to Accommodating
Individual Interests   123

Summary   124
Action Steps   125
References You Can Use   125

PART THREE:
Designing the Curriculum   127

8   Prescribing the Appropriate Curriculum   129

Differentiating Curriculum for the Gifted   129
Choosing Modifications That Are Right
     for You   134
Sample Curricular Plans   138
Student Outcomes from Appropriate
     Curriculum   141
Summary   141
Action Steps   142
References You Can Use   142

9   Models for Developing Curriculum   143

Role of Models in Planning Curriculum   143
Bloom's Taxonomy of Objectives
     for the Cognitive Domain   144
Clark's Integrative Education Model   148
DeBono's CoRT Thinking Model   151
Gallagher's Model for Content Modification   153
Krathwohl's Taxonomy of Objectives for the
     Affective Domain   156
Parnes' Creative Problem-Solving Model   160
Renzulli's Enrichment Triad Model   163
Suchman's Inquiry Development Model   166
Treffinger's Model for Encouraging
     Creative Learning   169

Williams' Model for Implementing Cognitive-
    Affective Behaviors in the Classroom   172
Using Models to Adapt Curriculum for the Gifted
    and Talented   175
Summary   176
Action Steps   176
Resources You Can Use   177

10   **Putting It All Together: Case Studies   178**

Case Study: Mathematics   178
Mathematics Lessons That Challenge   181
Case Study: Language Arts   185
Language Arts Lessons That Challenge   190
Case Study: Science   193
Science Lessons That Challenge   196
Case Study: Social Studies   198
Social Studies Lessons That Challenge   201
Case Study: Arts   202
Arts Lessons That Challenge   205
Summary   206

PART FOUR:
Maintaining the Programs   207

11   **Troubleshooting   209**

Students with Problems   209
Dealing with Other Educators and Parents   214
Administrative Participation   218
Program Evaluation   221
Summary   230
Action Steps   230
References You Can Use   231

12   Beyond the Regular Classroom   232

Full Programming for the Gifted
  and Talented   232
Alternative Program Configurations   234
Pull-Out Programs   234
Full-Time Programs   239
Highly Gifted Students   241
Summary   244
Action Steps   244
References You Can Use   245

Appendix   247

References   259

Index   267

Preface

Educating gifted and talented students in regular classroom settings is a controversial topic. There are those who firmly believe this placement to be totally inappropriate. They hold the position that the gifted should be in special settings with other students like themselves and have resources available that go beyond those typically found in the regular classroom. Although there is some defense for this position, it is weakened by the fact that most gifted students *are* in regular classroom settings at least part of their school day. Many are there for the majority of their time. *Gifted Students in Regular Classrooms* has been written in order to bring appropriate educational experiences to gifted students where they are—in regular classroom settings.

Programs for the gifted that are conducted in regular classroom settings (be they formal or informal) should be viewed as part of an overall programming effort for this population. However, regular classroom programs are not sufficient to meet the needs of the gifted population in and of themselves; they are an important part of a programming mosaic that offers options from which students and teachers may choose. Such an approach strengthens the overall general educational program without competing with it.

How, then, do educators begin to meet the needs of these students who learn more quickly and at greater depth than the rest of their classmates? How do educators respond to the unusual requests for information these students so often seek while still maintaining control and quality instruction for the other students? Possible strategies that can be used to address these dilemmas are many, but they must be based on an understanding of what the gifted and talented are like, how they can be recognized, the types of programs in which they flourish, and the curricular modifications they need.

These four topics provide the focus for this book; each is integral to a comprehensive understanding of the gifted, which will result in educational decision making for the gifted being at its best. In order to give the reader the necessary information to address these factors, the book is composed of four major parts. Part One: Establishing the Framework acquaints the reader with the characteristics of gifted and talented children, the mythology that surrounds them and often impedes their receiving needed services, definitions upon which programs are based, programs that are responsive to student needs, and classroom environments that will enhance the learning of the students. Part Two: Selecting the Programs describes programs responding to each of the learning characteristics that distinguish the gifted from their age peers—the pace at which they learn, the depth at which they learn, and the interests they exhibit. Guidelines are also presented for developing a program mosaic from which programs may be selected. Part Three: Designing Curriculum makes recommendations for differentiating curriculum for the gifted within the regular classroom without creating a separate set of lessons. It describes models that can be used to develop curriculum for the gifted that will not segregate them from the other students in the classroom. Case studies are presented in the different subject areas, explaining how teachers have overcome problems common to educating gifted children. The last section, Part Four: Maintaining the Programs, tackles some of the issues that can undermine and weaken these efforts. Dealing with student problems, parents of gifted children, other professionals, and administrators are among the topics addressed. The book closes by discussing full service programming for the gifted and the students for whom the regular classroom setting will not work.

It is my hope that *Gifted Students in Regular Classrooms* will provide guidance to teachers and program planners who are grappling with the problems inherent in mounting meaningful educational programs for all students and will give affirmation to those who are already engaged in student-centered educational practices. The well-being of the students in our charge must be the basis upon which we make our decisions and conduct our classrooms. Hopefully, the result will be students who thrive and grow into their abilities and dreams.

PART ONE

Establishing the Framework

The first section of this book contains four chapters that outline the fundamental bases upon which most programs are designed, including those for gifted and talented students. In the regular classroom or in special programs, students exhibit a range of abilities that should be addressed in a comprehensive manner. In order to do so, the program planners and implementers must have a basic understanding of the many characteristics of giftedness, the wide range of interests and behaviors the gifted may display, comprehensive assessment procedures for student selection and program placement, the process of building program mosaics that reflect the abilities and instructional needs of the students, and the environments in which students are most likely to have successful learning experiences.

Without using this basic knowledge, programs for the gifted within the regular classroom may fail. It is true that most gifted and talented students spend the majority of their time within this setting, but it is also the case that too many are not receiving adequate learning experiences and are frustrated and impeded in their growth. Therefore, it becomes the teachers' duty to assure that all students within their classrooms are receiving programs that are equal to their abilities.

The first step in the process is to understand who the gifted are and who they are not. Many myths have arisen over the years that have led to misguided beliefs such as, "The gifted will make it on their own and do not need special programs" and "Gifted programs are elitist." Neither of these positions is accurate and must be dispelled as part of the programming process. The necessity for differential programming and their role in it will then become clear to the educational staff. Chapter 1 addresses these issues and what must be done to assure equitable experiences for all students.

Understanding gifted students leads further to the realization that the gifted are a very heterogeneous population. Bringing them educational opportunities from which they can profit begins with an assessment of their strengths and weaknesses, the topic for Chapter 2. Resulting profiles of ability are part of a model for assessment, which includes student selection, program placement, and program and student evaluation.

When there is a gap between the assessed abilities of the students and the educational opportunities available to them, program development must take place. Chapter 3 considers the topics of differentiating programs for the gifted so that students can be well served within the regular classroom programming structure.

Assessment procedures and program structures are meaningless unless students feel that the environment in which they learn is safe for them to grow, explore, and question. Building environments conducive to learning is the focus of Chapter 4. Student-centered decision-making processes and self-directive learning approaches are the underpinnings of creating circumstances in which students learn how to learn and develop the skills needed to be lifelong learners.

Knowing the wide range of characteristics that gifted students may exhibit, how to assess their capabilities, and methods for designing programs and environments that will enhance their learning will give the educator a strong framework upon which educational decisions can be made. Knowing the right questions to ask in the process is central to a successful end product—providing students with the opportunity to learn in the ways and at the levels that are commensurate with their abilities.

1

Gifted Students: Who They Are and What They Need

It takes only a very few days in a classroom to become aware that there are a variety of abilities in the students we teach. Some learn very quickly with little effort, while others seem to struggle just to understand the basics. How can educators respond to the challenge that such ranges of ability present? How can they do the best possible job, making sure that all the students receive the types of instruction they need?

These are tough questions and ones that educators grapple with all their professional careers. The tasks can be made less difficult by learning more about how students differ and how to respond to their varying needs. Gifted and talented students require attention, for these students are not readily understood. "In all my years of teaching, I have never had a 'gifted' child in my class" and "It shows favoritism to put these students in 'special programs'" are among the comments often heard when discussing the plight of the gifted. However, neither is the case! There are gifted and talented students *throughout* our school systems who are in dire need of programs that are suited to their abilities. In order to deliver such programs and alter these misconceptions, it is first necessary to understand what is meant and not meant by the term *gifted.*

WHO ARE THE GIFTED? DISPELLING THE MYTHS

The misconceptions that have been held over the last century about the nature of giftedness have led to a mythology that surrounds persons of high ability. These myths can result in flawed educational decision making. One of the earliest myths was "genius is next to insanity." In other words, the smarter you are the more likely it is that you will also be a bit crazy. Following years of study (Terman, 1925), it has become very clear that this is *not* the case. The highly accomplished among us are not more likely to have psychological problems; in fact, they may have fewer. This is just one myth among many; let us now look at additional myths and actualities about the gifted and talented.

MYTH: Gifted students are a group of like individuals.

ACTUALITY: Gifted students vary greatly in their abilities, personalities, and interests.

There are no definitive lists of characteristics that indicate that people are gifted. Rather, the characteristics vary within the group as much as they do between the gifted and their age-peers. This is a very heterogeneous population. Not all gifted students are Einsteins, Mozarts, or Edisons, displaying eccentric or supernatural abilities. Most are students who have abilities that surpass those of other persons the same age and, therefore, are in need of educational programs other than or in addition to those typically offered at their grade levels. A fixed set of characteristics for the gifted and talented does not exist. Each student is an individual with his or her own strengths and weaknesses, likes and dislikes, quirks and flaws, and each should be judged on his or her own merits, accomplishments, and potential.

MYTH: Gifted children are "better."

ACTUALITY: All students in a classroom are of equal value.

All students in a classroom are of equal value. To believe that gifted children are "better" is to do a disservice to all the students in the class. It is not unusual to hear the objection to special programs for gifted and talented students based on the premise that taking the "good" students from the classroom will jeopardize the entire group. This sounds as if there are "good" and "bad" students in each class. The abilities of students do not make them better or worse as individuals; each child in a class is of equal value as a person. Each has the same right to be respected and to receive an appropriate educational experience. Gifted students are different, but their abilities do not make them inherently better individuals and they should not be treated as such as it makes other students question their own worth.

MYTH: Gifted students will make it on their own.

ACTUALITY: Gifted students need the guidance of teachers.

Many people believe that it is not necessary to focus on the education of gifted students because they will make it on their own, regardless of what schools do. Although they may appear to be achieving, it cannot be assumed that gifted students, when left to their own devices, will achieve at a level commensurate with their abilities. This fact has been a point of discussion for eighty years. Marland (1972) expressed this belief in his report to the Congress of the United States when he was the United States Commissioner of Education. His report states:

> Large scale studies indicate that gifted and talented children are, in fact, disadvantaged and handicapped in the usual school situation. Terman observed that the gifted are the most retarded group in the schools when mental age and chronological age are compared. Great discrepancies existed during his study (1904), and continue to persist today . . . (p. 26).

Since gifted students are usually able to display large amounts of information at any time, it is assumed that they possess the strategies necessary to be able to learn on their own. In fact, a gifted student may not know what a thesaurus is or how to locate information in the library, have difficulty deciding on a topic for an independent study, or be unable to reconstruct how he or she arrived at the correct answer to a complicated mathematics problem. Gifted students need to be given the opportunity to learn how to learn. Without such instruction, we cannot assume they will be able to use such skills when needed.

MYTH: Gifted students are perfect.

ACTUALITY: Gifted students have strengths *and* weaknesses.

Gifted students may be perfectionistic, but they are never perfect. Some frequent misconceptions about gifted students are that they do not make mistakes, always complete their work on time, never need remediation, and always have a positive attitude toward school. As with all children, the gifted vary in these behaviors. It is unrealistic to assume that they will constantly perform at their highest possible levels. Gifted students rarely have equal ability in all academic areas, they do not always behave as we may wish, and their attitudes toward school may range from enthusiastic to very negative. Gifted students do make mistakes; they may be behavior problems, underachieving, or handicapped in some manner. Just because these students are not perfect in all aspects of their lives does not mean that they are not gifted and/or talented, and they should not be disqualified, on that basis, from receiving programs commensurate with their abilities.

MYTH: "Early ripe, early rot."

ACTUALITY: Gifted students' abilities do not "burn out."

The belief that the performance levels of gifted students level off may be referred to as the "early ripe, early rot" theory of child development. This position holds that students who display precocity at a young age will eventually begin to lose their advantage, and their performance levels will more closely approximate that shown by their classmates. When gifted students are provided with appropriate programs that include challenging experiences and opportunities to learn new things, this phenomenon does not take place. However, when gifted students do not receive appropriate programs, there is evidence to suggest that they may lose much of the advantage that they have when they arrive at school (Ness and Latessa, 1979).

MYTH: Gifted students like to be called *gifted.*

ACTUALITY: Gifted students feel they are basically like other students and have not been "given" anything.

It will surprise many people to learn that gifted students do not like to be called *gifted.* They find the label to be a detriment both socially and emotionally. This is particularly the case when they reach the middle school or junior high school years and the peer group gains increasing importance. Gifted students report that they do not feel as though they have been "given" anything. Rather, they feel that they are regular people who happen to learn differently and sometimes enjoy different types of activities than their classmates. They do not like to be separated from their peers or made to be an example (positive or negative) for the rest of the class. By doing so, teachers position them for peer sanctions, an event that can lead to the gifted students being less inclined to show their true abilities for fear of social ramifications.

These mythological beliefs have contributed to a condition in our schools and society in which gifted and talented students are often underserved. By understanding the actualities of giftedness we can see that this population, although unique in many ways, is in need of the same basic considerations we should afford all our students. Getting the facts straight about these students, then, becomes a necessity; the next step is to understand just what giftedness really is.

DEFINITIONS OF GIFTEDNESS

Over the past century, the meaning of the term *gifted* has changed from a single-dimensional (high IQ) definition (Terman, 1925) to one in which multiple abilities and intelligences are recognized (Guilford, 1956; Taylor; 1968; Sternberg, 1982; Gardner, 1983). This transition has opened the door to greater understanding of students and their needs in schools. It is clear that there are many students who, by virtue of their exceptional abilities, require programs that are beyond those typically offered to them. When such a case exists, the process of terming students *gifted and/or talented* can commence.

There are a number of definitions employed to describe people who are gifted and/or talented. These definitions usually recognize that giftedness is a multidimensional trait since there are *many* different areas in which students may have exceptional abilities. These capabilities are reflected in the definitions that are most commonly adopted for the operational and funding purposes of programs for the gifted and talented.

United States Department of Education definition. The most commonly used definition of *gifted and talented* is stated in the Educational Amendment of 1978 (P.L. 95–561, IX (A)). It is a multidimensional definition based on Marland's *Education of the gifted and talented, Volume 1. Report to the Congress of the United States by the U.S. Commissioner of Education* (Maryland, 1972). This definition, as revised, reads as follows:

> (The gifted and talented are) ... children and, whenever applicable, youth who are identified at the preschool, elementary, or secondary level as possessing demonstrated or potential abilities that give evidence of high performance capability in areas such as intellectual, creative, specific academic or leadership ability or in the performing or visual arts, and who by reason thereof require services or activities not ordinarily provided by the school (U.S. Congress, Educational Amendment of 1978 [P.L. 95–561, IX (A)]).

There are a number of interesting facets to this definition. It notes that there are many areas in which a student may be gifted. Furthermore, it recognizes by its words, "demonstrated or potential abilities," that not all students display their abilities at all times, thereby allowing programs to be constructed for high potential/low or average performance students, such as gifted underachievers. Finally, it calls for specific programs to be instituted to meet the needs of these students by stating, " ... and who by reason thereof require services and activities not ordinarily provided by the school."

All or part of this definition is used by over 94 percent of the states (Council of State Directors of Programs for the Gifted, 1986). In addition, many school districts use this definition for guiding their program development and establishing guidelines for program eligibility. However, critics point out shortcomings of this model. Renzulli, Reis, and Smith (1981) list three: failure to include nonintellective (motivational) factors; unparallel factors, with two relating to abilities and three to processes; and the misuse of the definition by persons who treat the categories as if they were mutually exclusive.

Renzulli's Three-Ring Conception of Giftedness. The Three-Ring Conception of Giftedness (Renzulli, 1978) is based on studies of creative and productive individuals. These data show three interlocking traits that are evident in this type of person: above average ability, creativity, and task commitment (see Figure 1-1). When these abilities converge in one person, the result is an individual who is exceptional in performance and a significant contributor to society. It is Renzulli's belief that these are the factors that should be considered when determining which students are

Figure 1-1   Renzulli's Three-Ring Conception of Giftedness

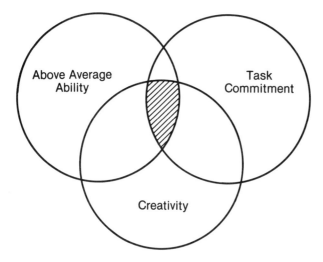

Source: J. S. Renzulli, S. M. Reis, and L. H. Smith, *The Revolving Door Identification Model* (Mansfield Center, Conn.: Creative Learning Press, 1981), p. 19. Reprinted with permission by Creative Learning Press, Copyright © 1981.

eligible for a program for the gifted. His definition of giftedness (Renzulli, 1978) is:

Giftedness consists of an interaction among three basic clusters of human traits—these clusters being above average general abilities, high lovolo of task commitment, and high levels of creativity. Gifted and talented children are those possessing or capable of developing this composite set of traits and applying them to any potentially valuable area of human performance. Children who manifest or are capable of developing an interaction among the three clusters require a wide variety of educational opportunities and services that are not ordinarily provided through regular instructional programs (p. 261).

This model is based on the premise that there are many ways in which the gifted and talented may demonstrate their abilities and that these demonstrations may come at different times and under varying circumstances. Thus, Renzulli calls for the identification processes to be ongoing and the programs to be multifaceted. The inclusion of the noncognitive factor of "task commitment" sets this definition apart from past definitions of gifted and talented students.

Gardner's Theory of Multiple Intelligences.   Gardner (1983) posits that there are "intelligences" rather than a single intelligence. Seven distinct intelligences are described in this theory:

... intelligence should be considered as a constellation of at least seven different competencies—linguistic, logical-mathematical, spatial, bodily-kinesthetic, musical, inter-personal and intra-personal (Hatch and Gardner, 1986, p. 148).

This theory, which results in profiles of ability, allows a person to be gifted in one area and average or below average in others. Although similar to the Department of Education's definition of giftedness, this is a *theory of intelligence,* with factors based in the author's research. However, it does provide a useful basis for discussing the nature and identification of giftedness.

Gagne's Differentiated Model of Giftedness and Talent.   An attempt to integrate the above models has been made by Gagne (1985), author of the following definitions:

> *Giftedness* corresponds to competence which is distinctly above average in one or more domains of ability.
>
> *Talent* refers to performance which is distinctly above average in one or more fields of human intelligence (p. 108).

He elaborates:

> Talent, which is defined in the context of a large or narrow field of human activity, expresses itself through a set of behaviors linked to this field of activity. . . . Giftedness is somewhat different in that abilities are generally identified using more unidimensional and standardized measures so as to connect together in the purest form possible those individual characteristics which "explain" the observed performance (p. 108).

Gagne shows underlying abilities that, when coupled with the catalysts of environment, personality, and motivation, can result in the demonstration of high-level performance in talent areas (see Figure 1–2). Thus, he combines the notions of multiple intelligences, personality factors, environment, and talents into one model of giftedness and talent.

Critical Points

You can now see that there is no agreement as to an absolute definition of giftedness and talent. Over the past thirty years, however, the notion of multiple abilities and multiple intelligences has gained wide acceptance. These are the critical points to remember when developing a definition of giftedness for program planning:

1. There are many intelligences.
2. Intelligences will vary in the extent to which they are developed and show strength.
3. Consideration of giftedness and talent should encompass multiple ability areas.
4. Developing, as well as developed, abilities should be considered.
5. High levels of ability may require programs beyond those typically provided in schools in order to nurture and develop students' abilities fully.
6. The definition that is adopted by a school district or for a particular program serves as the basis for the development of student selection and program design procedures.

Figure 1-2   Gagne's Model of Giftedness and Talent

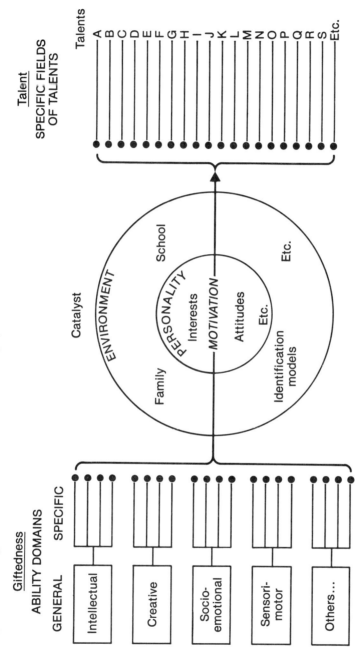

Source: F. Gagne, "Giftedness and Talent: Reexamining a Reexamination of the Definitions," *Gifted Child Quarterly*, 29 (1985): 109. Reprinted with permission by National Association for Gifted Children, Copyright © 1985.

11

WHY EDUCATORS SHOULD BE CONCERNED

Incidence

Gifted and talented students are everywhere—in every community and in every classroom. Keeping in mind the multiple ability notions of intelligence and the U.S. Department of Education's definition, which states that the gifted are those students who "(possess) demonstrated or potential abilities that give evidence of high performance capability ... and who by reason thereof require services or activities not ordinarily provided by schools," it becomes apparent that there is a myriad of students who fall into these categories. Some set the number at 2 to 5 percent of the population (Council for Exceptional Children, 1978); others are more inclusive, identifying 15 to 20 percent of the school population as students who can potentially benefit from special programs (Renzulli, Reis, and Smith, 1981).

Regardless of the definition of giftedness to which one adheres and regardless of your specific teaching assignment, the fact is that every teacher probably has students in the classroom who could benefit from some type of differentiated programming because of the advanced abilities they possess. Whether or not they have been officially identified, or a designated program for the gifted and talented exists in your school, it is the responsibility of educational professionals to make sure that these students are receiving a proper education commensurate with their abilities.

This can be complicated and tricky to accomplish. One of the problems often encountered is a feeling by a faculty that there are *no* gifted and/or talented students in their school. They fail to realize that giftedness can be situationally specific and is relative to the environment. If a student displays abilities that transcend the other students in the class, that student may need some type of accommodation to have an appropriate education. The student does not have to score 95 to 99 percent on a standardized achievement test to merit such consideration. Rather, *the performance level of the student judged within the context of the environment should lead to the decision of whether or not alternative programming is needed.* Again, there is no absolute state of giftedness. There are gifted behaviors and situations in which students need differential treatment due to their advanced abilities, talents, and interests.

Current Programming Patterns

Another overwhelming reason why educators should be actively concerned about gifted and talented students is that the vast majority of such students are in regular classroom placements. This has historically been the case and continues to be the placement of choice in a preponderance of districts due to such factors as philosophical positions, convenience, and/or default. In the Council for Exceptional Children's 1977 *Survey of the States and Territories,* it was found that approximately 33 to 53 percent of the gifted students in the thirty-two states that had programs for the gifted at that time were receiving *any* type of special services. Although that number has increased over the last decade, the levels of service are still far below the incidence and need levels. Apparently, most gifted and talented students are in typical classroom placements.

Even when programs are instituted for the gifted and talented, the programs of choice tend to be those that center around the regular classroom. The Richardson Study Survey (Cox, Daniel, and Boston, 1985) reports that the five most frequently instituted programs for the gifted across the country were: (1) part-time special classes, (2) enrichment, (3) independent study, (4) resource rooms, and (5) itinerant teachers. All five of these approaches center around the regular classroom. In each instance, students are in the regular class for all or part of the week—yet, their abilities are with them *all week long.* Part-time programs exist in abundance, but giftedness and talents are full-time capabilities. Therefore, provisions for these abilities must be thought of in the context of the entire school week, not just in the hour or two the students typically happen to be in a program for the gifted and talented.

Student Well-Being

The classroom teacher is one of the most influential persons in the students' school lives. Teachers hold a great deal of power within the classroom and have tremendous impact on the lives of their students. When eminent people are asked who influenced their lives the most, they usually respond that it was a teacher or a parent (Goertzel and Goertzel, 1962; Bloom, 1985). Thus, teachers play an integral role in the development of student abilities and talents.

These influences can be both positive and negative, however. Therefore, it becomes important for teachers to learn how to handle the wide range of abilities found in the average classroom in such a way that all students flourish. The gifted and talented students need guidance and direction as well as skill development. Independent studies and tutoring students of lesser ability will not sufficiently compensate for academic requirements that are below students' achievement levels. Teachers must develop the skills of managing the learning of children of all abilities if students are to survive school in a healthy manner.

Student well-being is based on teacher attitude as much as teacher skill. The gifted require teachers who value student abilities and encourage excellence and achievement. They need instructional leaders who will understand the costs as well as the benefits to being exceptional. Such compassion and understanding are vital to the gifted as they attempt to develop their abilities to the fullest extent. Gifted students are not free of problems; they are children who face a different set of problems. The teacher is in a unique position to be of assistance as these students work through the difficult issues they face.

WHAT CAN BE DONE?

What can educators do to make sure that their gifted and talented students receive appropriate educational experiences? The list is truly endless, but there are four guidelines that will serve you well in thinking about gifted students in regular classroom settings. They provide the philosophical underpinnings for this book.

1. *Accept all children as individuals with differing abilities.* We all know that there are many levels of student ability within a classroom. Recognizing this fact and designing instruction to respond to it are giant steps toward meeting the needs of gifted and talented students. Looking for the behaviors of students that may indicate exceptional ability is the beginning stage for providing appropriate programs for the gifted. But programs for these students *must* be considered within the context of appropriate programs for *all* students.

2. *Establish student-centered classrooms.* Classroom decisions should be based on the needs of the students. Allow students to become part of the team by enfranchising them with decision-making power. They are the ones who must ultimately be responsible for their own learning, so why not give them the power to do so? Running a student-centered classroom involves making students the center of the decision-making process. This seems only reasonable since schools exist so students can learn.

3. *Plan models of instruction that allow individual differences to be accommodated.* There are methods of instruction that will allow students to respond to instruction at their own levels of expertise. Such approaches to teaching are valuable because they accommodate the many ability levels within the classroom without designating who the slow and rapid learners are. Choosing the appropriate model for the given circumstances is the hallmark of an excellent teacher. Having many approaches available and using multiple methods to teach should result in students learning through their various learning styles and at their highest possible levels.

4. *Remember that gifted students are not "better"; they are just "different" in their abilities, needs, and interests.* Try to avoid placing a value judgment on the abilities of students. We do not do a favor for gifted children by placing them on a pedestal for other students to emulate. They are students with their own needs and problems who require the same compassion and care as the other students in the class. Their needs may be different, they are no less urgent than those of students with lesser abilities.

SUMMARY

Giftedness is a multidimensional trait seen through the behaviors of students who signal potential or actual performance levels that are at an exceptionally high level. Gifted and talented students are found throughout our schools and classrooms, as that is the placement of choice in most school districts. Therefore, it becomes the task of the regular classroom teacher to meet the needs of these students through whatever means necessary. Strategies do exist to accomplish this feat and will be discussed in later chapters. From the onset, however, it is important to keep in mind that there are many students in our classes with exceptional abilities who require differential programs for the full development of those abilities. It is the classroom teacher who is the vital link to assuring that such programs exist and flourish for the students who need them.

ACTION STEPS

1. Choose or write a definition of giftedness and/or talent that fits your purposes and philosophical position. Keep this handy for future reference, as it will be the basis for assessment, program, and curricular planning. Remember to take multiple abilities into account and to provide for students who both display and have the potential to display levels of achievement that surpass their peers.

2. Inventory your own attitudes. Do you believe that any of the myths discussed in this chapter to be actualities? If so, try to go a step beyond recognizing these biases and begin to change your attitudes. This can be done through reading publications on the topic of gifted and talented students and by talking with experts, the students themselves, or their parents to find out exactly what it is like to be unusually adept.

3. Begin to evaluate the regular classroom settings. Are multiple

ability levels being addressed within the instructional program? If so, in what ways can improvement be made? If not, what changes should be made? Begin to construct a written plan of action to bring an equal education to all your students. Write down your thoughts and put them in a folder along with the definition of giftedness that you wrote. You may want to refer to these later as you learn more about providing programs for the gifted and talented in the regular classroom.

REFERENCES YOU CAN USE

Bloom, B. (Ed.). (1985). *Developing talent in young people.* New York: Ballantine Books.

Clark, B. (1983). *Growing up gifted* (2nd ed.). Columbus, OH: Merrill Publishing Company.

Gallagher, J. (1985). *Teaching the gifted child* (3rd ed.). Boston: Allyn and Bacon.

Renzulli, J. (1978). What makes giftedness? Reexamining the definition. *Phi Delta Kappan, 60*(3), 180–184, 261.

Treffinger, D. (Ed.). (1982). *Gifted Child Quarterly* (Special issue on the myths in educating the gifted), *26*(1).

2

Finding Gifted and Talented Students

The task of identifying which students are gifted and/or talented can paralyze an educator if the fundamental procedures are not known. We worry about matters such as missing some students whose needs for special services are not apparent, the impact that designating a few as "G&T" will have on the other students, and our own competence at making such decisions. These are fears that must be and can be dispelled.

Whenever the task of identifying students for differential programming is undertaken, there is the possibility of an imperfect procedure, resulting in students being improperly identified or missed. This should be seen as a reason to proceed carefully but not as a reason to dispense with the process altogether. Students may be missed, as procedures can be imperfect and student abilities are not always evident when we are looking! It is important to begin the assessment process on the best information available and to amend the procedures as needed. If students are, in fact, missed, they can be added at a later date.

Students know who the "bright" students are. Despite our efforts to muddy the situation, students have a fairly accurate notion of where they stand in relationship to their classmates in matters of academic, social, and physical abilities. What becomes harmful to students is when they are treated differently because of their advanced or retarded abilities. All students deserve the same chances to learn and know; none are "better" or "worse" because they learn more or less quickly. If all students are treated with respect, identifying some as gifted and/or talented should not have overwhelmingly deleterious consequences. The students do not have to know that they or their peers have been identified. But the teacher has to know which students need special programming and then make sure that those programs are delivered.

Teachers *can* determine who the gifted and talented students are in their classrooms. Although the research evidence points out the difficulties teachers have in making these designations (Pegnato and Birch, 1959; Jacobs, 1971; Borland, 1978), Gear (1978) found that when teachers are given training on how to identify the gifted they are twice as effective in determining which students qualify as when untrained. Without such training, teachers do appear to have the tendency to nominate students for programs who are like themselves, get good grades, and are not behavior problems. This can lead to students being inappropriately identified. All gifted and talented students are not like their teachers, do not get top grades, and do not act in a manner that teachers feel is appropriate. Therefore, it becomes imperative that teachers do receive some guidance on how to determine which students are gifted and/or talented.

CHARACTERISTICS OF GIFTED AND TALENTED STUDENTS

Chances are that your first inkling about which students are gifted and/or talented will come from a student's question or remark, or an observation that you make. All educators have had the sensation of intrigue when a student makes a particularly astute observation or gives an especially inspired performance. These moments of insight are important and should lead to further investigation of the student's aptitudes and abilities.

For the classroom teacher, these moments can come at any time. During a third grade social studies lesson on Australia, a teacher was standing at the world map, showing the students where the continent of Australia was located. Without being assured of a response, the teacher asked the students, "Why do you suppose that people in this little country (England) so far away from Australia and Australians speak the same language?" The students were given time to ponder the question and one of the students (previously thought to be quite average) answered, "Perhaps they have a similar ancestry." His insight gave the teacher a clue to his actual abilities, which had been underestimated up to that point. The judgment of whether or not this child was "gifted" was not made and was not appropriate at that time. However, the judgment that this student was one who merited further consideration and observation *was* made and *was* appropriate.

It is essential, then, to know the range of characteristics that gifted and/or talented students may display. From this information, the teacher can begin to observe students in a more objective manner, relying less on guessing and instinct. The sections that follow outline some of the characteristics of gifted and talented students and should be read with two cautions in mind. First, the lists of characteristics are not exhaustive. These are *among* the characteristics of gifted and talented students that teachers may observe. Second, these characteristics cannot be applied as a litmus test for giftedness. Students should not be expected to show all of these characteristics. Any one or cluster should be enough to indicate that the student merits further investigation for differential programming. The lists are best used to give teachers general guidelines for observation and consideration from which they can begin to view students as being or potentially being of exceptional ability.

Cognitive Characteristics

Cognitive characteristics are those that involve the ability to think. These attributes are often displayed in the classroom situation but are not confined to that locale. The manifestation of any one or group of these characteristics should indicate to the teacher that the student may have potentially advanced abilities. Among the cognitive characteristics that distinguish gifted students are:

1. *An advanced ability to manipulate symbols.* This trait (Gallagher, 1985) may be seen in children who read early or are precocious at reading music or playing with numbers. It is also apparent through the large and advanced vocabularies many of these children display.

2. *Unusual ability to remember.* Memory is not a problem with these students. They have ready recall of facts. If the teacher promises students five minutes of free time on Friday, the gifted will certainly be among those students who remember that statement and remind the teacher (most likely every day until Friday!).

3. *Large storehouses of facts.* The advanced ability to remember enhances the power of these students to have a large number of facts at their disposal. They generally know a great deal about a number of things. If there is an area in which they have particular interest, it is likely that they will know the topic in depth.

4. *Unusually deep levels of comprehension.* Not only do these students know and remember facts, they also understand the concepts and relationships present in fields of knowledge at levels that are advanced for their ages.

5. *Seeing generalizations readily.* Their ability to comprehend shows itself in the ability to generalize beyond what is presented to larger concepts and connections. This often results in gifted students working in academic areas two to three grade levels above their age-peers.

6. *Advanced ability to concentrate.* Gifted students are capable of concentrating for extended periods of time on investigations of interest to them. However, if the area is of little interest, concentration levels may be low. Although we often see gifted students

riveted to their work, attending with great diligence, the scattered impatient attention of disinterest is also among their attributes.

7. *High levels of curiosity.*   Constant questions are a hallmark of the gifted. These students display keen interest in their environments and what makes things work. They also enjoy solving puzzles and playing games.

8. *Ability to learn quickly.*   When interest in a topic is there, these students have the ability to learn very quickly. Their learning is characterized by fewer repetitions to learn facts and concepts and by knowing information that is beyond what is normally expected. One trial is often enough to learn a concept. When belabored with additional trials and examples beyond those needed for mastery, the gifted can become impatient, bored, and careless in their responses.

9. *Varied interests.*   The interests of the gifted may be varied in nature or sophistication. Many gifted students have numerous interests and advanced abilities in each. Others identify one area of particular interest and probe it thoroughly. The interests they do display are often those characteristic of older children or adults.

10. *Uneven cognitive and physical ability.*   Many gifted students are frustrated in their attempts to demonstrate their abilities because their unusual capacity to think does not correspond with their abilities to write, draw, act, or speak. This discrepancy of abilities may make it difficult to measure effectively and accurately the actual abilities of the students.

Affective Characteristics

Affective characteristics are those that involve students' feelings, emotions, and personalities. In these areas, too, teachers may find that gifted and talented students differ from other students who are the same age. It cannot be assumed, however, that advanced cognitive ability is always in tandem with advanced skill in affective areas. Many gifted and talented students have asymmetrical profiles of ability in which the cognitive and affective abilities are not similarly strong and advanced. Whereas a sixth-grade student may have the cognitive capability of a high school student, the emotional responses may very well be those of an emerging adolescent. Among the affective characteristics displayed by these students are:

1. *Sensitivity to themselves, others, and their environment.* Gifted students are very aware of their environment and the

people who are in it. This awareness is coupled with sensitivity to the feelings of others and the events in that environment.

2. *Preference to be with adults or older children.*   Even from an early age, parents report that their gifted children have preferred to play with older children more often than with their age-peers. Teachers find that their gifted students prefer to work and discuss ideas with them, rather than the other students in the room. People tend to gravitate to their mental age-peers; gifted students do this naturally, too.

3. *Intensity.*   One can feel the intensity emanated from a gifted student who is working on a topic of interest. The intense concentration, perseverance, and commitment to the task is obvious in many areas of interest, not just those involved in "school learning."

4. *Perfectionism.*   This is one trait found in gifted people of all ages, from the very young to the elderly. There is often an inner motivation to be perfect or as near perfect as possible. The results can be high performance levels or total inability to perform for fear of failure.

5. *Leadership ability.*   Gifted students are often looked to by other students for guidance unless the gifted students are so deviant from their age-peers that they are considered to be "weirdos" or "nerds."

6. *Moralistic.*   A strong sense of right and wrong is often found in this population. They have a deep sense of conviction and can be found going to bat for what they believe and for those who they consider to be mistreated. Convincing them that there are gray areas in judgments may be a difficult task.

7. *Resourcefulness.*   The ability to bring many resources to bear on a problem is characteristic of the gifted. They may be able to solve a problem through more than one procedure, find an unusual way to proceed in a problem area, or suggest a new solution to an old problem.

8. *Advanced sense of humor.*   Gifted students often display a sense of humor unusually sophisticated or insightful for their ages. These are the students who are likely to understand the teachers' jokes, use puns, and conjure up riddles of their own.

Characteristics of Creative Students

Students with creative abilities may or may not display many of the characteristics listed above. They are often a "breed apart" and usually are not as well liked by teachers as students who are more conventional in their thinking and behaviors. This alternative sense of values and unconventional thinking and behaviors can lead to the underestimation of the abilities of these students. In addition to the characteristics listed above, you may find the following in highly creative students:

1. *High intelligence.* Although creativity and intelligence are often thought to be separate abilities, they do seem to go together. The more intelligent a student is, the more likely it is that the creativity level will also be high (up to an IQ level of 120) (Yamamoto, 1965).

2. *Natural drive to explore ideas.* This zest and unbridled curiosity can result in both endearing and disturbing qualities in a creatively gifted student. On the one hand you may find the student vigorously pursuing exciting new concepts; on the other hand you may find that this pursuit may result in ideas that seem radical, outlandish, bizarre, and totally inappropriate.

3. *Ability to see things wholistically.* Creatively gifted students tend to learn in a wholistic manner. They prefer to get the whole idea first and then break it down into parts. Unfortunately, they often find that concepts are presented in steps or parts rather than as a whole. This is a prime example of a student's learning style being in conflict with a teaching style.

4. *Challenging of the conventional.* By nature, creativity is generating ideas that are new. In order to do so, that which is conventional must be challenged. Although such activity is the lifeblood of a progressive society, those who do the challenging are often regarded with disdain. Thus, creatively gifted students can have trouble coexisting with their parents, teachers, siblings, and peers.

5. *Independent thinking.* These students prefer to think for themselves. They will not be content in taking an authority figure's "word for it"; instead, they will seek out their own answers. Again, although this can result in new and innovative ideas and products, it can also be highly threatening to those in authority.

6. *Playfulness.* Creative students tend to be playful in their thoughts, actions, and products. They see humor and can generate it throughout their work. They are not afraid to take risks, and sometimes they do things for the sake of seeing the result or others' reactions.

Characteristics of Special Populations

The impact of certain environments, cultural mores, and handicapping conditions may result in characteristics in the gifted other than those listed above. When looking at the behaviors of students in order to develop impressions of ability, it is important to keep in mind that many factors can and do affect the way children act and think, and the activities in which they choose to engage. Therefore, it is essential to take into account these factors when analyzing the characteristics of the gifted.

Since different cultures have different values, students from cultures outside of the mainstream may exhibit their abilities in different ways. For example, in some cultures girls are not encouraged to speak their beliefs; this lack of verbalization should not be seen as an indication of low intelligence. Instead, factors other than verbalizing should be taken into account when assessing the abilities of these students.

Handicapped students face many barriers in having their abilities recognized. Emotionally handicapped students may have their abilities hidden by their inappropriate behaviors when teachers mistakenly believe that in order to be gifted students should act in acceptable ways. The inappropriate behavior is not an indication of lack of intelligence and should be disregarded (to the extent possible) when assessing ability. Similarly, gifted learning disabled, hearing impaired, physically handicapped, and visually impaired students often show their abilities through alternative means. In the case of gifted learning disabled students, abilities may be hidden due to their ability to get acceptable grades, which may hide the disability *and* the ability. Often it is the advanced ability to compensate for the learning disability that is resulting in the satisfactory grades!

It is also becoming evident that gifted girls may deviate from ideal behavior patterns. Too often they choose not to show their abilities or to work at levels calculated to be at "socially acceptable" levels. They are still handicapped by society's gender-specific expectations and patterns of progress that may force them into careers, classes, or achievement levels other than those they might otherwise select.

ASSESSING FOR A PURPOSE

Once you have familiarized yourself with the many and varied characteristics of gifted students, it is time to address yourself to the question, "Why should I be concerned with who the gifted and talented students are?" There are many possible answers to the question but one remains paramount: *It is important to determine who the gifted and talented students are in order to provide programs that are appropriate to their needs and interests.* This can be accomplished without affixing the label of *gifted and talented,* however. If that designation is a philosophical or political problem, one can simply dispense with the label and proceed to determine student abilities. The overall purpose of assessment, formal or informal, should be to determine student *profiles of ability* that can be used to make programmatic and curricular decisions.

These profiles can be viewed as representations of students' strengths and weaknesses from which teachers can make educational decisions. Students who show unusual ability in any area may become part of a *talent pool*. This talent pool can then be drawn upon to find candidates for specific programs or alternative placements within or outside the regular classroom.

Students from the talent pool with profiles showing high ability in academic areas such as reading, math, science, and writing (in excess of two to three grade levels above the norm) might be considered eligible for a full-time class for gifted students, a special school, or grade acceleration. A student with a profile indicating outstanding musical ability might be tapped for an artist-in-residence program with the conductor of the local symphony. Students reading two grade levels above the norm, but with more typical levels of performance in the other academic areas, might be placed in an advanced reading group, be a part of a multiaged reading group, or travel to another class that has reading instruction at the students' level.

It is through the assessment process that the ability and achievement levels of students can be determined, profiles of ability can be prepared, and educational decisions can be made. *Labeling is secondary to the generation of data for appropriately placing students in programs commensurate with their abilities and interests.*

MODEL FOR ASSESSMENT

The purpose of an assessment process is to gather information that can be used to make meaningful evaluations and decisions affecting the education of these students. In order to accomplish this task, purposeful multifactored assessments should be undertaken. In multifactored assessment: all students are considered eligible for the procedure; multiple assessment instruments are used in each area being assessed; instruments are chosen to measure each student's strengths and weaknesses; assessment is in the child's primary language; and trained personnel conduct the assessments.

In addition to these guidelines, it is wise to view the assessment process as ongoing. You can never predict when a student will be at peak performance levels or unusually slow in a response. Also, students do not always show their potentials and abilities at an early age. A continual plan of assessment is your safeguard against having inaccurate, incomplete, or misleading data on a student.

Assessment processes for gifted and talented students should start early. Witty (1953) states, "Studies show that gifted children who develop most effectively are those whose ability is recognized early and who are encouraged to take part in stimulating, individually suitable activities in school and home" (p. 313). The findings of Bloom's study of 120 highly talented individuals, reported in *Developing Talent in Young People* (1985), support this earlier notion. He found that the identification and nurturance of talent at an early age had profound effect on later talent development. It is quite clear that early recognition of ability is integral to successful dovolopmcnt in later years.

Assessment Model

Identification is just one step in a comprehensive model for multifactored assessment of the gifted and talented (see Figure 2-1). In order to gather the types of data necessary for broad programming decisions, information must be accumulated that goes beyond that needed for program placement decisions. Engin and Parke (Parke, 1981) have proposed a

Figure 2-1   Model of Multifactored Assessment for the Gifted, Based on the United States Department of Education's Definition of Giftedness and Talent

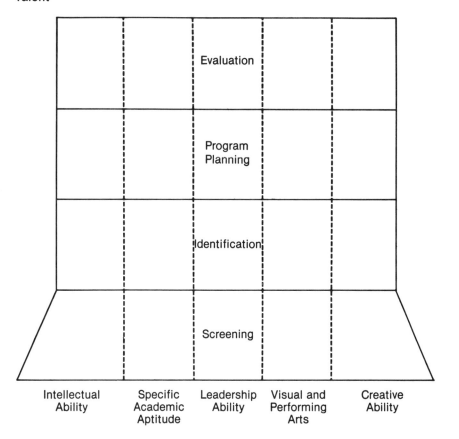

model consisting of four steps and including the five areas of giftedness set forth in the Gifted and Talented Act of 1978 (P.L. 95–561). These steps are screening, identification, program planning, and evaluation.

The first two steps, screening and identification, are classic program placement steps (Cronbach, 1970; Anastasi, 1976). During this time, information is assembled to determine student profiles of ability and to which programs students' abilities are best suited. The program planning step is one in which the data are gathered to determine the design of the program and curricular practices through which the students will learn in the most efficient and effective manner. Evaluation, the final step, is when individual and program success are measured and scrutinized for possible change.

Steps in the assessment model.   The four steps in the assessment model are designed to accomplish three purposes: select students for programs by matching student profiles to existing or new programs; design programs based on student needs and abilities; and evaluate the success of the programs and the achievement of individual students.

The first step in the multifactored assessment process is *screening,* which is used to gather broad information about the strengths and weaknesses of students with the purpose of finding *general* indicators of ability. At this time, potential is equally important as performance, and *any* known indicators of ability are sought. These data are used to begin the process of developing profiles of student ability from which placement decisions can be made. Again, the goal is to find the indicators of potential ability and actual high-level performance in order to amass the broadest possible signs of talent and to be as inclusive as possible. This is generally accomplished through the use of a variety and combination of techniques such as: teacher, parent, or student nominations; group intelligence tests; achievement test scores; awards; grades; and activities (see Table 2–1). Students who show potential for high achievement or actual achievement levels are noted are then designated as members of the *talent pool* and become eligible for special programming.

Another frequent use of the talent pool data is to identify programs that need to be introduced into a school system. By reviewing the data available and comparing it to the programs offered, gaps in programming can become known, and those people responsible for program development can begin the process of eliminating them.

The purpose of *identification,* the second step in the student selection phase of the assessment model, is to distinguish which talent pool students meet the criteria for any given program. This is accomplished by reviewing the data from the screening phase and determining which students show promise for the program under consideration. These students are then further assessed, as needed, to determine which students will

Table 2-1   Assessment Steps and Recommended Instrumentation

Assessment Step	Purpose	Instruments
Screening	Look for potential/ indicators of ability Gather wide range of data Establish talent pool Determine need for new programs	Nominations by: teachers parents students Group IQ tests Achievement tests Grades Awards
Identification	Gather in-depth data Match students to programs Make placement decisions	Criterion-referenced tests Individual IQ tests Products Portfolios Auditions
Program Planning	Determine the "how" and "what" of instruction	Observations Placement tests Learning style inventories Interest inventories
Evaluation	Measure program and student success	Tests/Products Interviews Observations Surveys

best profit from the programming experience. For example, students may be needed for an advanced language arts program. In this case, the talent pool students are reviewed in order to determine which show the most potential for high performance in language arts. This may be seen through standardized achievement test scores, teacher nominations, and/ or grades. The students who do show promise can then be assessed in greater depth to identify those who have abilities in line with the purposes of the class. Criterion-referenced tests, portfolios of writing samples, and interviews may be among the measures used for this purpose. Placement committees are often convened to make these decisions and determine what criteria will be used for selection.

Once it has been determined which students need differential instruction, the third step of the assessment model is employed—*program planning*. In this stage, assessment data gathered during the student selection process is augmented by further measures (as needed), in order to select and design the types of learning experiences best suited to the students. Again, we typically see the use of criterion-referenced placement tests, interviews, learning style and interest inventories, and observations. These data are analyzed to see in what ways the learning experiences of the students can be enhanced.

The final step, *evaluation,* is one in which assessment data are used to determine if the special provisions are successful and if individual student progress is satisfactory. This may necessitate further data collection but can be built on existing data from the other assessment steps. From these data, program planners and teachers can decide if modifications need to be made, if students are properly placed, if additional classes are needed, or if different types of strategies should be employed.

GATHERING ASSESSMENT INFORMATION

Before you begin the task of gathering assessment data, it is wise to determine the steps that will comprise the process. Although assessment procedures for the purpose of student selection vary from district to district, there are some basic guidelines that are followed when program planners begin this process. They are:

1. Determine the purpose of the assessment. Why are you doing it and what types of students do you hope to find?
2. Decide on the types of assessment data that will be collected. These should conform to the principles of multifactored assessment and the purposes of the procedure.
3. Determine from whom the assessment information should come. Do you want to see student work? Is it important to ask other teachers or parents about prospective students?
4. Consider the limitations of the procedure for special populations. Devise alternative methods of analysis or data collection as deemed necessary.
5. Conduct the assessment procedure and collection of data.
6. Make final student selections based on program purposes, criteria established for selection, and student profiles of abilities.
7. Interview students and/or parents to see if they wish to participate in the program and to familiarize them with its scope and content.
8. Compile the final roster of program students.
9. Create a plan for ongoing student assessment.

Types of Assessment Information

When you begin the process of locating the gifted and talented students in your classroom, you will want to identify different types of information that will help you toward that goal. It is usually recommended that more than one type of measure be used and that data are collected from more than one source. In this way, you can be more certain that your information reflects the students' actual abilities. This process of gathering multiple measures from multiple sources is called *triangulation.*

For most programming decisions, data are collected through the use of instruments from *each* of three categories: tests, nominations, and student products. There are various types of instruments in each of these categories that can be employed.

Tests. Tests (see Table 2-2) are generally of three types: norm-referenced, criterion-referenced, or inventories. Each type of test can be used for student selection purposes. Norm-referenced tests are those that are normed on a cross-section of the population so that individual student scores can be compared to the range of scores typical of the distribution of scores for students of the same age. Achievement tests (*Iowa Test of Basic Skills, California Test of Basic Skills, Stanford Achievement Test*) and IQ tests (*Stanford-Binet Intelligence Scale, Peabody Picture Vocabulary Test, Otis-Lennon Mental Ability Test*) are examples of norm-referenced measures. The scores are usually reported in stanines, percentiles, grade-level equivalencies, and/or standard scores. From these data it may be determined, for example, that a student is reading three grade levels above the norm or that the vocabulary score of the student exceeds 98 percent of all other fourth graders.

Criterion-referenced measures are those in which students' scores are assessed against a predetermined criteria for success, without concern for the students' score in relationship to a norm. Teacher-made tests are usually of this variety, as are placement tests. The primary reason for giving this type of test is to see what information students know and the level of expertise they have gained. These scores are generally reported through ratios (12/15), number of items correct (+12), or number of items wrong (−3). Data from criterion-referenced tests may show that students have mastered the content of a unit of study before it has been taught or that remediation is needed.

Learning style and modality inventories are tests that determine the manner in which students learn. There are a number of different tests available (Torrance's *Your Style of Thinking and Learning,* Kolb's *Learning Style Inventory,* and Swassing and Barbe's *Learning Modality Test*), each with its own categories of learning styles. These tests can give you

Table 2-2   Listing of Tests Commonly Used in Student Selection
Procedures for Programs for the Gifted and Talented

Tests of Potential

Individual
   Goodenough-Harris Drawing Test
   Peabody Picture Vocabulary Test—Revised
   Raven's Progressive Matrices
   Stanford-Binet Intelligence Scale
   Weschler Intelligence Scale for Children—Revised (WISC—R)
   Weschler Pre-School and Primary Scale of Intelligence (WPPSI)

Group
   California Short Form Test of Mental Maturity
   Cognitive Abilities Test
   Otis-Lennon Mental Ability Test

Tests of Achievement

California Achievement Test
Iowa Test of Basic Skills
Metropolitan Achievement Test
Peabody Individual Achievement Test
SRA Achievement Series
Stanford Achievement Tests

Tests of Creativity

Creative Product Scales
Khatena-Torrance Creative Perception Inventory
Remote Associations Test
Thinking Creatively with Sounds and Words
Torrance Test of Creative Thinking—Figural
Torrance Test of Creative Thinking—Verbal

---

an indication of whether the student learns best through visual, auditory,
or tactile experiences. In addition, inventories have been designed to determine such factors as whether students prefer to work alone or in small
groups. Interest inventories are given in order to be aware of the types
of activities that students prefer. These measures can give the teacher
clues as to the topics that will be of interest to the students and those
with which they are already familiar.

Nominations.   Nominations to programs are usually found in the form of a checklist of behaviors. These can be given to teachers, parents, peers, or the students themselves. Nomination forms allow the respondents to assess the designated student on the factors listed on the checklist. Although this information is more subjective than the testing data, it is nevertheless useful in spotting students who may have special abilities. Last year's teacher may have information on a special project the student completed that was exceptional; parents can tell you about what the child does in his or her free time and when the child began to read. The types of information that can be accumulated in this way are limited only by the questions that are asked. Figures 2–2 and 2–3 show examples of nomination forms.

A nomination form is constructed by determining a list of student characteristics that will indicate if a student belongs in a particular program. A nomination form for a program that deals with creativity should include items that reflect a student with creative ability. For a fast-paced mathematics class in which students will be accelerated, the checklist should include indicators that a student can handle the pace *and* is prepared for the higher level content. By matching the characteristics to the program, the nomination forms can give program planners important information about the potential students.

Often, nomination forms are developed by program planners. However, there are commercial forms available that are also widely used. The *Scales for Rating the Behavioral Characteristics of Superior Students* (Renzulli, Smith, White, Callahan, and Hartman, 1976) and *GIFT* (Rimm, 1976) are two such inventories. When using commercially available checklists or adapting one from another school district, be certain that it reflects the purposes of your assessment. If it does, use it; if it does not, discard it, adapt it, or make your own.

Nominations are generally used in the screening phases of the student selection process. They are good indicators of overall student ability. However, they can be inaccurate if the person completing the form is misinformed or misrepresents the student. Therefore, it is essential that individuals be trained in using the form properly and that nominations be used in conjunction with other measures.

Student Products.   Assessment data in this category are collected throughout the student selection steps. Products that are often used include: grades, awards, science projects, portfolios of writing or art, audition video tapes, and independent study projects. The types of products that can be used are endless; they need only conform to the purpose of the assessment and the type of information you are seeking. When selecting students for a painting program at the local museum of art, you may wish

Figure 2-2   Sample Teacher Nomination Form to Program for the Gifted and Talented

---

Teacher Nomination Form

Student _____ ID # _____ Birthday _____
Address _____ Teacher _____
School _____ Grade _____ Date _____

This student is being considered for the gifted and talented program in our school. Would you please take a few moments to complete this form? Your cooperation is greatly appreciated!

Please rate the student on the following characteristics on a 0–3 points scale.

(0) NEVER   (1) RARELY   (2) SOMETIMES   (3) ALMOST ALWAYS

Characteristic   Rating

---

1. Displays a great deal of curiosity about many things.   _____
2. Displays a keen sense of humor.   _____
3. Learns quickly and easily.   _____
4. Is persistent in completing tasks of interest.   _____
5. Asks many questions about a variety of subjects.   _____
6. Knows about many different things.   _____
7. Has a large vocabulary that is used correctly.   _____
8. Has a good memory.   _____
9. Has a high motivation to learn.   _____

Write additional comments on the back of this page.

---

to have students submit samples of their own painting. Advanced classes in creative writing may call for a collection of poems or short stories to be judged. When looking for students who would profit by a program in which they must be skilled in handling equipment, an audition with that equipment would be appropriate.

Various scales have been developed to assess student products (see Figure 2-4). These are rarely standardized; however, some do contain information about their reliability and validity along with directions for proper use. When constructing your own evaluation scale, be sure that the dimensions upon which the product will be measured are consistent

Figure 2-3   Sample Parent Nomination Form for Program for the Gifted

---

Parent Nomination Form

Student _____   Date _____
School _____   Birthday _____
Nominator _____   Grade _____

Why do you think your child should be nominated for the program for gifted and talented students? _____
_____
_____

Please check the degree to which the following items describe your child.

Characteristic	Little	Some	A Great Deal
1. Has lots of ideas.			
2. Read before entering school.			
3. Has a large vocabulary.			
4. Likes to play with older kids.			
5. Is involved in a lot of activities.			
6. Asks many questions.			
7. Is able to concentrate for long periods of time on tasks of interest.			
8. Enjoys solving puzzles and games.			
9. Has collections.			

Write additional comments on the back of this page.

---

with the purposes of your evaluation. If you are looking for originality, make sure that that ability is assessed. If potential for exceptional performance is a factor of interest, the scale should consider it (with or without a measure of current performance levels).

SAMPLE ASSESSMENT PLANS
Assessing for General Ability

If you are interested in assessing the overall abilities of students, design a multifactored assessment that will give you indications of the overall *potential* and *performance* levels of the individuals. This requires that

Figure 2-4   Creative Product Scale—Art

Worker _____   Rater _____

Introduction: While it's relatively impossible to evaluate an art product with objectivity, the following group of elements and principles of art should transcend cultural, geographic, sex, and age barriers as grading tools. They are absolutes which may appear in total or in part of a painting, sculpture, or craft product regardless of the sophistication of the producer. Consequently, a Leonardo Da Vinci, a Papuan native, or a Cass Tech art student are all aspiring toward the same composite ideal of elements and principles while expressing their individual concepts.

The evaluator should be forewarned that the number 10, or unique category, is synonymous with masterpiece and should therefore be used with cautious reservation. A masterpiece can only be rendered by a master artist, the work has to be universally recognized, it must have a life of its own, be technically perfect, comprise past, present and future tendencies, and have staying power. Any additional comments you wish to make please put them on the back of this sheet.

PLEASE CIRCLE YOUR RATING

	DEVELOPING			ADEQUATE			COMPETENT	EXCEPTIONAL	UNIQUE
1. UNITY	1	2	3	4	5	6	7	8	9	10
2. LINE	1	2	3	4	5	6	7	8	9	10
3. SHAPE	1	2	3	4	5	6	7	8	9	10
4. VALUE	1	2	3	4	5	6	7	8	9	10
5. VOLUME	1	2	3	4	5	6	7	8	9	10
6. FORM	1	2	3	4	5	6	7	8	9	10
7. TEXTURE	1	2	3	4	5	6	7	8	9	10
8. COLOR	1	2	3	4	5	6	7	8	9	10
9. CONTRAST	1	2	3	4	5	6	7	8	9	10
10. HARMONY	1	2	3	4	5	6	7	8	9	10

Source: Detroit Public Schools. Reprinted with permission by Detroit Public Schools, Copyright © 1983.

you use various assessment instruments to collect these data. Table 2–3 displays one such plan for assessing overall student abilities in academic, creative, and artistic areas.

Assessing for a Reading Program

When designing an assessment procedure to measure student performance in reading, you will want to concentrate on factors that indicate percocity in this area. The reading level of the student, vocabulary, outside reading habits, and standardized test scores are among the factors you may wish to review through assessment. Table 2–4 shows an assessment system designed for the purpose of selecting students for an advanced reading program.

Assessing for a Mathematics Program

An individualized mathematics program will require an assessment procedure that looks at both mathematical ability and the ability to work on one's own. Therefore, the corresponding instrumentation must take both factors into account. Mathematical ability can be measured through tests and grades from previous years; the ability to work on one's own may be measured through teacher nominations, observations, or student inventories (see Table 2–5).

Table 2–3   Assessment Plan for Student Selection Based on General Intellectual Ability

Assessment Purpose:	To identify Grade 5 students with general intellectual ability.

Assessment Step	Procedure/Instrument
Screening	Teacher nominations Group IQ Grades, Awards, Projects Achievement test scores (full battery)
Identification	Individual IQ Student inventory Interview with student

Table 2-4   Assessment Plan for Student Selection for an Advanced
Reading Program

Assessment Purpose: To identify Grade 3 students who would profit from
reading with students at a higher grade level and have reading levels that
exceed third grade.

Assessment Step	Procedure/Instrument

Screening	Achievement test scores in:
	  Vocabulary
	  Reading Comprehension
	Teacher nomination

Identification	Criterion-referenced placement test in reading Oral reading Interview with student

Table 2-5   Assessment Plan for Student Selection to a Fast-paced
Mathematics Program

Assessment Purpose: To identify Grade 7 and Grade 8 students for a fast-
paced mathematics program who have demonstrated high achievement in
mathematics.

Assessment Step	Procedure/Instrument

Screening	Achievement test scores in:
	  Mathematics Computation
	  Mathematics Concepts
	  Mathematics Applications
	Teacher nomination
	Grades in mathematics

Identification	Criterion-referenced placement test in math Student interview Parent interview

Assessing Musical Talent

The assessment process designed to find students with musical talent also necessitates the use of multiple measures. The purpose must be determined at the onset. Do you want students who may develop into fine musicians, students who already display a high level of ability, or both? How you answer that question will determine the type of process used. Table 2-6 is a sample assessment procedure in which students are expected to have already achieved highly in their talent area.

DEVELOPING PROFILES OF ABILITY

Once you have gathered the assessment data on the students, you will want to begin the process of developing profiles of student abilities. These profiles are the basis for the talent pool and are the pictorial representation of the students' strengths and weaknesses. It is by reviewing these profiles that a placement committee or an individual teacher can determine which students are in need of special programs and which types of programs should be available.

A computer disc or a file folder can be the housing for the profiles. They should appear in a standardized format so that information can be found and interpreted easily. There should be space for the results of the ongoing assessment procedures, placement decisions, evaluation of student performance, comments, and student data (see Figure 2-5). This information can be kept in a central location so that it is available to educational staff members throughout the students' tenure in the school system.

Table 2-6   Assessment Plan for Student Selection to an Advanced Vocal Music Program

Assessment Purpose: To identify Grade 6 students for an advanced vocal music class.

Assessment Step	Procedure/Instrument
Screening	Music teacher nomination *Measures of Musical Ability Test* *Music Achievement Test*
Identification	Audition Student interview

Figure 2-5   Sample Student Profile of Ability Chart

STUDENT PROFILE OF ABILITY

Name _____ School _____ Address _____ Birthday _____ Phone _____	

Assessment Data: Test   Score   Date

IQ
Achievement
Other

Nominations
Products
Other

Placements: Program   Date

Student Evaluations:

Comments:

MAKING PLACEMENT DECISIONS

Placement decisions can be made in a variety of ways—by a placement committee or by an individual teacher, counselor, or principal. Regardless of how the decision is made, there still should be criteria established for making the decision. For instance, if you wish to determine if any students could profit from a program in which advanced readers go to another grade for reading in order to receive instruction at their reading level, the teacher of the sending and receiving classrooms should be involved in the decision-making process. When making decisions about which students should be placed in a full-time segregated program for the gifted, a committee of teachers, administrators, program personnel, parents, and technical staff might be established.

Placement decisions are generally made through one of four techniques. The first is the *case study approach* in which the data on each candidate are reviewed by a placement team, and those students thought to be most qualified are placed in the program. The second technique, the *matrix approach* (Baldwin, 1977), is one in which the student performance levels on the assessment instruments are given numerical equivalents that are added together for an overall student score. The score for each student is computed in this manner and the scores of all the students are then rank ordered. Students with the highest scores are placed in the program. The third approach, *standard score approach* (Feldhusen, Baska, and Womble, 1981), is similar to the matrix approach, as it converts scores on assessment instruments into numbers that can result in a single numerical rating for a student. The difference is that in this approach student assessment scores are converted into standard scores and then added together. The fourth approach is far less formal and simply involves the teacher looking at the assessment information and making judgments for program placements. This could be termed the *eyeball approach*. A student who is assessed as reading three grade levels above her or his current placement is given the opportunity to try a book at that level; a student who shows great interest in the life cycle of a butterfly is encouraged to conduct controlled experiments on the topic as part of an independent study.

These four techniques should be considered when determining how placement decisions will be made. The different methods are all effective; however, the circumstances and purposes of any particular assessment procedure may make one or a combination of approaches preferable to the others.

SUMMARY

When undertaking an assessment procedure, it is essential that the purpose of the assessment be known. By establishing the purpose of the assessment at the onset, you can focus on what it is you need to find out. It is best to proceed using a multifactored assessment process in which you gather information through a number of measures and in more than one way in order to establish a talent pool through student profile charts. Once you have established the assessment's purpose and the manner in which the data will be collected, you can proceed with the actual data collection, analysis, and program placements. However, assessment does not end there. Rather, you can use the data amassed in the student selection procedure for program planning and evaluation purposes.

Although all teachers are concerned that a placement process may miss some students who should be part of a program, do not let this keep you from beginning. Remember that you can always add students to programs at a later date; this is the primary reason why assessment practices are ongoing.

ACTION STEPS

1. Familiarize yourself with the characteristics of gifted and talented students. You can do this by reading about the gifted or by watching the students in your class. Take special note of the ways in which they differ and the ways in which they are alike.

2. As you observe the students, notice which of them display some of these characteristics. Complete one of the sample nomination forms in this chapter for those students. Do the same for two additional students who you feel may have special abilities.

3. When you have decided to institute some type of special programming and before beginning to gather data, determine your purpose for the assessment process. Are you focusing on developing student profiles? Is there one subject in which you want to work? Do you wish to find achievers and/or students with the potential to achieve at high levels? Does your assessment conform to your definition of giftedness?

4. Review the assessment data that you already have on hand about the students, such as standardized test scores, interest inventories, product assessments, and grades. What additional pieces of information will assist you in your decision-making process? What other types of information can you reasonably attain?

5. Now use the assessment model presented in this chapter to plan the assessment of the students.

6. Conduct your assessment and analyze the data, including that which is extant. Remember—fancy analysis is not necessary. You need only collect the information and do the analysis necessary to make the decisions needed.

7. Determine which students fulfill the purposes of the assessment. Talk with them and their parents (if appropriate) to see if they wish to be involved in the new programming efforts.

8. Make plans for ongoing assessment, keeping in mind that not all students show their stripes when we are looking and that assess-

ment data can also be used for the purposes of program planning and evaluation.

REFERENCES YOU CAN USE

Anastasi, A. (1976). *Psychological testing* (4th ed.). New York: Macmillan.

Buros, O. (Ed.). (1983). *The ninth mental measurements yearbook.* Highland Park, NJ: Gryphon Press.

Gardner, H. (1983). *Frames of mind.* New York: Basic Books.

Martinson, R. (1974). *The identification of the gifted and talented.* Ventura, CA: Office of the Ventura County Superintendent of Schools.

VanTassel-Baska, J., & Strykowski, B. (1986). *An identification resource guide on the gifted & talented.* Evanston, IL: Center for Talent Development.

3

Planning the Programs

Planning programs to accommodate gifted and talented students should commence under one circumstance only: If the needs of these students are not being met by an existing program, then an alternative program designed to address their needs should be instituted. Gifted students have unique abilities that may necessitate such a step, as it is the right of all students to have educational programs that will meet their learning needs.

Each child in the regular classroom has a unique learning schema, preferring to work alone or in small groups, to write a response to a question or answer orally, to take direction from the teacher or grapple with a problem alone. If you observe students as they work, you will find that they all have their own learning characteristics. These varying characteristics are what necessitate building programs with sufficient flexibility to accommodate multiple approaches to the learning process.

LEARNING CHARACTERISTICS
OF GIFTED STUDENTS

Many lists of characteristics exist that describe the population of gifted learners as a whole; one such list appears in Chapter 2. You may have observed many of these characteristics in the classroom. You may have noticed, in particular, that the learning characteristics of the gifted tend to differ from their chronological age-peers in three important ways (Maker, 1982).

First, gifted students tend to learn more quickly than other students. The *pace* of their learning is advanced. They can absorb information at a faster rate and process it efficiently. This is one reason that many gifted students seem to have minds like a sponge. They learn a great deal of information quickly and they rarely miss much. Second, gifted students are often able to comprehend information with greater *depth* than their classmates. They tend to ask the questions that show insight or understanding of more universal concepts. More than one teacher has been shocked at the understanding displayed by some six- and seven-year-olds about world conflict, death, or the monetary system. Finally, gifted students are often distinguished by *interests* that are different from others of the same age. Interests may be shown in areas more typical of older students or adults. A walk through a high school science fair will quickly demonstrate the wide variety of interests enjoyed by the student body.

These three primary characteristics are enhanced by others which complement them and add to the variance in the way these students learn. Dunn and Griggs (1985, p. 43) report that learning styles of gifted students, when considered as a group, can be characterized by the following descriptors; "(a) independence (self learners); (b) internal or external control; (c) persistence; (d) perceptual strengths; (e) nonconformity; (f) task commitment; and (g) high self motivation." They further comment that these categories of behaviors will vary with individual students and can only be used as indicators of group tendencies.

It quickly becomes obvious that gifted students come to their educational experiences with different credentials than most students, and they will likely require programs that allow them to work at their own pace, explore topics in greater depth, and pursue their own interests in addition to those topics covered by the conventional curriculum. The difficulty for the teacher comes in trying to establish programs that will be sufficiently flexible to meet the needs of *all* students in a classroom without segregating or isolating individuals and groups of students who are members of that class.

DIFFERENTIATING
THE EDUCATIONAL PROGRAM

Differentiated educational programs are necessary for all students because each student has unique learning needs and styles. Any educational experience will not be equally beneficial for all students. In fact, it is not equal education to have all students receiving the same experiences. It is far more defensible to establish programs that have the flexibility to respond to various needs, interests, and learning styles of students. This *cannot* be accomplished if only a single program is in place. If all the students in the class are doing the same math problems or reading the same basal reader, it is most likely that the educational needs of some students are not being met—it may be the students of more advanced skill or those in need of remediation. Regardless, the needs, abilities, and interests of the students should determine their educational program.

It is essential for the educator to think in terms of a *multiple programming approach* in which options are available to the teacher and/or student to develop an individualized program based on the student's profile of abilities, achievements, needs, and interests. The programming options should include various ways to make a classroom program more flexible in the delivery of educational experiences to students. By so doing, all students, not just the gifted, will be better served with programs that facilitate learning to a greater degree.

For the gifted student, then, the teacher will need to pay particular attention to those aspects of the program that influence the pace at which students learn, the depth that they are allowed to explore a topic, and the opportunity to pursue or incorporate their own interests into their studies. Questions similar to the following may arise: What options are available to a child who is reading at the second-grade level while enrolled in kindergarten? What options are available for a first-grade student who can multiply and divide accurately? What options are available for the sixth-grade math student who is able to begin the study of algebra? What can you do for the fifth-grade student who is involved in dissecting frogs at home and is aggressively studying anatomy on her own? If a teacher is not in the position to answer these questions with reasonable alternatives, then attention needs to be given to how the educational program can be differentiated to accommodate the individual learning profiles of students.

Differentiating programs for the gifted can begin by remembering the following guidelines for program planning:

1. The program should be characterized by its flexibility to respond to the individual needs of students.
2. Program options should be in place so that the varying skills, abilities, and interests of the students can be accommodated.
3. Patterns for grouping students should be based on the unique needs of the students and should allow students to progress at their own pace.
4. Decision making should be based on student needs. Individualized program planning should take place for all students.

SELECTING PROGRAMMING OPTIONS

Selecting programming options to institute in the classroom involves three steps. Each is essential to this decision-making process. The first step is to determine the academic, social, emotional, and physical needs of the students in the classroom. Among the questions to be investigated are: What is the range of ability the students display in reading? Are there students who have problems socializing with the other students? Do all the students complete their work at the same time, or are some students faster or slower than the norm? A look at the abilities and needs of the students will lead you to the next step in the process of selecting appropriate programming options. The next step is to establish learning objectives for all the students in the class. The objectives for gifted students may be similar to those for the rest of the class, but will differ in that the gifted students have unique requirements for appropriate programming. After you have investigated the needs of the students and have established objectives for their educational experiences, you can then begin the third step, selecting programming options that will address these needs and objectives in a comprehensive manner.

Step 1:   Determining Student Needs

The needs of students can be determined through a number of methods. Some involve formal assessment procedures whereas others are very informal and subjective in nature. Regardless of the types of procedures selected, the purpose is still the same: Construct a profile of student abilities, achievements, needs, and interests from which program placement decisions can be made. It is critical that profiles be established for *all* students in the classroom. When the objectives are written and the program design is determined, they must reflect the needs of all students working in that environment, not just the gifted students. It is the intent of this program planning process to develop programming options that will facilitate the learning of all the students in the regular classroom, not just a few. Program designs must not discriminate among children unfairly or isolate certain students from the rest of the class, socially or physically. Establishing a sound program design will assure that individual needs and differences are addressed and that learning is encouraged.

Various types of instruments can assess the needs and abilities of students. Tests of ability or achievement used in the assessment process for program placement can be reevaluated (see Chapter 2). Criterion-referenced tests, such as the placement tests provided by many textbook publishers, can provide a great deal of information regarding student levels of achievement in subject areas. A look at the accumulative record file on a child may very well result in information that will prove useful in determining current levels of functioning and past activities. More informal methods, such as observations and interviews, can yield equally important information, particularly as you investigate the social and emotional developmental factors. Interest and learning style inventories can also be useful tools for determining student needs and preferences. Parent questionnaires can produce clues to the abilities and interests of the students that may be exhibited outside of school. When these data are accumulated and profiles of individual students are completed, the information should be synthesized into a classroom profile to be used in determining the types of programs and curricular accommodations that are needed (see Figure 3-1).

Figure 3-1   Student Profile Chart

Student Name:	Student Number:
Grade Level:	Teacher's Name:
Date Profile Completed:	

Grade Level Equivalency   Test

Curricular Area:

Reading
   (see attached skill chart)

Math
   (see attached skill chart)

Spelling
   Book level completed _____

Writing Proficiency

Handwriting Proficiency

Special Interests:

Special Talents:

Awards:

Projects:

Extracurricular activities:

Step 2:   Establishing Student Objectives

Objectives for students are written so that the students and the teacher have a basis upon which to make decisions about the students' educational experiences. They are the guides to program planning and the foundation for curricular decision making. Some objectives will be the same for all the students in the class; others will vary depending on the profiles of the students. Objectives should reflect the unique composition of each student's profile, the total class profile, and the following six basic rights that should be afforded to all students.

- *All students have the right to learn at their own pace.*   Those students who learn more quickly should be allowed to move through material at a faster pace. It is also the right of students who learn more slowly to progress at a rate that will allow them to learn with the greatest effectiveness.

- *All students have the right to receive instruction that is at their achievement levels.*   Materials and methods of instruction should be determined by the abilities and achievements of the students, not the grade level to which they are assigned. A third grader capable of reading at a fifth-grade level, should be receiving fifth-grade materials and reading experiences.

- *All students should be given the opportunity to develop independent thinking skills.*   Students must be prepared to make decisions on their own. They cannot learn to think independently if they are not given the opportunity. Problem-solving techniques, inquiry, and higher level thinking skills are strategies that can benefit all children in a classroom. They should be integrated into the classroom through the program design, curriculum, and interpersonal interactions.

- *All students should be prepared to be lifelong learners.*   Objectives must be established in such a way as to give students the responsibility for learning and the tools to learn on their own. This will mean designing programs that allow students to make decisions and experience the consequences of their decisions. As well, this will necessitate that students become partners with teachers in the decision-making processes of the classroom. Their learning commenced before they began school and it will continue long after their formal schooling ends.

- *All students should be allowed multiple means of expressing what they know and how they feel.*   Young children who have cognitive abilities that surpass their physical abilities must be given outlets to express their ideas that will not be hindered by an inability to write or speak. Children who can express themselves through artistic display should be given the opportunity to do so. By developing divergent modes of expression, children are better able to use all their abilities and develop new ones.

- *All students should be encouraged to develop a respect for themselves and others.*   Schools can play an integral role in teaching children about themselves and those around them. By treating students with respect, we model appropriate behavior. By helping them gain insight into their behaviors and those of others, we assist them in understanding that all people are different and each deserves to be treated in a respectful manner.

Keeping these rights for all students in mind, individual and/or group objectives should be written to outline the types of learning experiences that are needed and the methods that will facilitate learning in the most effective and efficient manner. These objectives should address the academic, social, emotional, and physical needs of the students. Objectives typical for gifted students take into account their special need for accommodating the pace at which they learn, the depth at which they are capable of comprehending, and the unique interests they display (see Tables 3-1 and 3-2). Kaplan (1974) lists ten basic areas on which objectives can be built. They are:

- Awareness of environmental and academic learning opportunities;
- Leadership;
- Academic achievement;
- Interpersonal relationships;
- Self-awareness;
- Creativity;
- Research skills;
- Abstract thinking processes;
- Basic skill mastery; and
- Career and vocational opportunities (p. 39).

Actual objectives listed for any individual may include many but not necessarily all of these areas. Each area should be considered, however, in the process of generating the objectives. Objectives are central to the program planning process as they provide the focus for instruction. As the program develops and student abilities change, objectives must evolve also. They should be reviewed periodically and modified as necessary.

Table 3-1   Typical Objectives for Gifted Students

The student will:

1. Develop divergent modes of expression.
2. Develop the ability to think critically.
3. Develop the ability to solve problems by using multiple resources.
4. Develop the ability to learn independently.
5. Master basic skills needed to study at advanced levels.
6. Develop curiosity and learn strategies to pursue questions and interests that arise.
7. Develop an awareness and acceptance of personal abilities.
8. Develop a love of learning for the intrinsic pleasure that it can bring.
9. Develop any special talents and skills to the highest level.

Table 3-2   Typical and Accelerated Learning Objectives
in Length, Height, and Distance

Typical Objectives

The students will be able to:
1. Point to the longer/shorter-item.
2. Point to the longer/shorter-same length item.
3. Write line length to the nearest inch.

Accelerated Objectives

The student will be able to:
1. Write line length to nearest eighth inch.
2. Convert up to 10 feet to inches.
3. Write solutions to story problems.

Step 3:   Choosing Program Options

There are many administrative arrangements for delivering programs for gifted students. In choosing programming options to fit a particular set of circumstances, it is best to think in terms of combinations of programs rather than a single configuration. If you offer only one type of program, you can be assured that the needs of some of your students are not being met. It is far more valid to construct a mosaic of programming options from which to choose when making program placement decisions for students.

The range of programs recommended for gifted students is quite broad. The Pyramid Project (Cox, Daniel, and Boston, 1985) proposes program options that extend from more typical programs to programs appropriate only for the highly gifted learner (see Figure 3-2). As you climb the pyramid, the programs become more separated from the regular classroom and more segregated in their design. This is a reflection of the increasing difficulty teachers experience in trying to meet the needs of students in a regular classroom environment as abilities of gifted students become more and more advanced beyond those typically displayed by their classmates.

Program options can be combined or offered alone. For example, a school district may choose to have programming for gifted students strictly in a resource room arrangement with students coming to the program one-half day per week. Or the district may choose to employ a cluster grouping concept in addition to the resource room program, in which a group of gifted students are placed in a class, with provisions for a resource teacher to assist the regular classroom teacher in delivering their educational programs.

The types of program options used should be a reflection of the needs and abilities of the students, along with the objectives that were established from student profiles. The goal is to have all students in the classroom receiving appropriate programs that allow them to learn at their

Figure 3-2   Pyramid Project Program

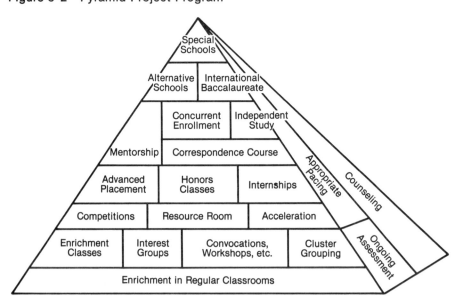

Source: Gifted Students Institute, Fort Worth, Texas. Reprinted with permission.

own pace, their own depth, and take into account their individual interests.

THE ROLE OF CREATIVITY IN PROGRAMS FOR THE GIFTED

Enhancing creativity is considered to be an integral component of many programs for gifted and talented students. When looking at the goals of programs or student objectives, creativity is usually mentioned as a priority. When thinking about student-centered programming within the regular classroom environment, it should also be seen as an important piece of the mosaic.

This does not mean, however, that creativity should be viewed as separate from the other subjects and processes we teach (Parke, 1985). Rather, creativity should permeate and enhance the classroom through such factors as accepting attitudes, open-ended questions, explorations, and choices. Thirty minutes of "creativity time" is not enough. Thoughtful attention should be given to how creativity relates to classroom activities at all times.

In *Megatrends: Ten New Directions Transforming Our Lives* (Naisbitt, 1982), our society is depicted as moving from one in which industrialization is paramount to one in which information processing is key and either/or decisions are becoming ones in which multiple options are sought. Preparing students for this type of future society has ramifications for school systems today. Our students need to learn how to use their resources to the fullest, work cooperatively, find innovative answers to questions, and not block their own creative abilities. Remaining cognizant of the role creativity can have in this pursuit and integrating creative expression and problem solving throughout the curriculum can help students be better prepared for the world in which they live.

PATTERNS FOR GROUPING GIFTED STUDENTS IN THE REGULAR CLASSROOM

For philosophical or pragmatic reasons, many school districts choose to place gifted students within the regular classroom structure. Historically, this is where gifted students have received their educational programs. For some of these students this may not be an overwhelming handicap. However, to avoid underserving them, careful attention must be given to assuring that the programming in such an environment is done properly and that differentiated programming is occurring.

In order to meet these goals, attention must be given to the grouping patterns that will respond to the student and class profiles of ability. Six configurations are often found, singly or in combination, in classrooms with gifted students. These options are cluster groups, interest groups, skill groups, multiaged classes, grade skipping, and telescoping.

Cluster Groups

Cluster grouping is a procedure in which a group of high-ability students is placed together in a classroom. This type of grouping assumes that a teacher is more likely to build challenging programs if a number of students will benefit rather than just a few. A typical cluster may number as few as four students and as many as ten. Students within the cluster are an integrated part of the class, but may have some different learning opportunities and materials with which to work. Teachers have more latitude to adjust the pace and depth of learning when they are dealing with more than one student at a time. By grouping these students together, they also have the social/emotional advantage of being in contact with other students like themselves who have similar interests and abilities.

Cluster grouping differs from the typical grouping patterns in that all teachers may not have the same distribution of student ability levels in their classes. The traditional method of rank ordering students as to their achievement levels and then assigning them to classrooms so that all teachers have the same balance of abilities becomes obsolete (see Table 3–3). In its place, a grouping procedure emerges that has the top students in clusters (in one or more classes) and the other students evenly distributed, based on their ability (see Table 3–4).

As stated previously, the advantage to this type of system is twofold. First, teachers have a defined group of students of similar ability for which to plan a program. Therefore, the students are more likely to receive accommodations that will meet their needs. Second, the students have others like them within the classroom. It is important for gifted students to have the opportunity to interact with their peers as it gives

Table 3–3 Traditional Grouping Procedure Using Student Ranks

| | | Teacher | | |
A	B	C	D	E
1*	2	3	4	5
6	7	8	9	10
11	12	13	14	15
16	17	18	19	20
21	22	23	24	25

*Number 1 ranking student

Table 3-4   Cluster Grouping Procedure Using Student Ranks

		Teacher		
A	B	C	D	E
1*+	5	6	7	8
2+	10	11	12	13
3+	15	16	17	18
4+	20	21	22	23
9	25	26	27	28

*Number 1 ranking student
+ Cluster group member

them a more accurate view of their own abilities and an assurance that there are other people like them in the world.

Interest Groups

Groups can also be established based on the interests of students. The purpose is to allow students who have similar interests to explore them together. For example, students who are interested in miming may work together on their art. Those who are interested in computers may meet to write programs. Students who are adept at writing and journalism may belong to a group that writes a classroom newspaper.

Interest groups are often used in conjunction with other types of groups, such as cluster groups and skill groups. They serve an important function in the regular classroom, providing a forum in which students group themselves according to interests rather than abilities. Students who are in the cluster groups may find that interest groups give them the opportunity to integrate themselves into the mainstream of the class, as all the students have a chance to work and meet together.

Skill Groups

Skill grouping can appear in concert with cluster and interest groups. They are established based on the academic needs of the students in the class. There is always a range of achievement levels in any classroom, whether it has the more typical mix of students or is a classroom solely for gifted students. It is not unusual to find gifted students with uneven skills and in need of remediation!

The teacher bases the skill groups on some type of assessment procedure, depending on the type of skill being addressed. For example, third-grade students may be tested on skills ranging from short vowel sounds and syllabication to character development and main idea. When an accurate assessment is made of the skills the students have and have not mastered, a class profile can be assembled from which the skill groups can be drawn (see Table 3-5). All students who have not mastered the short vowel sounds can work on that skill. Other students who know the short vowel sounds should not have to spend their time working on a skill they have already mastered. Rather, these students should be in other skill groups, studying topics they have not mastered, such as syllabification and contractions (see Table 3-6).

As with interest groups, skill groups give the students opportunities to work together. Gifted students have varying skills and may need to be in a skill group studying at or below grade level. For instance, a child in a cluster group may not know his math facts, and computes problems by counting on his fingers. Since it is important that this child learn the facts and commit them to memory, an appropriate placement would be to assign this student to a group in which the students are memorizing their math facts.

Students do not remain in the same skill groups all year long. Rather, when a student has mastered skills to the teacher's and student's satisfaction, he or she is ready to move to another skill. Students may find that they are in more than one skill group at a time. Or they may be placed in the same skill group on more than one occasion if the teacher is rotating skill groups and finds that certain students either do not know the skill or have not retained the information from the last time the group was assembled.

Table 3-5   Class Profile of Reading Skills

	Students					
Reading Skills	Bob	Jan	Sue	Jim	Ted	Ben
Recognizes and uses:						
1. Initial consonants	+	+	+	+	+	+
2. Final consonants	+	+	+	−	−	−
3. Blends	+	−	−	+	+	−
4. Long vowels	+	+	−	−	+	+
5. Short vowels	−	−	−	−	+	+
6. Double vowels	−	−	−	−	−	−
7. Silent consonants	+	+	+	−	−	−
8. Syllabication	−	−	−	−	−	−
9. Contractions	−	−	−	−	−	−

+ = Mastered skill
− = Instruction needed

Table 3-6   Skill Groups Drawn from Class Profile

Final Consonants	Short Vowels	Blends
Jim	Bob	Jan
Ted	Jan	Sue
Ben	Sue	Ben
	Jim	

Multiaged Classes

Multiaged classes can be of two types. The first type is assembled by having students from more than one grade assigned to one class. This may be a "split-grade" arrangement, in which a teacher has students from two contiguous grades in the same class, such as a second/third-grade combination. Or the class may be made up of students from a number of grades, such as a first/second/third-grade combination.

The second type of multiaged classroom arrangement is found when the typical class structures are in place and teachers have students in the class who are at the same grade level. In this design, when a student needs instruction at an advanced or lower level, that student travels to the appropriate grade classroom for instruction. A fourth-grade student may go to the sixth grade for reading, and a seventh grader may go to the high school for an algebra class.

This type of grouping, again, allows students to receive instruction at the level that is appropriate for them. The disadvantage most frequently cited is that the scheduling of these arrangements is often difficult. The fourth-grade teacher may not have math at the same time or for the same amount of time as the sixth-grade teacher. The seventh grader may have to find her own transportation to and from the high school and may find that the algebra classes are conducted during her regular class's reading time. Cooperation among faculty members is necessary to employ this type of grouping efficiently.

Grade Skipping

Grade skipping is a way to group a child with students who more resemble the student's abilities than do the age-peers. This is accomplished by allowing the student to skip a particular grade and advance to the next. For example, a precocious first grader may be advanced to third grade; the second-grade year is omitted, allowing the child more educational experiences in keeping with his or her abilities.

Problems commonly associated with this technique can be minimized if certain guidelines are followed. First, if grade skipping is being seriously considered, it is important that the child be functioning at the 75 percent or above in the class *into which* the child is moving. Students who are used to performing at the top of the class should not be put in a situation where they will be average. This can be psychologically harmful to the student. In addition, social and emotional development should also be considered, along with the physical development of the child. This evaluation is best done by a psychologist who is familiar with high-ability children. Third, the time most conducive to skipping grades without trauma is when a natural break in the class patterns occurs. If a school district has a middle school that begins in fifth grade, then skipping a third grader to fifth might be a reasonable move. Since all the students are developing new peer groups, the child who has skipped a grade will seem less out of place. Another method to consider is early entrance, wherein a four-year-old begins kindergarten or a five-year-old goes directly to first grade. Again, the peer group is established at the onset. Finally, if grade skipping is advised, it should be done on a trial basis. If the students are not flourishing in the new environment, they should be allowed to return to the class level originally skipped.

Telescoping

Many of the problems inherent in grade skipping are eased by telescoping, a procedure in which a student enters into a mixed grade situation with the understanding that two years of work will be completed in one (see Table 3–7). A student may be assigned to a fourth/fifth-grade split. The student comes into the class as a fourth grader and leaves at the end of one year with the fifth graders. This is possible because most students who are eligible for such consideration are already quite advanced for their age and probably already know most of what is being taught at their level. Care must be taken in this instance to assure that time is spent learning the fourth/fifth-grade skills that the student does not know so that no gaps appear in the student's skills.

One of the advantages most frequently mentioned regarding this approach is that the student maintains a peer group, as the students with whom the child is being advanced are already friends and classmates. The

Table 3–7   Grade Skipping and Telescoping Compared

	Student Grade Progression						
Grade skipping	K	1	2	3	5	6	7
Telescoping	K	1	2	3/4	5	6	7

student is not arriving into an unknown world full of strangers who think she or he is an anomoly.

Grouping, then, is one way to begin thinking about ways to educate gifted children appropriately in the regular classroom. These six grouping techniques are administrative arrangements that can be employed to facilitate the learning of children and the teaching of the educators. When properly done, grouping can result in students receiving instruction at the levels reflecting their abilities and in teachers organizing their classrooms to meet individual needs of students. It is this *student-centered* approach to teaching that allows students to engage in educational experiences in a way that will result in full and comprehensive programming.

INDIVIDUALIZATION AS A FRAMEWORK FOR PROGRAM PLANNING

With grouping as the base, individualizing is one of the primary frameworks upon which programs for gifted students in regular classrooms are built. In order to begin the process of educating students when a range of abilities exists, you must make a philosophical commitment to educating individual children with individual needs, rather than educating a mass of students termed, for example, "fifth graders."

Schools exist for the purpose of educating our youths. In order to be effective in this pursuit, we cannot forget the needs of the students we are instructing. Therefore, it becomes imperative that a student-centered approach to learning is adopted. This may sound self-evident, but the mechanics of delivering programs that are student-centered are difficult at best. Those people who are involved in the decision-making processes must be committed to this philosophy. Teachers must be trained to become managers of learning as well as oracles of knowledge. Schedules must be devised that allow flexible pacing for students. Materials need to be acquired that will allow students to pursue their broad interests at their own levels of ability. These conditions are not easily realized, but they are essential components to educating students in a student-centered environment.

Individualization Defined

The word *individualization* is often misused and misunderstood. Clark (1983) simply defines individualization as "a way of organizing learning experiences so that the rate, content, schedule, experiences, and depth of exploration available to all students stem from their assessed needs and interests" (p. 215). This does *not* suggest that each student must be doing something different than her or his classmates at all times. Rather, it outlines a process through which educational decisions are made—by assessment of individual needs and interests from which learning experiences are organized. These may appear in the form of large or small group instruction, if more than one student or the entire class is in need of the same experience. Or it may result in students working on their own for part of the day.

What Is Individualized?

Blackburn and Powell (1976) cite five facets of an educational program that can be individualized: (1) the rates at which students progress through their work, (2) the actual learning alternatives, (3) the schedule, (4) the content of the instruction, and (5) the depth of exploration that is allowed. These areas correspond closely to the learning characteristics of gifted children that necessitate differentiating programs (see Table 3-8). This compatibility makes individualization of programs a highly defensible alternative for programming for these students.

Aspects of an Individualized Program

Dunn and Dunn (1975) have made great contributions to the practice of individualizing programs for students. They suggest that there are thirteen aspects of individualized programs. There are many such lists in the literature on this topic, but the Dunn and Dunn listing is one of the most inclusive. It mentions the following:

1. Diagnosis (teacher, student, cooperative, team);
2. Prescription (teacher, student, cooperative, team);
3. Publicly stated objectives (teacher, student, cooperatively or team prescribed);
4. Alternative resources through which to learn;

Table 3-8 Correspondence Between Areas that Can Be Individualized and Learning Characteristics of Gifted Students

Area to Be Individualized	Gifted Students' Characteristics
1. Rate	Learns more quickly
2. Learning alternatives	Wide range of interests
3. Schedule	Learns more quickly
4. Content	Understands with greater depth/ Wide range of interests
5. Depth of exploration	Understands with greater depth

5. Alternative or optional activities;

6. Self-pacing;

7. Self-leveling;

8. Self-assessment and/or cooperative assessment, teacher and/or team assessment;

9. Self-selection of learning methods;

10. Objectives and prescriptions based on student abilities and interests;

11. Opportunities for student creativity incorporated into prescription;

12. Criterion-referenced evaluation; and

13. Performance-based evaluation (student demonstration of knowledge through means other than written tests) (p. 48).

Many of these aspects to individualized instruction appear in methods typically employed in the classroom, such as learning activity packages, contracts, programmed learning packages, computer-based tutorial programs, work-study experiences, mentorships, and commercially marketed instructional programs. Combining many approaches to individualization will most likely be necessary when building programs with multiple options. This variety serves only to strengthen a program, as it makes the program more flexible and responsive to student needs, abilities, and interests.

Advantages to Individualization

The greatest advantage to individualizing programs for students is that it allows them to receive instruction that is appropriate for their abilities in content and pace, achievement levels, and interests. In addition, individualizing programs for students allows the teacher more freedom to attend to the individual learning needs of the students. Dunn and Dunn (1975) list the following additional benefits accrued through individualizing educational programs:

1. Provides for student success rather than failure;

2. Builds self-image;

3. Permits peer interaction that causes retention;

4. Decreases student dependence on the teacher and initially transfers it to peers and eventually to self;

5. Provides for problem-solving experiences;

6. Develops internal motivation rather than peer competition; and

7. Develops critical analysis abilities (pp. 48–49).

The advantages to individualizing programming are many. It allows students an opportunity to take charge of their own learning and gain the tools to become life-long learners. The gifted students in the classroom must learn how to rely on themselves to gain information because much of their learning will be accomplished on their own. It is unrealistic to expect teachers to know everything the gifted students know or want to know. However, teachers can provide students with the tools to learn on their own. Certainly, allowing for individualization in the classroom is one way to begin this process.

INDIVIDUALIZED EDUCATIONAL PLANS (IEPs) FOR THE GIFTED

One strategy that has been proposed to plan and manage instruction for the gifted is the Individualized Educational Plan (IEP). It contains the following information about a student: student name, school, address, phone; current performance levels; annual goals for each area of special programming; short-term objectives for each goal; an evaluation plan for each goal; and date and signatures of all parties involved. Some IEPs also include information about support services and ancillary staff involvements. This document is usually brought to a meeting at which the teachers, administrator, psychologist, parents, and (sometimes) the child discuss the plan and approve its intent and contents.

IEPs have received mixed levels of acceptance among those people who work with gifted students. Many have found them to be a useful planning and management tool. In fact, in *The State of the State's Gifted and Talented Education* (Council of State Directors of Programs for the Gifted, 1986), it is reported that eleven states require IEPs for assessment and placement purposes. Although the use of this technique seems to be growing, there are still those people who believe that IEPs are too constricting for the gifted and that their use aligns gifted education too closely with special education.

ASSEMBLING THE MOSAIC

Devising a program schema for gifted and talented students is much like assembling a 2,000-piece jigsaw puzzle or an intricate stained glass window. Each piece is vital to the completed product; if pieces are missing, the entirety is marred. If visualized, the programming efforts for these students would look much like a mosaic. That is, they are composed of many parts of differing hues, intensity, and shapes, but when placed together a harmony emerges that is pleasing and tranquil to all who view it.

In order to construct a mosaic of program options that has these traits, balance must be attained between the key elements. First, the programs must be based in an environment that is conducive to learning and that respects the varying abilities of the students. This environment should include teachers who understand and have compassion for gifted students and who are willing to allow the students to enter into the process of decision making in a student-centered approach to living.

Second, a balance must be achieved between programs that will deal with the pace at which students learn (generally accelerated courses of study), the depth at which they learn (usually enrichment opportunities), and their unique interests. All are essential to the harmony of the mosaic for gifted and talented students. Too often, programs are heavily weighted in one direction. Either they deal only with acceleration or enrichment, or they are so intense in academic areas that they ignore the arts and extracurricular activities such as drama, gymnastics, and computer club. For the best results, many possible configurations for programming should be available, with the actual courses students take based on their own profiles of ability.

Finally, a balance must be struck between what a student can handle cognitively, emotionally, and physically. There are many instances in which a student has been pushed beyond the limit and has either failed, stopped participating, underachieved, or (in the extreme) become suicidal. Program mosaics must make room for students to work at comfortable (yet challenging) levels. For some students, highly rigorous, demanding, accelerative programs will be fine. However, for others, more conservative programs that include a smattering of accelerated options, along with enrichment opportunities, will suffice nicely. When dealing with young children, this balance is especially important. With these students, physical abilities often lag behind cognitive abilities, and being engaged in options that require them to write or draw beyond their abilities may lead to disaster. In one instance, a ten-year-old student was involved with radical acceleration and was taking his courses at the high school. He was able to comprehend the language and science courses fine, but he began to have headaches and was soon bedridden. The doctors determined that the child was physically exhausted by trying to keep up with the older students, carrying heavy textbooks and studying for prolonged hours. This is an obvious case of a student's program being out of balance. Programming options were being employed, but the results were not acceptable.

As you begin to think about programming for the gifted and talented students in regular classroom settings, remember that you should develop a mosaic of programming possibilities from which actual student programs can be matched to profiles of ability. Balance is essential to the success of the programs. What works for one student will not necessarily work for another. Having the capability to respond in many ways to the unique needs of students will allow you to provide educational experiences that will enhance the students' learning and your own satisfaction as an educator.

SUMMARY

Planning programs for gifted students in regular classrooms requires many decisions to be made. These decisions are based on the needs, abilities, and interests of the students, as well as institutional requirements. However, it is critical that the needs of students take priority and that decisions are made based on what those needs are. This requires familiarity with the students involved and a commitment to their individual programming needs.

Profiles of student needs serve as the basis for program planning. These profiles should suggest multiple programming options, or programming mosaics, that will accommodate the pace and depth at which these students learn, as well as their interests. Grouping patterns and individualized program prescriptions that can best serve the students can then be outlined. Gifted students have unique learning needs that necessitate differentiated programming. These needs result in challenges for classroom teachers—to provide the types of programs needed for the students without making them feel different and without segregating them from the class in some way. When the gifted and talented are in the regular classroom, they need to feel a part of the class, not apart from the class; it is up to the classroom teacher to make sure this happens.

ACTION STEPS

1. Review the programs that are currently available to students within and outside the regular classroom. Is there sufficient range to accommodate the educational needs of your students?
2. Make a list of these programs, adding a short description of each. Use this for reference in program planning when matching student profiles to programs.
3. Closely scrutinize the regular classroom offerings to determine the extent to which they allow individual student growth, flexible pacing, in-depth investigations, and interests to be pursued.
4. Spend some time thinking about the extent to which you feel prepared to open the regular classroom to student exploration and shared responsibility for learning.
5. Choose a group of three to five students and review their assess-

ment data. Are their current programs sufficient? What is needed? Begin to plan comprehensive programs for them.

6. Expand the number of students receiving individualized programs as much as you are comfortably able.

REFERENCES YOU CAN USE

Cox, J.; Daniel N.; & Boston, B. (1985). *Educating able learners: Programs and promising practices.* Austin, TX: University of Texas Press.

Dunn, R., & Dunn, K. (1972). *Practical approaches to individualizing instruction: Contracts and other effective teaching strategies.* West Nyack, NY: Parker Publishing Company.

Juntune, J. (Ed.). (1986). *Successful programs for the gifted and talented* (2nd ed.). Circle Pines, MN: National Association for Gifted Children.

Kaplan, S. (1974). *Providing programs for the gifted and talented: A handbook.* Ventura, CA: Office of the Ventura County Superintendent of Schools.

Renzulli, J., & Reis, S. (1986). *The schoolwide enrichment model: A comprehensive plan for educational excellence.* Mansfield Center, CT: Creative Learning Press.

Renzulli, J., & Smith, L. (1979). *A guidebook for developing individualized educational programs for gifted and talented students.* Mansfield Center, CT: Creative Learning Press.

4

Developing
an Environment
for Learning

When it has been determined that program options for the gifted students will include some based in the regular classroom, it becomes essential that you establish a classroom environment that allows all students in the class to feel free to learn and to have the means to learn in their own ways. The environment in which learning takes place is critical to the success of learning. Students are more likely to ask questions in an environment where it is safe to wonder. They are better able to solve problems and to take responsibility for making their own decisions when they have been taught the techniques for doing so. Lifelong learners are more apt to develop in an environment that values learning and teaches students how to make use of materials, resources, time, and their own talents to explore topics of interest to them.

The old adage, "Actions speak louder than words," holds true when we talk about classroom environments. The physical setting may be in a brightly lit, cheerfully decorated room. However, if the students are not allowed to ask questions or explore topics of interest to them, they are not going to feel free to learn. When students are penalized for asking seemingly tangential questions, they are less likely to take that risk in the future. If students are criticized for trying a new approach to an old problem, they will not feel as free the next time to allow their minds to wander and create original thoughts. When gifted students are established as "fine examples" for their classmates and placed on a "they can do no wrong" pedestal, they often feel less inclined to display academic precocity because they fear the hostility of their peers. When they are isolated from others under the guise of individualization or afforded special privileges due to their abilities, they are more likely to be ostracized by the rest of the class.

The environment sets the stage for what can be either successful placement or frustration and difficulty. To increase the chances of the former, the classroom environment should be structured in such a way that the gifted are an integral part of the class yet able to learn at their own ability levels. This will require that the teacher display attitudes of acceptance for individual differences and have managerial expertise in establishing procedures which neither segregate nor inhibit students. It is with this philosophy in mind that the rest of this chapter is presented. The techniques described are those that will establish an environment in which all students can learn within the same structure and still remain a part of the group.

SHIFTING THE FOCUS OF LEARNING TOWARD STUDENTS

Central to successful programs for gifted students is a student-centered learning environment where decisions are made for the benefit of the students and made with their assistance, to the extent possible. In order to make a shift from the traditional teacher-centered structure to a more student-centered approach, some basic alterations must be made in the learning and instructional procedures. In a student-centered environment, the following features are incorporated.

1. *The student is a partner in curricular decision making.* This is accomplished by allowing students options for skill development and an opportunity to determine how part or all of their time is spent. Contracts, conferences, learning packets, and learning centers are all methods that can encourage students to take a more active role in their instruction. After all, it is the students who are ultimately responsible for their own learning. Educators will facilitate this by allowing them the opportunity to learn how to handle this process.

2. *Seating patterns facilitate learning.* In the student-centered environment, the seats in the classroom are arranged so that learning can take place easily and comfortably. This will most likely involve arranging groupings for small and whole group activities, along with places for individualized work and learning stations (see Figure 4–1). When you enter a student-centered classroom, you may find a skill group working at the chalkboard on a vocabulary lesson, students scattered at their desks working on their contracts, and a few students working at the listening center taking their spelling test. The teacher is most likely work-

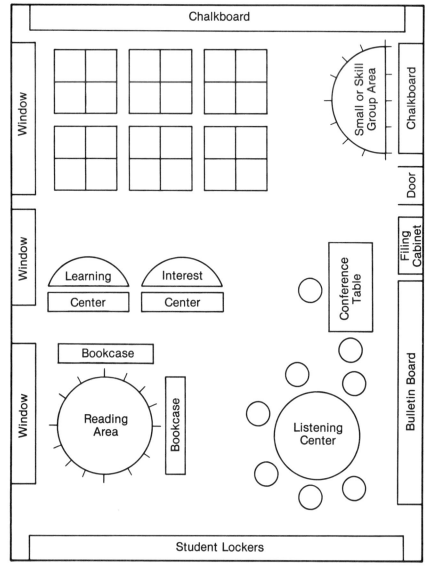

Figure 4-1 Seating Pattern to Facilitate Learning

ing with the skill group, while keeping an eye on the rest of the class.

3. *There is activity and a reasonable level of noise.* It is impossible to conduct a student-centered class without having some activity and degree of noise present in the room. In this type of structure, not all students are doing the same thing at the same time, therefore, movement is often required. Students need to learn how to move about the room without disturbing others. When small group and individualized learning is taking place, it is frequently necessary to have discussions between students as they work on joint problems or answer questions for one another. This will result in voices being heard in the classroom other than the teacher's. In this type of environment, student discussion is encouraged as long as it is appropriate to the task at hand and kept at a reasonable level.

4. *Individualized plans for learning are developed and executed.* A student-centered environment cannot be conducted without attention to the individual learning needs of students. This necessitates the use of individualized learning plans, IEPs, or contracts for all the students in the class. These plans are based on the abilities, achievement levels, and interests of the students. Student time is spent working on learning activities from which they will profit.

5. *Decisions are made mutually by the teacher and student when appropriate and possible.* If one of the goals of education is to teach students to be independent learners, then they must be given the opportunity to practice making decisions and taking responsibility for their learning. This can be accomplished only if students are allowed some control over what they learn and how they learn it. Teachers can extend this opportunity to students by allowing them a part of the decision-making processes in the classroom. This can start by establishing mutually agreed upon class rules, and may be carried through to student-generated learning activities, student self-pacing, and student self-evaluation activities.

By opening up the classroom to the students, the students are given a chance to take responsibility for their own learning and teachers are allowed the opportunity to focus on the learning of individual students. When decisions are made and structures are established within the classroom with the students in mind, student learning is more apt to take place in a way that will benefit the entire body of students.

SELF-DIRECTED LEARNING:
ONE APPROACH TO JOINT DECISION MAKING

It is the position of Treffinger (1975) that "the goal of primary importance in the education of the gifted and talented is to *cultivate self-directed learning.*" He sees this goal culminating in students having a higher motivation to learn, increased abilities to apply learning that takes place in school, and more complete involvement in their learning.

The goals of self-directed learning are designed to foster self-direction and to give students the opportunity to participate in planning goals and objectives of instruction, diagnosing individual needs, and the evaluation of their progress. The student goals are to:

1. Function effectively in one's total environment with peers, teachers, parents, and other adults;

2. Make choices and decisions based on self-knowledge of needs and interests;

3. Assume responsibility for choices and decisions by completing all activities at a satisfactory level of achievement and in an acceptable time frame;

4. Define problems and to determine a course of action for solutions; and

5. Evaluate one's own work and being able to answer the question, "How well can I do what I want to do?" (Treffinger and Barton, 1979, p. 3).

In order to accomplish these goals, the teacher must first recognize that students can be independent. Teachers must also value self-direction, be willing to learn new skills themselves, and learn how to react to children (Treffinger and Barton, 1979). With the goals in mind, then, self-directed learning is based on a basic instructional model (see Figure 4-2). This model of instruction begins with the identification of goals and objectives. After these are determined, entering behavior is assessed and

Figure 4-2 Basic Model of Instruction for Self-Directed Learning

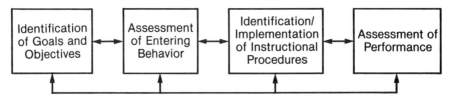

Source: D. Treffinger, "Teaching for Self-Directed Learning: A Priority for the Gifted and Talented," *Gifted Child Quarterly, 19* (1975): 52. Reprinted with permission by National Association for Gifted Children, copyright © 1975.

instruction is implemented. This is followed by an assessment of the performance of the students. Self-directed learning is fostered in students by engaging them in each of these phases to some degree. Treffinger (1975) proposes steps (see Figure 4-3) that can be taken in each of these areas in order to move toward self-directed learning. It is likely that teachers

Figure 4-3   Steps Toward Self-Directed Learning (S-D-L)

Goals and Objectives

Teacher-directed:	Teacher prescribes for class or for pupils.
S-D-L, 1st Step:	Teacher provides choices or options for pupil.
S-D-L, 2nd Step:	Teacher involves pupils in creating options.
S-D-L, 3rd Step:	Learner controls choices, teacher provides resources and materials.

Assessment of Entering Behavior

Teacher-Directed:	Teacher tests and makes specific prescription.
S-D-L, 1st Step:	Teacher diagnoses, provides several options.
S-D-L, 2nd Step:	Teacher and learner use diagnostic conference, tests employed individually if needed.
S-D-L, 3rd Step:	Learner controls diagnosis, consults teacher for assistance when unclear about needs.

Instructional Procedures

Teacher-Directed:	Teacher presents content, provides activities, arranges and supervises practice.
S-D-L, 1st Step:	Teacher provides options for learners to employ independently, with learner's own pace.
S-D-L, 2nd Step:	Teacher provides resources and options, uses student contracts which involve learner in scope, sequence, and pace decisions.
S-D-L, 3rd Step:	Learner defines projects, activities, etc.

Assessing Performance

Teacher-Directed:	Teacher implements evaluation and grades.
S-D-L, 1st Step:	Teacher relates evaluation to objectives, gives student opportunity to respond.
S-D-L, 2nd Step:	Peer-partners used in providing feedback, teacher-student conferences for evaluating.
S-D-L, 3rd Step:	Student self-evaluation.

Source: D. Treffinger, "Teaching for Self-directed Learning: A Priority for the Gifted and Talented," *Gifted Child Quarterly, 19* (1975): 52. Reprinted with permission by National Association for Gifted Children, copyright © 1975.

will feel comfortable at different steps of the process; what is imperative is that teachers find what *combination* of steps works best for them.

Self-directed learning can serve as a model for teachers who wish to design a system for incorporating students more fully into the decision-making processes in the classroom. Although different teachers may employ self-directed learning concepts to differing degrees, moving toward the goal of a self-directed class should result in experiences for students that will enhance their ability to learn.

MANAGING LEARNING IN A STUDENT-CENTERED CLASSROOM

The structure of the classroom procedures should be taken into account when establishing an environment that will stimulate student learning. These structures should allow students the opportunity to experience the processes of learning in addition to the content presented. Our objectives include:

- Students will have the opportunity to learn at their own pace.
- Students will receive instruction that is at their achievement level.
- Students will be given the opportunity to develop independent thinking skills.
- Students will be prepared to be lifelong learners.

It is essential that teachers give students the chance to develop these skills and make these opportunities an integrated part of their daily classroom experiences.

When these objectives are coupled with the practical problems of trying to manage an individualized learning program, tools are needed to organize the structure of learning and mechanisms to monitor and direct the learning activities of the students are essential. Contracts, conferences, management sheets, and student product folders form a management system for this approach to learning. All students can profit by using these tools. Gifted students will benefit greatly and have the capability to use the tools to direct a great deal of their learning. By having the entire class involved in varying degrees, no student appears different from the rest and all students have the benefit of learning the skills it takes to self-monitor, self-direct, self-pace, and self-evaluate their learning.

Contracts

Contracts are written agreements between teachers and students that outline what students will learn, how they will learn it, in what period of time, and how they will be evaluated. Some contracts are detailed learning packages, others are simply plans for learning. Regardless of how detailed a contract is, the purposes are the same. They are to allow students the opportunity to plan with the teacher their own learning, to begin to take responsibility for that learning, and to discover their capabilities to learn on their own as they direct their activities.

The students, then, can use a contract to direct their learning, plan daily activities, self-pace, and self-evaluate their work. Contracts allow the students to engage actively in the decision-making process, directing their course of study. The teacher's role changes from that of content expert to the manager or facilitator of learning—providing the materials, guidance, direction, and quality control function as students learn to take more responsibility for their own work.

Management contracts are developed for the purpose of directing student activities (see Figure 4-4). They tell the student what work should be completed in a given time frame. The content and the schedule are mutually determined by the teacher and the student, usually at a Contract Conference, which is held on a regular basis. At that time, students contract for their work by suggesting what they propose to do and how that will be accomplished. The teacher can set minimum levels of performance that students must meet, and may help the students analyze their capabilities as they plan.

The contract for a second-grade class may serve to illustrate these points. In this class, students have the possibility of contracting in three areas: Reading, Spelling, and Mathematics. All students contract in Reading and Spelling. The students in the cluster group also contract for Mathematics. Once a week, on a rotating basis, the students meet with the teacher to review their work for the week and to prepare a contract for activities in the upcoming week. Cluster group students may be expected to contract for a minimum of three stories per week, along with one spelling lesson and five skill pages in math. The other students may be expected to complete two stories and one spelling lesson per week. Either group can contract for more, but not less. It is up to the teacher and the students to decide on individual contract specifications. Although all students are working from the contract base, they are not all doing the same lessons or the same learning activities. Depending on the rate at which they learn and the interests that they hold, performance levels will vary between students, gifted or not. These differences are tolerated as long as suitable performance levels are maintained.

When instituting contracts in the classroom, it may be best to begin with a few students at a time. Contracts do require new management skills for both the teacher and the students, so it may be beneficial to experiment with a small but manageable group at the beginning. Short, focused contracts are preferable at this initial stage. As students learn to use contracting, they will be better able to handle longer and more com-

Figure 4–4   Sample Management Contract

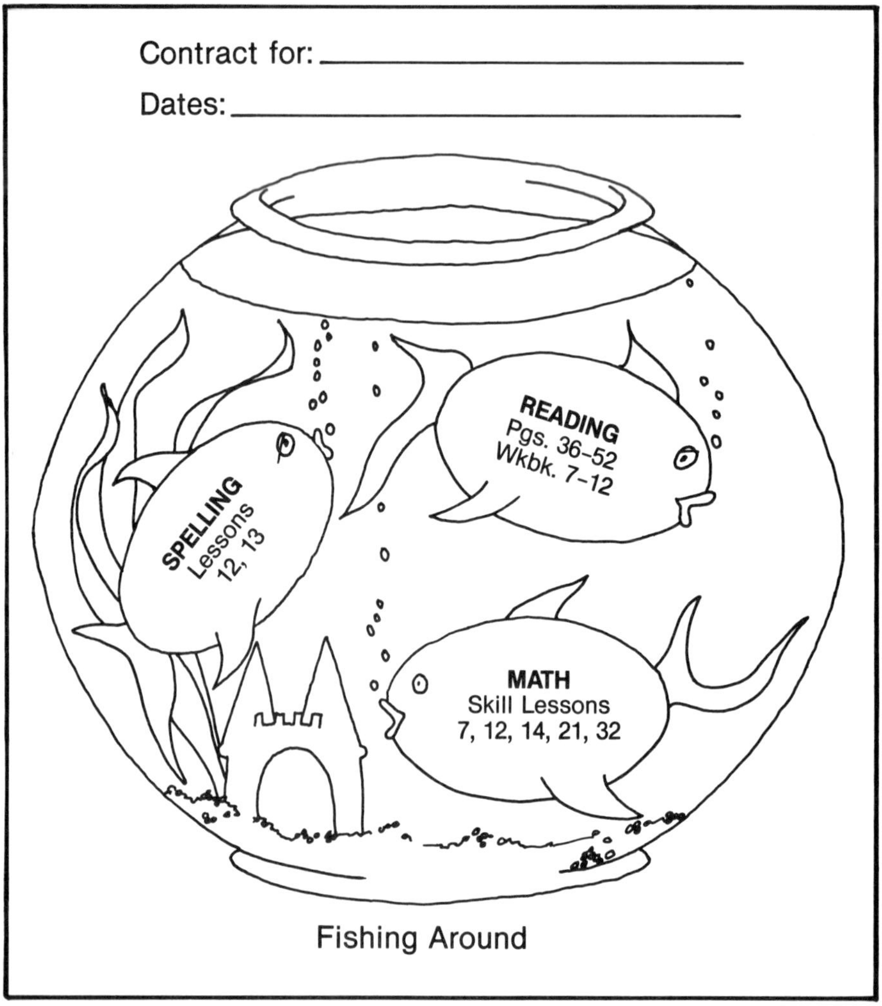

Contract for: _____

Dates: _____

SPELLING
Lessons
12, 13

READING
Pgs. 36–52
Wkbk. 7–12

MATH
Skill Lessons
7, 12, 14, 21, 32

Fishing Around

plex contracts. The teacher will gradually be able to manage increasing numbers of students working in this individualized fashion. This gradual involvement will most likely yield the best success for all involved.

Conferences

Whereas contracts provide the structure for the students to manage their learning, conferences provide the formal monitoring function and a regular time at which teachers can meet individually with students on a predetermined basis. Conferences can be used for many purposes.

Monitoring student work is a primary function served by conferences. During the time spent with the students, the teacher must make sure that the students understand the content they are responsible for on their contracts. Since different students contract for varying amounts of work, the conference time needed for monitoring will also vary. Reading workbooks can be checked, oral reading listened to, comprehension questions asked, vocabulary tests given, mathematics tests reviewed, or independent studies discussed during this time (see Figure 4–5). The teacher should be able to spot any potential trouble areas, tutor the student in skill-deficit areas, and reward the good work that the students have produced. Conferences are a time for intensive work and review. They also give the students and teachers an opportunity to assess the students' work formally and to double-check on the informal monitorings that have occurred during the rest of the week.

Planning future work is another function that conferences can serve for teachers and students. They provide the time for the students and teachers to review what the students have accomplished during the week, and write the contract for the next week. The time can be used to help the students gain understanding of their capabilities, as they review their progress. The conference is a time for the students to determine, with the teacher's guidance, if they are attempting to do a reasonable amount of work in a week, too much, or not enough. Planning involves evaluating

Figure 4–5   Sample Oral Reading Checklist

SKILL	DATE						
Even pace							
Clearness							
Expression							
Obeys punctuation							
Finger pointing							
Comprehension							
Comments:							

past performance and determining a course of action for the future. Students are likely to find that it will take time to understand their capabilities fully, and they will need the assistance of the teacher in making planning decisions. Planning for the week in the curricular areas should be formalized by writing down the agreed upon work on the form. Conference time used to plan independent studies or individualized learning activities should also result in a written agreement for the week's work. The teacher will want to keep a record of these forms. In this way, the students will have a reference source to remind them of their plan, and the teachers will have a guide for their own planning of resources and time allotments.

Finally, conferences can give the students and the teacher the opportunity to talk together. Conferences should never be so task-directed that the participants lose the chance to talk informally about what is on their minds. Although this time is not for formal counseling, it can be used to discover what concerns and triumphs students may be experiencing, and how the teacher can help them overcome any problems. The time can be used as a one-on-one exchange of ideas and can serve as a chance to become more involved in helping the students know themselves, evaluate their capabilities, and make decisions.

Management Sheets

Management sheets are forms that the teacher can devise to give the students a vehicle through which they can self-pace and self-track their work (see Figure 4–6). They are used as the students progress through their work in order to answer the question, "What do I do next?" A well-constructed management sheet will outline the progression of work so that the students can answer that question by simply consulting the form.

It is most helpful to have management sheets prepared in advance for the areas in which the students are contracting. For example, if the students are using contracts for their reading, they will need management sheets for the books they are reading. Mathematics will also require that a sheet be constructed by chapter, book, or skill. Independent investigations will proceed more easily if a management sheet is constructed for the study, outlining a plan of attack for the project.

Management sheets are brought to the conferences and are used as a reference point for the week's planning. If the minimum number of stories that students are to read is two, then the teacher and students can go to their management sheets and block off those stories on the form. If the students finish that work prior to the next scheduled conference time, the management sheet will show what work follows, so the students can proceed on their own. If an open-ended contract is being used, the

Figure 4-6   Sample Management Sheet for Mathematics

Name:

Page	Directions	Items	Number	Score	Miss More Than	Do	Number	Score
256	Study example at top of page. Then complete problems.	1–15	15		2	16–30	15	
257	Read story problems carefully!	Even 2–20	10		1	Odd 1–19	10	
258	See teacher for lesson.	1–25	25		3	Study Sheet #52	15	
Test #11	Get test from box. Hand in test with folder. Do not continue until test is graded.	1–25	25					
259	Study review problems on page.	1–20	20		1	21–32	12	

management sheet provides the plan for the progression of skills and the work that will take place on a daily basis.

Management sheets free the teacher from writing the assignments on the board everyday, and are a far more subtle way of allowing students to work at varying levels without calling attention to that fact. All students in the classroom have management sheets; however, some may be for more advanced work. They also allow students the opportunity to learn how to make decisions about their learning. Each day when they begin their work, *the students* must decide what they will do; the teacher does not give them this information. When they have completed the work assigned through the contract and conference, they make the decision about what they will do next. If they decide to continue on to another story in the reading book or the next math page, they have the information in front of them that tells them what comes next. The responsibility is the students'—the management sheets allow them to exercise that responsibility more fully.

Student Product Folders

A weekly accounting of the students' activities at the conference time is not sufficient monitoring for most teachers. Since the students are creating work daily, they feel the need to look at it daily. This is easily accomplished by having students compile a product folder during the course of the day. It should include their management sheets, contracts, independent study plans, and any other papers that they have worked on or completed. For example, you might find a notebook paper with self-corrected math problems written on the page, skill sheets that you assigned to the small group on syllabification, and a book report in the making. When these are turned in at the end of the day, you can review them and return them for the next day's work, corrected and with comments. This serves the monitoring function on a daily basis and gives the students a convenient way to organize their work and get timely comments on it.

TEACHER'S RESPONSIBILITIES
TO ENVIRONMENTAL CONCERNS

The teacher plays a central role in establishing the environment in the classroom. It is the teacher who must see the students as individuals and treat them with respect; it is the teacher who must adopt the position that all students are of equal value and deserve an education commensurate with their abilities. This will mean providing materials at appropriate levels, high or low, and activities that will further student learning. It also requires the teacher to construct an environment in which different levels of learning can take place without students feeling different because they are at the high or low end. Teachers must adopt the attitude that learning is an ongoing and fun experience. The classroom becomes the laboratory for learning and is interactive with the students. Materials are housed in such a way that the students can find and use them and learning can take place. Quiet areas and areas where talking is permitted are established. Areas to display work are prominent and students may place their own work there for others to see. This accepting attitude is critical for learning. An accompanying environment is necessary for students to take advantage of that attitude in a real way.

The teacher's role becomes one of *facilitator* of learning. No longer is it the responsibility of the teacher to give students all the information they will need to know through lecture alone. Rather, the teacher is responsible for providing direction through conferences, contracts, management sheets, and discussions. In addition, the teacher should provide the materials for the students or help the students identify the resources they will need; serve as the quality control monitor over the students' work and plans; and be their ombudsman in matters that require some negotiation or confrontation.

STUDENTS' RESPONSIBILITIES TO ENVIRONMENTAL CONCERNS

Students also have responsibility for making the environment in their classrooms one in which learning can flourish. They play an active role in setting the tone for learning and they affect the conditions under which instruction takes place. Three areas of responsibility are in the forefront. First, the students must be cooperative. They must commit themselves to each other, the teacher, and the classroom in a way that is respectful and productive. Most students are quite willing to be a part of the group, cooperate with the other students, and interact meaningfully with others during the course of a day. When cooperative spirits are missing, it is very difficult to function in the manner that is necessary for learning. If cooperation is a behavior that is unfamiliar to them, students should be taught how to do so.

Second, the students must actually take responsibility for their own learning. It is one thing to provide the circumstances under which they can do so; it is an entirely different matter to really get them to do it. Students are often conditioned to look to the teacher as the curricular leader and sole decision maker in the classroom. Giving them that responsibility may initially be greeted with some skepticism by the students. But they will soon come to understand that it is a power they had all along. It cannot be ignored that some students would rather not take responsibility for their own learning due to laziness or fear of the consequences. These students need to be gently but firmly nudged to take a progressively more active role. For the conditions of learning to be stimulating to the students, they must understand that they are the primary participants and hold the keys to learning.

The last critical responsibility of students to the environment is that of maintaining the classroom in a reasonable fashion. When students are actively using the classroom, the materials, and the space throughout the room, they must be responsible for its upkeep. Giving students individual jobs can make this task easier, but it does not replace the responsibility each student has to making sure that the work spaces are orderly and that materials are returned in useable condition for the next student. Chaos and messiness will work against the learning process. Organized chaos, on the other hand, may help!

SUMMARY

The environment in the classroom envelops all else that occurs within its walls; it permeates all that we do and it has a powerful impact on the students. What we do and say reflect the attitudes we bring to the students. Some attitudes block the learning of children, whereas others facilitate the learning process. It is critical that teachers who have gifted students in their classrooms adopt attitudes toward these students that are accepting of individual differences while allowing for the growth of all students.

The physical environment is also integral to providing an atmosphere in which learning can flourish. It should be designed so that students can use the space in a manner that is profitable to them. Materials, books, and seating arrangements are among the areas that must be considered and made responsive to student needs.

Classroom structures are also important. With the goals of teaching children to be lifelong and independent learners so central to the mission of the class, it is imperative that they be given the opportunity to learn the skills necessary to do so. Allowing students to be responsible for their learning is the first step in this process.

ACTION STEPS

1. Take stock. What kind of environment do you find in the regular classroom? Is it accepting of individual differences? Do students feel free to explore, take risks, and be themselves? If you are not sure, ask them through a survey or opinion poll.

2. If students are not included in the decision-making processes,

consider doing so. Let them know that it is they who are responsible for their learning.

3. Try using contracting with a few students. See how it works with them, then add a few more.

4. Select a subject area and begin to design management sheets. Mathematics is a good place to start. Commit yourself to completing the task for one subject area this year. Add another next year. (Reading is a logical follow up.)

5. Sit back and enjoy the progress the students are making in their learning and self-management skills.

REFERENCES YOU CAN USE

Clark, B. (1986). *Optimizing learning.* Columbus, OH: Merrill Publishing Company.

Dean, D. (Ed.). (1982). *Helping teachers manage classrooms.* Alexandria, VA: Association for Supervision and Curriculum Development.

Elkind, D. (1981). *The hurried child: Growing up too fast too soon.* Reading, MA: Addison-Wesley.

Galyean, B. (1983). *Mind sight: Learning through imaging.* Long Beach, CA: Center for Integrative Learning.

Webb, J,; Meckstroth, E.; & Tolan, S. (1982). *Guiding the gifted.* Columbus, OH: Ohio Psychology Publications Company.

PART TWO

Selecting the Programs

Creating a "fit" between the student profiles of ability and the programs available for the gifted and talented is among the most important tasks that educators undertake in making program decisions for these students. Gifted and talented students have a large variety of educational needs that correspond with the range of abilities and interests they display. One type of program cannot hope to meet all the requirements of these students. Therefore, mosaics of programming options should be built from which students and teachers may choose the programs that best suit individual profiles of ability.

The mosaics should include programs that correspond to the learning characteristics of the gifted. Among those that most distinguish this group are: they learn more quickly, in greater depth, and exhibit interests that differ from their age-peers. The three chapters in this section describe the types of programs that build on these characteristics.

Flexible pacing is a key provision of successful programming for the gifted in regular classrooms or special programs. These students tend to learn more quickly than other students, need fewer repetitions, and finish their work ahead of the other students in their classes. In order to avoid behavior or attitudinal problems and to assure meaningful learning occurs, some provision must be made so that students can learn at their own rates and at the levels at which they are capable. Chapter 5 lists such programs and tells how they contribute to assembling a programming mosaic.

Varying the depth at which students can learn is another way to differentiate programs for the gifted, which is the topic of Chapter 6. These students have the capability and desire to know about topics in depth. Some of the ways in which they are identified are their propensity to ask questions, the fervor with which they pursue information about topics in which they have interest, and their tendencies to maintain steadfast in their areas of interest across their lifetimes from being avid collectors as children to being equally dedicated to vocations and avocations as adults. Finding ways to allow such exploration within the classroom is a challenge that teachers of the gifted face daily. To make this process easier, Chapter 6 presents suggestions for program configurations.

Chapter 7 discusses programs that will provide structures through which students can pursue their interests. The topics typically of interest to gifted and talented students more closely typify topics of interest to older students. Therefore, it becomes incumbent on the teacher to find ways to accommodate this tendency while maintaining the more traditional academic components of their programming efforts.

Combining these types of programs into a mosaic of options will bring balanced educational experiences to the gifted. One approach is not sufficient, for the students differ in what they require and the types of programs from which they can profit. Establishing options in each of the categories will assure that each student's programming needs will be more fully met.

5

Adjusting the Pace of Learning

One of the first qualities noticed about gifted students is that they learn new information very quickly. Skills that normally take a week to present may be fully understood after one class period. Assignments designed to last for two weeks may be completed overnight, or a learning center that is planned for six weeks of use may be finished in a week's time. These students are often heard asking the familiar question, "What do I do now? I've finished my work."

One way to respond to that question is by instituting programs within and outside of the regular classroom setting that will allow students to work through their assignments at their own pace. This is called *flexible pacing*. The ideal situation exists when an entire school is set up to facilitate the pace at which students learn. In such settings, teachers cooperate to combine their expertise and materials so that the students have access to whatever they need. Team planning is often found, along with joint filing cabinets and materials cupboards. Rarely is there a certain topic, unit, or reading book that is the sole domain of a particular teacher or grade level. Principals are the key people in encouraging this type of sharing and interaction among teachers and staff, for it is they who set the climate for instruction in their schools.

If such a climate does not exist, gifted students can still receive instruction at an appropriate pace. However, under these conditions, it is the classroom teacher (along with the support staff and all the materials that can be mustered) who takes the major responsibility for assuring that flexible pacing exists. Although the options for programming in this situation are more limited, they are nonetheless useful to the students. Implementing a solid program will help avoid the predictable outcomes seen in students who are stifled in their learning. Some become bored and will not try even when challenged; they are content to work in materials at grade level and avoid those that make them think or learn new concepts. Others become careless in their work; assignments that should be easily completed in accurate form are done sloppily and are filled with errors. Teachers and parents become confused when these bright students miss math problems that are easily within their levels of ability, or when students simply "forget" to complete a report that was assigned a month ago. There are other highly able students who say nothing and go along with the set pace, even though it can be at great expense for them. In each of these instances, the gifted students are adapting to an environment that does not allow them to flourish, plodding along at a pace that is too slow. They respond by losing interest, doing the minimal amount of work needed to get by, becoming behavior problems, or by simply acquiescing and becoming like the more average students for whom the pace is appropriate. By employing the concept of flexible pacing, students are able to work at a pace that is comfortable to them, use materials geared to their instructional levels, and continually be challenged in their learning.

Gifted and talented students are not alone in their need for flexible pacing of instruction. All students learn at differing paces and in differing ways. Therefore, consideration should be given to the pace of instruction for all the students in the class. It is very likely that accommodations are already being made in most classes. The question to be posed and pondered is if that flexibility is great enough or if some students are being held back from learning at the pace at which they are capable. A listing and description of programs that can introduce flexible pacing into the regular classroom environment follows. Beginning with one or a combination of options can start the process of flexible pacing in the classroom and insure that gifted and talented students will not be frustrated or bored by instruction that is too easy or too slow. The result can be students who are active and self-directed in their learning.

PROGRAM OPTIONS FOR FLEXIBLE PACING

Flexible pacing is more than just a means of moving students through subjects at an accelerated pace. It is the mechanism through which information is delivered at the students' instructional levels *and* at a pace that is appropriate for them. The following list of program designs is not inclusive, but it does reflect the basic patterns that are used to accomplish the goal of managing the learning of students in such a way that the pace at which they learn is their own.

Programs within the Classroom

Curriculum compacting.   Renzulli and Smith (1979) introduced the idea of curriculum compacting in order to provide gifted students with a mechanism through which they could cover the regular classroom curriculum in a faster or different manner. "In its simplest form, compacting consists of determining through formal and informal assessment procedures the curricular content areas that some students have already mastered or might be able to master through modified approaches to instruction" (Renzulli, Reis, and Smith, 1981, p. 78). There are three phases to this program: assessment of skill levels, strategies to cover curriculum, and alternatives for enrichment and/or acceleration (see Figure 5-1).

When a teacher has a student who has already mastered much of the content that will be taught or who can go through the materials more quickly than the other students, curriculum compacting can be used to assure that the student will not have to spend time on content that is already known and can use that time to better advantage. Careful assessment of student skills is the first step in determining if the student has mastered the content under consideration. If that has been done, as measured through a form of criterion-referenced testing, then alternative plans can be investigated. Options could include the student using other materials or being involved with other activities in the same content area, progressing to more difficult objectives and skills, remediating skills that need extra work, or doing assignments in another area. Thus, curriculum compacting can be used effectively for both acceleration and enrichment purposes.

In one instance, a student who was particularly adept at science and involved with an extensive experiment looking at factors that influence the life span of a fruit fly, was scheduled for a unit on the research process. The teacher chose to use curriculum compacting to determine the extent to which the student should be engaged in the unit. After assessment, it was obvious that the student had mastered the content of the unit and had produced extensive examples of applying the content to his own experiments. Therefore, his responsibilities during the unit included working as a lab assistant to the teacher, in which he was required to perform demonstration experiments for the class, prepare the materials, log the outcomes of the experiments, and spend time furthering his own investigations, through an independent study process, either on his fruit fly research or another topic of his choosing. The only stipulation made was that he document the manner in which he adhered to the scientific process.

Self-Instructional Programs. Another technique that can be used within the regular classroom to adjust the pace of learning is through self-instructional systems. Programmed instruction, computer-assisted instruction, correspondence courses, and learning packets (or learning contracts) are a few of the methods available. There are some distinct advantages to including these procedures among the programming options for the gifted. They result in flexibility in both the pace of instruc-

Figure 5-1   Curriculum Compacting Form

Individual Educational Programming Guide The Compactor		
Name _____ Age __ Teacher(s) _____ School _____ Grade __ Parent(s) _____		Individual Conference Dates and Persons Participating in Planning of IEP __ __ __ __
Curriculum Areas to be Considered for Compacting. Provide a brief description of basic material to be covered during this marking period and the assessment information or evidence that suggests the need for compacting.	*Procedures for Compacting Basic Material.* Describe activities that will be used to guarantee proficiency in basic curricular areas.	*Acceleration and/or Enrichment Activities.* Describe activities that will be used to provide advanced level learning experiences in each area of the regular curriculum.

Source: J. Renzulli, S. Reis, and L. Smith, *The Revolving Door Identification Model* (Mansfield Center, Conn.: Creative Learning Press, 1981), p. 79. Reprinted with permission from Creative Learning Press, copyright © 1981.

tion and the topics that can be introduced and mastered by the students. Parke (1983) found that primary-aged gifted students can self-instruct mathematics successfully when using a management system to assist them. Language arts areas have also been successfully taught through such methods.

Programmed instruction currently appears most often in the form of computer-assisted instruction. Whether in workbooks or on a computer monitor, the strategy is the same. Students are introduced to distinct bits of information to learn, practice trials are presented, and performance levels are assessed. As students master skills, they advance to more diffi-cult and complex skills, and remedial loops are employed when mastery has not been attained. The rate at which they move through the material is determined by their own level of competency. Many commercial pro-grams are available and are in abundance in schools today. Gifted stu-dents can be seen sitting at computer terminals working feverishly at multiplication tables or reading stories to determine the main idea. Work-ing on these high-interest, immediately reinforcing programs keeps the students rapt in their work and highly motivated to learn more difficult concepts. The biggest problem teachers face when working with com-puter-based programs is tearing students away from the machines and finding time for all students to participate.

Correspondence courses, long available for adult learners, are now available for students of middle-school age. These are usually sponsored through universities or colleges for students of exceptional ability who do not have access to certain courses within their geographic area. They register for the correspondence course and receive materials through the mail which they complete and return to the sponsoring institution. Reac-tion and comments are returned to them throughout the course time. The assignments, along with telephone and computer conferences and tutor-ing, are used as means of monitoring progress. Exams and papers are often required as proof of mastery, and pass/fail or satisfactory/unsatis-factory grades are usually given. Classes in history, literature, mathemat-ics, and languages are among the typical course offerings. Some home schools do accept these credits, but usually students who choose to take advantage of such learning opportunities do so on their own time without expectation of credit toward graduation.

Learning packets, or learning contracts (as they are sometimes called), are another means of self-instruction. Generally, they focus on an individual topic or skill that the students learn through a progression of steps and activities (see Figure 5–2). Dunn and Dunn (1975) list the fol-lowing components of a learning packet:

1. Diagnostic test;
2. Behavioral objectives written for the child;

Figure 5-2   Sample Management Form for Learning Packet

Learning Packet

Name _____   Date _____

Topic _____

Objectives:

1. _____

2. _____

3. _____

Resources for You to Use:

_____

_____

Activities to Complete: Date Due: Evaluation:

_____   _____   _____

_____   _____   _____

_____   _____   _____

How You Will Report Your Progress: When:

_____   _____

_____   _____

How You Will Evaluate Your Work:

_____

Signed:

_____   _____
Student   Teacher

3. Resource alternatives;
4. Activity alternatives;
5. Reporting alternatives;
6. Self-assessment inventory;
7. Teacher assessment; and *if necessary*
8. Enrichment or review materials (p. 33).

Learning packets can be used with curriculum compacting or with management contracts in subjects that need remediation or that are areas of expertise or interest. Regardless, students have control over the pace of instruction, and all students need not progress at the same rate.

The gifted students' abilities to be self-directed enhance their capability for this type of program. Be advised that gifted students should not be involved in self-instructional programs to the exclusion of all other types of instruction. They also need to be part of the classroom. Self-instruction should be seen as only one part of their programming.

Advanced Materials.   By making use of materials more advanced than those commonly found at grade level, teachers have long dealt with students who learn more quickly. Keeping a stockpile of intriguing books, puzzles, games, and manipulatives will leave the teacher prepared to respond to the "What do I do next?" questions. One teacher kept a learning center in the back of the room titled "Stumpers" in which she rotated challenging laminated file folder activities for the students. When they were done with their work, they always had that center as an option. The activities were constantly changed, so the challenge was always fresh. Having stimulating materials at the students' disposal gives them the opportunity to find their own learning and direction through their many discoveries.

One key to making this approach a success is to assure that the materials are available to the students. By letting them know what is available and how to use the resources and equipment, they can investigate on their own without worrying about interrupting the teacher with questions or for permission. The media specialist, librarian, special teachers, and parents can be your allies in providing materials with special interest and enticement.

Programs Involving the Whole School

Continuous Progress Curriculum.   The ultimate program for managing the speed at which students learn is continuous progress curriculum. In this program, instruction is delivered in such a way that students move through the curriculum according to their assessed skill levels rather than their grade levels. This form of individualization is based on regular assessment of skill levels and is diagnostic-prescriptive in nature. Students engaged in this approach to learning take placement tests to determine their skill level, and from these tests and teacher judgments, the curriculum is planned. There are no "third grade" skills or "fifth grade" materials. Everything is fair game for everybody; the only requirement for using certain materials is that the students' skills warrant the use.

After the students have been assessed and the skills that need to be learned are determined, skill groups or individual assignments are established for instruction. As students master one skill or a group of skills, they proceed to other skills that, based on the ongoing assessments, need their attention. They go as far as their abilities will take them without regard for traditionally defined limits of grade level instruction. Management sheets (see Figure 4-7), contracts, and conferences are often found in this program in order to manage the students' progress. Individual skill cards, listing the skills in the assessment and those that have been mastered, are also essential. They provide the means through which subsequent teachers or team members know of the students' skill levels (see Figure 5-3).

Obviously, this is a program that takes coordination beyond a single teacher. Full school involvement is usually necessary; the materials and assessments need to be pooled so that every teacher has access to them. Also, there is a great need for a student tracking system that enables subsequent teachers to know the skill areas that have been mastered by the students so that further instruction can be planned.

Figure 5-3   Sample Skill Card in Spelling

	Instruction Level		
Skill	Mastery	Instructional	Frustration
Alphabetical Order			
Building Words			
Compound Words			
Homonyms			
Prefixes			
Suffixes			
Vocabulary Development			

Fast-Paced Classes.   Some gifted students are best served in subject-based classes that move at a fast pace. These classes are only for students who have advanced knowledge in the subject and are able to handle the rigor of dealing with information quickly. Acceleration in content *and* speed are found in these classes, therefore, students must be prepared for the intensity of the experience.

Fast-paced classes are run in a variety of ways. Some are organized on an individualized basis, using management sheets and allowing students to go through the materials as quickly as they wish, getting tutoring as indicated by tests or themselves. Other fast-paced classes are run on a more formal basis, with the teacher giving demonstrations and assignments based on the lesson of the day. Many are sponsored by school districts or consortia and are offered on a pullout basis. Colleges and universities also hold these classes in the summer or on Saturdays.

In this arrangement, extensive homework is the norm. Students are expected to dedicate a great deal of time and effort to the course in and out of class. Thus, it becomes imperative that the students and the parents know the requirements of the class prior to enrolling. This can best be handled in an interview situation or through a parent meeting. Still, there will be students who find the demands of the course more than they wish to handle. These students should be given the option of dropping the course, following a meeting with the student and his or her parents.

Most fast-paced classes seem to fall into the areas of (but should not be limited to) mathematics and computer science, and are usually not attempted until students reach the seventh or eighth grade. In a few unusual instances, elementary-aged students may be eligible. An example of such programming can be found in the mathematics classes offered through the Talent Search program (Stanley, Keating, and Fox, 1974). In this program, junior high school students are placed in advanced classes based on their high scores on the *Scholastic Aptitude Test.* A typical class progression might have students in the seventh grade taking seventh and eighth grade mathematics during the same academic year. Eighth grade mathematics is then a course in Algebra, accelerating the student one year in mathematics. Another series of classes often found combines Algebra I and Algebra II into a one-year course of study, giving students time to take five high school years of mathematics.

Again, this type of program is only for a select population who has the ability and motivation to be part of such an environment. It is one method to accommodate the speed at which some students learn. Be cautioned that it also takes very special teachers to instruct these classes, for the challenge of teaching these students is great.

Early Admission.   Another strategy that can be used to expedite students' learning is through early admission. These programs have procedures by which students qualify for entry into school at an earlier age or higher grade than normal. Early admission is not a means to move through curricula faster, as are the other programs that have been discussed; it is merely a devise for starting students into school at an earlier age. The rationale for this approach is: If gifted students begin school at an earlier age, they will already be grouped with students who are of a more similar mental age; thus, they will be involved with curricula and programs that are more in line with their abilities. In this schema, for example, following a comprehensive assessment battery with a psychologist, a particularly precocious four-year-old might be allowed to enter kindergarten, or a five-year-old might go directly to first grade without spending a year in kindergarten.

Early admissions are not offered in all school districts, and are rarely publicized in the ones that do. All available programs consist of a formal application process, intensive screening through assessment batteries, psychological evaluation and recommendation, and interviews with the prospective students and their parents. There is controversy as to whether such programs are in the best interest of the students, as they do make intellectual and physical demands on the students that may be quite challenging. To add to the uncertainty, testing students at such a young age is a questionable practice, as the results on the instruments are less reliable. However, for a few students of high ability and advanced development, this strategy can result in appropriate placements, and it may avoid later need for grade skipping.

Multiaged Groupings.   Some grouping patterns or class configurations will enhance a teacher's ability to institute flexible pacing procedures. Multiaged classes is one such technique. Here, students from two or three contiguous grades are grouped into homerooms with teachers working on a team-teaching basis to provide instruction. Primary students (grades 1–3) may be grouped together in homeroom classes and then regrouped among those classes for instruction based on skill levels. Regardless of their ages, students who need instruction in a particular skill are pulled together for that work. This grouping pattern is highly compatible with continuous progress curricula. The gifted are more likely to be placed in instructional settings that are appropriately paced because there is a greater range of student abilities and, therefore, instruction.

Cross-level grouping is another way to assemble multiaged classes. These patterns are developed by instituting school-wide policies that allow students to leave their classrooms for part of the day in order to receive instruction from another teacher at a higher level. The high-ability first-grade reader may go to a third-grade class for reading, and the adept sixth-grade mathematician may take pre-algebra with the eighth graders. Such flexibility in grouping makes it possible for students to be placed in environments that are more compatible to the rate at which they can learn. Whole school cooperation is necessary, but not whole school participation. Such a program can also be organized between two teachers and be effective for the students involved.

ASSEMBLING THE MOSAIC

A facet of the program mosaic, then, should respond to the varying paces at which students learn. The gifted tend to learn quickly and are able to comprehend concepts with fewer repetitions than most students. Therefore, the types of programs they are involved in and the instruction within those programs may have to be more flexible in the way students proceed. Depending on the grade level in question, the characteristics of the particular school and classroom, and the needs of the student and teacher, different options can become part of the programming mosaic from which students and teachers can choose (see Table 5-1). These, too, may differ from classroom to classroom and year to year, depending on the situation at the time; however, an overall commitment to flexible pacing should be ongoing.

Whole school or district-wide plans for the programming mosaic should be in place, along with individual teacher plans. In that way, students will not be handicapped by uneven expectations and access to materials. Students who are allowed to progress at their own pace, only to be placed back in grade-level work the following year, experience a great deal of frustration. It is far easier on all concerned when a comprehensive strategy is in place that is adhered to by the entire staff and school

Table 5-1   Possible Program Combinations for Flexible Pacing

Grade Level	Progams
Kindergarten	Advanced Materials Cross-level Grouping in Reading Early Admissions
Third	Learning Packets on World Capitals Multiaged Classes Computer-Assisted Instruction (SRA Mathematics)
Sixth	Correspondence Course through Talent Search Computer-Assisted Instruction (Math, Computers, French) Advanced Materials Cross-level Grouping in Math and Reading

administration. This can be coordinated through a curriculum council, department heads, or at teachers' meetings. Whatever strategy is used, the plan and monitoring will result in students being free to learn at their own levels and at their own paces.

TEACHER'S RESPONSIBILITIES TO ADJUSTING THE PACE OF LEARNING

The basic responsibilities that teachers have toward adjusting the pace of learning are twofold: establishing the circumstances under which it can happen and establishing an attitude that will allow it. Hopefully, an accepting attitude is already in place, so the focus can be on the circumstances.

Finding resources and materials for learning is a large part of the responsibility that teachers hold in this area. The task is made more simple if the teachers are in a team-teaching or cooperative situation. In this instance it is a matter of locating, cataloging, and making readily accessible the materials that they jointly find. When there is no support available, the task is far more difficult. It can be helped along, however, with the assistance of the media and library personnel and other instructional specialists. Principals can be of great help in mediating the inevitable problems associated with introducing subject matter that is in the scope and sequence of another grade level.

Establishing management systems, like those described in Chapter 4, is another major component of what the teacher can do to assure flexible pacing. Such systems not only help the teacher know what each student is doing, but the students are also directed through the materials so that they know what to do. Keeping the information, such as assessment data, up to date can be time consuming, but it is important so that decisions can be made, based on the data, at any time.

Monitoring progress is another teacher duty. Determining if students are progressing too quickly, not quickly enough, or at a reasonable pace takes tracking. Observing students at work and meeting with them on a regular basis can help the monitoring process. Frequent criterion-referenced tests and student self-assessments can also aid in the monitoring function.

Cooperating with other professionals is essential to successfully instituting programs dealing with pace. It is vital to keep communication lines open to teachers in the contiguous grades into which some of your students might be sent for special classes or from whom you may wish to borrow some materials or equipment. Other staff people also play a central role and should be dealt with on a professional basis. You never know when you will need a special assist in developing a placement for a student or in procuring a special book for your library.

Keeping parents informed, the last teacher responsibility, is also important when programs are designed to take students through curriculum more rapidly. This can cause a strain on the students, and parents need to know what to expect and how the students are doing. Intermittent notes, calls, or meetings will do the job nicely, both when there are problems and when the students are doing well.

STUDENTS' RESPONSIBILITY
TO ADJUSTING THE PACE OF LEARNING

The major responsibility students have in programs that involve flexible pacing is to develop self-management skills. This can begin when students enter school and should continue throughout their schooling. The students must learn to monitor their own progress, evaluate that progress, make judgments as to how much time to spend in a given area, ask for help when they need it, and persist in studying when the material gets difficult. These are not easy tasks, but ones that are essential to becoming independent learners.

In addition, students have the responsibility to seek enrichment activities *as well as* accelerated activities. Some students fall into the trap of just wanting to go through the basal textbooks as quickly as possible without taking time to notice the nuances and explore subjects in depth. It may take encouragement (or strong tactics!) from teachers and parents to instill an appreciation for breadth. Nevertheless, the balance is important and should not be sacrificed for speed alone.

SUMMARY

Students learn at many differing paces. Gifted students, in particular, learn quickly and, with few repetitions, understand and can use concepts. When they are not allowed to progress on to new topics and skills, they can become bored and disinterested in their schooling. Therefore, it is important to include programs within a multiple options plan that will give students flexibility in the pace at which they learn.

Both school-wide and classroom-based programming options are available to this end. Each has its own purposes and serves the audience in its own way. Combining these approaches and matching them to the student profiles can result in many options for learning at paces that are appropriate for the students involved. Cooperation among teachers and with the administration is essential because flexible pacing invariably means teachers will be using materials and teaching skills that are typically the domain of another teacher or another grade level. However, when adjusting the pace of learning, student needs are paramount; traditional grade-level distinctions are secondary.

ACTION STEPS

1. Review the programs currently in place in your school district that can benefit the students. Do they allow students to work at their own pace or give you an outlet for advanced student placements?
2. Make a list of all the programs that will help you give students a flexibly paced program.
3. Assess classroom mechanics. Are students working at appropriate levels and at paces that are compatible with their ability? If not, make a plan for change and begin to make one alteration now.
4. Encourage co-workers to join you in a cooperative effort in this regard. Make plans for cross-level grouping, continuous progress curriculum, student exchanges, or joint filing cabinets for combining and sharing materials.
5. Meet with the curriculum planning committee and work with them to institute school-wide procedures for flexible pacing.

REFERENCES YOU CAN USE

Benbow, C., & Stanley, J. (1983). *Academic precocity: Aspects of its development.* Baltimore, MD: Johns Hopkins University Press.

Cox, J. (1982). Continuous progress and nongraded schools. *G/C/T,* 25 (November/December), 15–21.

Feldhusen, J. (Ed.). (1985). *Toward excellence in gifted education.* Denver, CO: Love Publishing Company.

Maker, J. (Ed.). (1986). *Critical issues in gifted education: Defensible programs for the gifted.* Rockville, MD: Aspen Publications.

Smith, L. (No date). *A seminar on creating and implementing a continuous progress program in your elementary school.* Englewood, CO: Educational Consulting Associates, Inc.

6

Varying the Depth
of Learning

The depth at which gifted and talented students are able to learn may vary from the other students in the classroom. Many of the characteristics that indicate giftedness relate to this ability. For example, gifted students may ask questions that show unusual insight into the subject matter being discussed. They readily see connections between seemingly unconnected concepts and are able to draw generalizations about their discoveries. Knowledge beyond that which would be expected is usually found in areas of interest to them, be it mammals or quadratic equations.

Not only do gifted students have the ability to comprehend at a greater depth than many other students, they also have a need to be given that opportunity. They complain of feeling stifled in environments that do not allow in-depth explorations and that concentrate only on basic skills. These students thrive when investigating topics of interest to them in great detail, and the insatiable curiosity they exhibit leads them through the maze of learning and results in their having unusual understandings and insights into their work.

As with flexible pacing, it is important to consider possibilities for varying the depth at which students can learn when planning programs for gifted and talented students in regular classrooms. Programming options should respond to the students' desire to learn some topics in greater depth than the rest of the class. Many options are in use and have been used successfully with this population for years.

Unlike some of the strategies for flexible pacing, a teacher *can* accommodate the different depths of learning without the cooperation of other people on the staff. Although it is generally profitable to enter into cooperative arrangements (in this case, too), an individual teacher can do many things to respond to the matter of learning depth. When cooperative efforts are possible, the learning of the students will ultimately be enhanced as the skills of many teachers are brought to bear on the students.

It is not just the gifted and talented students who will profit from a programmatic schema that allows variations in the depth at which students learn. Many students in a classroom will have the capability and interest to delve into topics in depth; programs that encourage this type of exploration should not be viewed as the sole domain of gifted and talented students. Any student who is capable and interested should be allowed to try the option and continue as long as the results of that trial are favorable. In this way, all students are receiving appropriate instruction to 'the depth at which they can learn, and the gifted and talented students are not set apart from the rest of the class through unnecessary barriers.

PROGRAM OPTIONS FOR VARYING THE DEPTH OF LEARNING

Among the strategies that a teacher can use to allow students to learn in varying depths are capitalizing upon currently available programs and augmenting those programs with new options. It is likely that there are already many activities occurring within regular classrooms that facilitate this effort. Teachers may allow students to do extra projects, read extensively on a topic, or conduct research projects. Special interest groups, such as a baseball statistics club, are a common result of such a program. Additional strategies are described in the following sections. These can be instituted in isolation or in tandem with other techniques for giving students the opportunity to immerse themselves in learning a topic in depth.

Programs within the Classroom

Questioning Techniques.   There are a number of ways to classify questions, but the most simple is to think of them as either *convergent* or *divergent.* Convergent questions have one right answer and when students make a response it is either right or wrong. "In what year was the Declaration of Independence signed?" is an example of a convergent question; there is only one correct answer to the question. Divergent questions, on the other hand, have more than one possible answer that can be considered acceptable. "In what ways would the United States be different if it were settled from the North rather than the East?" has no one right answer; rather, there are a number of correct answers (see Table 6–1).

Both convergent and divergent questions are needed in order to learn a topic in depth. Students must know the facts involved, but they must also have the opportunity to explore and manipulate those facts so new ideas and concepts emerge. To be able to do so requires that students be

Table 6-1 Convergent and Divergent Questions for Little Red Riding Hood

---

Convergent Questions
1. Where was the grandmother's house?
2. What kind of animal scared Little Red Riding Hood?
3. How did Little Red Riding Hood get her name?

Divergent Questions
1. What could Little Red Riding Hood have done to avoid meeting the wolf?
2. What would you do if you met a ferocious animal in the woods?
3. How would the story be different if Little Red Riding Hood met a turtle rather than the wolf?

---

given the chance to learn the skills involved with both convergent and divergent thought processes.

It is a relatively simple process to institute this type of program in the classroom. To determine what types of questions are currently being asked, either tape record and transcribe a lesson or request that a colleague write down the questions asked during a set period of time so that they can be analyzed. Classify the questions into convergent and divergent, and determine the ratio of one to another. Doing this periodically will give teachers data on how well they are keeping a balance between the two. Remember that *both* types of questions are needed for students to gain in-depth knowledge.

By writing questions in lesson plans or on index cards (to stick into books that are read aloud), a ready reference will be available for questioning. Teachers should also be aware of the test items they write and the wording of activities and assignments, as these usually require convergent responses only. Bringing additional divergent questions into the curriculum will give teachers an opportunity to observe the students' skills in responding to them. Different skills are needed when answering divergent questions and by giving the students that chance, new abilities will become evident and teachers will gain a better understanding of the true potential of the students.

Students also benefit when both convergent and divergent questions are asked in the classroom. As students learn a great deal from observation, they learn to ask better questions themselves. They also learn to enhance their abilities to reason, evaluate, speculate, and create—abilities that will assist them throughout their lives.

Independent Studies. When executed properly, independent studies can be an excellent program for varying the depth at which students learn. They provide a chance for students to inquire about topics of interest to them in a manner that allows extensive exploration. Independent studies have been used frequently with the gifted, but they have also been improperly used a great deal of the time. It is a misuse of student time when students are just told to study a topic of interest without developing any guidelines or directions. However, when direction is provided along with supervision and a plan for study, independent studies are an important part of the programming mosaic for the regular classroom.

Kaplan, Kaplan, Madsen, and Taylor (1973) list the following elements of a successful independent study program:

1. Student self-selection of what is to be studied;
2. Cooperative teacher-student planning of what will be studied and how it will be shown;
3. Alternative ideas for gathering and processing information;
4. Multiple resources which are readily available;
5. Teacher intervention through formal and informal student-teacher dialogues;
6. Skills integrated with the content area being studied;
7. Time specifically allowed for working and conferencing;
8. Working and storage space;
9. Sharing, feedback, and evaluation opportunities; and
10. Student recognition for his "expertise" and finished project (p. 111).

Keeping these elements in mind, the teacher and student can begin the process of preparing for the independent study. This is best accomplished through the use of a contract or planning form (see Figure 6–1). On the planning form, the student and teacher should write down the steps that will be taken to complete the study. Thus, a format is developed for the student to follow and a structure is established that will indicate when the study is completed.

A misguided independent study project came to light when a parent complained to a teacher that her first grader, who was studying the topic of computers, was becoming dissatisfied with the project and unhappy in trying to complete it. Upon further investigation it was learned that she had begun the project six weeks earlier and was without a plan—just an interest in finding out more about her father's profession. This scenario brings to light a number of commonly found problems with independent studies that can be easily avoided by keeping these guidelines in mind.

1. Limit the topic to an area that can be easily studied. Particularly with young children, choose topics about which information is readily available, but not so much that the student is swamped. The topic of

Figure 6-1   Sample Independent Study Form

Independent Study Form

TOPICS that interest me are:

1. _____

2. _____

3. _____

Circle the one that you will be investigating for this study.

QUESTIONS I want to answer:

1. _____

2. _____

3. _____

RESOURCES I will use:

_____

_____

REPORTING METHOD possibilities:

_____

_____

NEXT STEPS: _____

_____

Date to Be Done: _____

_____   _____

Student Signature   Teacher Signature

computers is too large for a student of any age—information is endless and the student will have trouble deciding what is germane to the study. Computer languages, choosing software, or computerized simulations are topics that will lead the students to the information they seek.

2. Complete a planning form with the student, which includes the topic to be studied, resources that will be used, questions to be answered, ways to report the data, and how evaluation will occur. This can be referred to during follow-up meetings to see if revisions are necessary.

3. Put a time limit on the study; do not allow it to go on indefinitely. Six weeks is too long for a first-grade student to be studying a topic on her own. For younger children and others who are not experienced in this type of program, it is best to keep the time frame relatively short. As students become more accomplished, the studies can become more complex and extensive in length.

4. Plan the resources that can be used before you start. Help students think of resources beyond the encyclopedia. They often forget that people can be resources for studies through interviews and that other audio-visual aids can give them information about their topics. Developing the strategies needed to procure information is one of the outcomes from this program, thereby making it an excellent way to teach students how to learn.

5. Keep the students thinking about a product for their studies. Encourage divergent products that go beyond the usual report and picture or map. Explore with the students such avenues for display as mobiles, dioramas, plays, stories, and simulations. A third grader who was studying Bigfoot hunted his prey while other students asked questions about the beast. At the end of the trail, he pulled down the window shade where he had placed a large picture of Bigfoot. A fourth-grade student who was interested in World War II planes made a filmstrip of his study called "Pacific Theater," and a younger student who studied real estate built and sold a house of her own design and making.

The possibilities with independent investigations are endless. Students can delve into topics at great length and study whatever their interest leads them to consider. While engaged in this process, they are also learning how to be lifelong learners and independent students who can pursue knowledge on their own.

Skill Grouping.   Organizing program curricula by using skill grouping is another way to vary the depth at which students learn in a classroom (see Chapter 3). When teachers employ this technique, they are acting on the assumption that all students are not at the same skill level; there is a built-in acceptance that the depth of learning needs to be varied. Grouping gives the teacher a chance to provide instruction to students at different levels of skill development. While one sixth-grade group of students is studying paragraph construction, another can be working on metaphor.

Skill grouping has benefits beyond that of facilitating the variation in depth of learning. It also provides a mechanism through which students of similar ability can be together during the course of the day. In the regular classroom, the gifted and talented students are often segregated by the type and level of work in which they are engaged. Pulling them together for a skill group brings them interaction with other students and gives them a chance to develop social and academic skills.

The number of skill groups a teacher uses at one time will depend on the needs of the students and the skill of the instructor. Some teachers will run as many as five groups simultaneously; others can handle only three. Regardless, it is important to provide this differentiation in instruction so that the students will have a chance to probe into topics at their individual levels.

Learning Centers. Another program configuration for varying the depth of learning is through learning centers. Centers are a common method teachers have been using for years to organize instruction. Most centers are for skill development or enrichment purposes. Skill development centers have goals and objectives upon which the activities and products of the center are designed. Interest centers are less directive and may have as their purpose stimulating student interests, imparting new information, or arousing curiosity and motivation. Both center types can be developed so that a broad range of abilities can be accommodated.

Charles (1976) lists eight components to a learning center: direction, objectives, task cards, samples/models, media, scheduling devices, record-keeping devices, and evaluation forms. By taking into account the varied levels at which the students will want to explore the topic of the center, the teacher can choose components that will allow diversity in student responses. For example, objectives for the center might include skill development beyond that which is for the immediate classroom level. Skill cards or activities can be developed so that they are of two types— mandatory and optional (see Figure 6-2). When the mandatory activities are completed, the basic skills of the center should have been developed; the optional activities, then, are for enrichment purposes and to give the students the chance to explore the topic more deeply. One way to encourage student probing is to give them the chance to develop their own skill cards or activities to include with those that are made by the teacher.

Learning centers are compatible with the philosophy of not segregating gifted students. Some students, though, may choose or be directed to complete different activities and develop more in-depth products. Creating separate centers for the gifted and talented students is a definite mistake. If that is done, it sends a clear signal to the rest of the students that they are not expected to do as well and it leaves the gifted students in the awkward position of being separated from their classmates.

Figure 6-2   Learning Center Activities

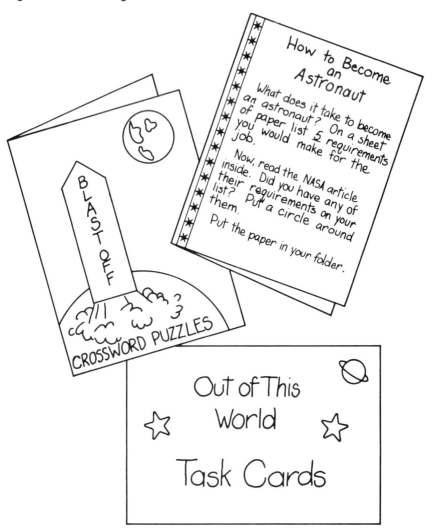

Basically, learning centers give teachers a vehicle for varying the depth at which students can learn while giving the students a chance to build many skills, both academic and social. Self-management, independent learning, creativity, critical thinking, self-evaluation, and new interests are among the outcomes of this program component which make it a very attractive part of the programming mosaic.

Programs Outside of the Classroom

Community Internships. Community internship programs are developed to let students experience real-world areas that interest them. The intensity and duration of the experience may depend on the age and sophistication of the students involved. In this type of program, students are matched with community volunteers and take part in the volunteer's activity or workplace as an assistant or observer.

The extent to which the students can become integrally involved will depend on the type of internship that has been arranged. Students working in a medical center with a surgeon will not be conducting surgery but may be able to sit in on a consultation or witness surgery from an observation area. Students who worked in a nursing home with the elderly (Slotnik, Reichelt, and Gardner, 1985) were more integrally involved with the patients' psychological well-being, as their roles were to talk with them while they developed skills involved with geriatric care.

Establishing and maintaining internship programs is a difficult proposition. Not all community placements are appropriate or receptive to having students work there. Screening of sites is necessary to determine if they can provide a learning experience for the students and if it has personnel who will be able to work with them. A visitation and interview with the people on the receiving end is a good idea because it familiarizes the program planner with the facility and people while providing an opportunity to explain the goals of the internship experience, the length of the program, and a bit about the students who will be coming. Follow-up visits or phone conferences should occur on a regular basis to monitor the experience. Students might keep a log of their experiences and reactions as a way of self-evaluating the program. After the internship is over, a letter of appreciation should be sent from both the students and the program director.

Obviously, this all takes a great deal of time. Developing a list of possible sites is taxing enough, but follow-through is also time intensive. However, the program does not need to take place on a grand scale! Community internships are not appropriate for all students at all times. Rather, only students with a definite desire to learn or experience a certain activity should be involved. Different students can be in the field at different times. Many programs ask students to submit plans of action for their proposed activity so that the program organizers can determine the extent to which the student is prepared to undertake the placement and if an appropriate placement can be found.

Participation in community internships gives students with the ability and desire to learn about a topic in depth the means to do so. They can become botanists, astronomers, chemical engineers, mechanics, florists, or teachers for a time and truly experience what it is like to hold that profession. Discipline is required to be successful in the internship experience, as is perseverance, curiosity, and intelligent inquiry. All these outcomes make the time needed to structure such an experience well worth it.

Simulations.   Simulations are contrived experiences concocted to represent real-life problems or situations in which actions need to be taken to solve problems. These can occur either in the classroom or outside the classroom as part of a special program (on or off campus). Participating in a simulation gives students the chance to immerse themselves into a situation and become an active player in it without truly having outcomes that are real.

There are many simulations used in schools and they provide an exceptionally fine way to vary the depth of learning. They usually require numerous players, thus the roles can be differentiated based on talents and interests. Students involved in the same simulation will have various experiences and will perceive the simulation differently. Therefore, placement of students into roles that are suited to their needs and abilities can result in their learning at their own levels.

In one popular simulation, the classroom is transformed into a community in which students assume different roles and responsibilities. The first goal is to establish the structure of the community with rules and ways to govern. Jobs are created along with salaries and banks to put them in. As a new need is found, the community-governing structure meets to find ways to incorporate the need into the existing structure. This type of simulation is a terrific civics lesson, but the impact is beyond social studies. Students learn to work cooperatively, solve problems, monitor themselves, evaluate one another, anticipate trouble, and plan for the future.

Simulations are available commercially in books, activity packets, and computer software. Using them is time consuming but they do provide a unique method of acquainting students with experiences in which they may not otherwise participate. Students may be uncomfortable in this type of activity as it requires dealing with the unknown and some amount of risk taking. Finding ways to deal with those feelings and successfully participate in the activity is yet another positive outcome that can occur.

Commercial Programs.   There are two commercially available programs of extremely high quality that will assist the teacher in varying the depth of learning for the students in the classroom. These are The Junior Great Books Program and Philosophy for Children Program. Both can be purchased and both have training packages available. They are unique in that they extend the ways in which students think while engaging them in inquiry and exploration of their own thoughts and ideas.

The Junior Great Books Program is available through the Great Books Foundation in Chicago, Illinois. It employs an inquiry approach that matches excellent literature selections with questions that can be answered in more than one way. The program can be used with elementary through high school students and involves the same inquiry technique throughout. Groups of about five to eight students, often advanced in language arts, are assembled and read from texts that contain approximately twelve selections. These students meet with a group leader (teacher, instructional aid, parent, administrator, National Honor Society member) who has received training in the inquiry process and who leads the students in their exploration of the selection. A guidebook, *Leader Aids*, is available from the Foundation as a source of questions to stimulate discussion. Most groups meet once a week, during or after school time, and cover one story at each session. The two factors that make this such an excellent program are the literature selections and the questioning approach (see Table 6–2). Discussion is generated easily as students are asked to respond to the leader's questions which are worded in such a way that there is more than one right answer. Students must develop a position on the question and support it by citing passages of the story. By so doing, they are learning to read with meaning and to probe beyond the surface of the stories.

Philosophy for Children (Lipman, Sharp, and Oscanyan, 1984), another inquiry-based program, is a product of the Institute for the Advancement of Philosophy for Children. Its purpose is to develop the thinking skills of the participants through reading thought-provoking stories, talking about the philosophical issues presented, and completing exercises relative to the content. A group leader is present, but she or he takes on a different role from the one in the Junior Great Books program.

Table 6–2   Inquiry Questions for the Junior Great Books Version of Robert Browning's "The Pied Piper of Hamelin"

1. Why does the author show us the Pied Piper's magic powers being used on both rats and children?
2. Who does the author think was most responsible for the children being led away?
3. Why did the people of Hamelin want to leave so many different kinds of records of what the Pied Piper did?

Source: Reprinted with permission by Great Books Foundation, copyright © 1975.

In this case, the leader is a facilitator, but is encouraged to lend a gentle hand in guiding the students, as it is recommended that the students take responsibility for their learning by leading their own discussions and activities rather than relying on the group leader. The leader can intervene, however, to organize the lessons, to keep conversations going, to bring to light the main ideas and themes of the stories, and to suggest activities (available in the Instructional Manual) to sharpen thinking skills.

Among the topics that the stories elicit are: What is culture?; Values as attitudes; Rules and freedom; Doubt; Are thoughts real?; and What makes you? The discussions and activities that these topics generate are then used to enhance the students' ability to develop new ideas and to sharpen critical thinking skills.

ASSEMBLING THE MOSAIC

This facet of the programming mosaic deals with the depth at which students learn, a capacity that varies depending on student ability, skill levels, and interests; therefore, these issues must be addressed when designing program options for the gifted and talented in the regular classroom. Many programming strategies respond to this need, some of which have been described in this chapter. Appropriate options for a particular student or class will depend on the resources available, time and personnel required, and the needs of the students. As with flexible pacing, the options need not be static or used by all the students. What is important is to have flexibility in the types of programs into which students can be placed based on their profiles of ability (see Table 6–3).

The "depth" mosaic pieces, when added to the "pace" mosaic pieces, begin to form a comprehensive programming approach to educating gifted and talented students. The next pieces will deal with student interests and will complete the picture. The character of this mosaic should vary from classroom to classroom and school to school as each has its own unique needs and assets. The quality of the program is insured by matching these two factors with students who are eager to learn as much as they can.

TEACHER'S RESPONSIBILITIES TO VARYING THE DEPTH OF LEARNING

When looking at programs where the depth at which students learn is varied, there are four basic teacher responsibilities that are readily apparent. The first of these is appropriately placing students in programs. Learning in greater depth requires certain skills; the teacher is in the best

Table 6-3   Program Combinations to Vary the Depth
of Learning

Grade Level	Programs
First	Questioning Techniques
	Independent Studies
	Skill Groups
Fourth	Junior Great Books
	Independent Studies
	Skill Groups
	Philosophy for Children
Sixth	Independent Studies
	Skill Groups
	Simulations
	Junior Great Books
	Internships

position to recognize these skills and then make placements accordingly. This responsibility requires teachers to know the true capabilities of their students and the requirements of the programs they seek to enter.

A second responsibility of the classroom teacher is preparing the students for these learning experiences. In order to be successful in many of these programs, students must have some independent learning skills. Additionally, particular programs or activities require special skills that the teacher should make sure are in place. For example, before students interview a subject for a newspaper column, they should know how to interview, write their questions beforehand, and have the skills to set it up. These skills are not typically taught as part of the curriculum, but are a definite part of the learning experience important to cub reporters.

Helping to find and identify resources is another task that falls into the teacher's (and students') responsibility area. In-depth learning requires the use of resources that may be beyond those normally found in the classroom. This is very time consuming and can be done in conjunction with other teachers, aids, or parents in order to ease the burden.

Finally, the monitoring of student progress is under the aegis of the teacher. Often, this type of program requires students to work alone or beyond the typical curriculum. Therefore, the usual monitoring systems and accountability procedures may not apply. Nonetheless, it is critical that students be monitored at all times. Student self-monitoring systems can be of assistance, but do not replace the teacher's continual formal or informal watch of the progress that is being made.

STUDENTS' RESPONSIBILITIES TO VARYING THE DEPTH OF LEARNING

The students' responsibilities to programs that aid in varying the depth at which they learn parallel the teacher's responsibilities to a great degree. These are: being prepared for the program requirements, actively finding new and unusual resources, developing a sense of direction for their studies, and persevering when the studies become difficult or complex.

Being prepared for program activities and requirements is central to the students' responsibilities in this area. When the depth at which learning takes place varies, so do the requirements and skills needed in the programs. The teacher can present the conditions under which these skills can be mastered, but it is up to the student to follow through.

Actively finding new and unusual resources is another responsibility of the students. In order to learn in depth, it will probably be necessary to go beyond the usual resources used at that grade level. Primary sources or firsthand observers of pertinent events may need to be located. Teachers should assist in this quest, but students also have a central role. It is an integral part of the learning that takes place.

Developing a sense of direction and inner locus of control is the third student responsibility and, hopefully, an outgrowth of this type of approach to learning. Through the self-monitoring process and explorations that take place, students can begin to establish lifelong interests and skills that will take them into their adult years and professions.

Last, in-depth learning is often challenging and requires that the students develop perseverance. Sticking to a difficult course of study or searching for an obscure reference can take a great deal of intellectual stamina. This is a trait that can be modeled, but basically it is one that needs to be developed. Student commitment to learning is very important and forms the core upon which perseverance can build.

SUMMARY

Gifted and talented students have the capability to learn in depth beyond what might be expected from their classmates. When they are placed in the regular classroom, it is up to the teachers or administration to develop programs through which this ability can be nurtured. Many programs are available and work successfully in conjunction with other programming mosaic components or the regular scope and sequence of skills.

Low-cost programs such as independent study, skill grouping, and asking challenging questions are just a few of the possible options. Many programs can be undertaken by the classroom teacher and do not require a great deal of assistance or budget to enact.

The benefits of this type of program to the students are many. Students are given a chance to pursue their interests, learn at the level at which they are capable, develop lifelong learning skills, and pursue ideas beyond the normal scope of study.

ACTION STEPS

1. Review the current programs that are available in your district, school, and classroom, and make a list of those that will help you vary the depth of learning for your students.
2. Match these programs to student names. Who might benefit from these programs? Are these students currently enrolled in the programs? How can you make them a part?
3. What additional options might augment your program in a meaningful way? List these.
4. Develop a plan to institute one new strategy before the end of the next term.
5. Meet with others and encourage them to develop further options so that the depth at which students learn can be varied throughout the school and the course offerings.

REFERENCES YOU CAN USE

Christenbury, L., & Kelly, P. (1983). *Questioning: A path to critical thinking.* Urbana, IL: National Council of Teachers of English.

Costa, A. (Ed.). (1985). *Developing minds: A resource book for teaching thinking.* Alexandria, VA: Association for Supervision and Curriculum Development.

Cruickshank, D. (1977). *A first book of games and simulations.* Belmont, CA: Wadsworth Publishing Company.

Kaplan, S.; Kaplan, J.; Madsen, S.; & Taylor, B. (1973). *Change for children.* Pacific Palisades, CA: Goodyear Publications.

Sund, R., & Carin, A. (1978). *Creative questioning and sensitive listening techniques: A self concept approach* (2nd ed.). Columbus, OH: Merrill Publishing Company.

7

Accommodating Individual Interests

Gifted and talented students often have interests that are different from their age-peers. They may be more advanced and similar to older students or be in entirely different subjects and activities. This being the case, it becomes important that the classroom teacher be aware of the varied interests and develop strategies to accommodate the differences.

During a science lesson about the heart, a second-grade teacher was surprised to learn that one of her students had a sophisticated understanding of the anatomy of the human body. Not only did he know about auricles and ventricles, he could also talk learnedly about cardiovascular fitness and the relationship between the heart, arteries, and veins. On further investigation, it was learned that the student had been interested in anatomy for years and had been encouraged in his studies by his parents. He had gone as far as to dissect a cow's heart on his own.

During a sixth-grade social studies lesson on the currencies of the world, one student began asking questions about the World Bank and its function in monitoring the world currencies. These questions resulted in a lengthy investigation of the agency and culminated in a family trip to Washington, D.C. to visit the offices of the World Bank and to see its operations firsthand. Questions led her through studies of mathematics, economics, politics, and bureaucracies more typical of high school and college-level studies than that of sixth grade.

You never know where the questions of students will lead or where their interests will take them. It is the wise teacher who makes an attempt at building from student interests in order to teach content and skills in the classroom. However, the interests of students are widely diverse and often change at a moment's notice. Therefore, the teacher must be equipped with strategies to respond to student interests while maintaining control of the curriculum and keeping students engaged in learning the skills they need.

To accomplish this, the teacher must establish an environment in the classroom that is flexible and will allow students to proceed in their learning through alternative avenues. Programming options are, again, the basis upon which the programming efforts are determined. Not all the opportunities need to be within the classroom environment. Outside experiences and resources can greatly enhance the program and lead to learning that would otherwise not take place.

The outcomes of accommodating individual interests for the gifted and talented in the regular classroom are many. These students are known for their desire to probe, question, and discover. They also are found spending great amounts of time studying the areas in which they are interested without being prompted by teachers and parents. They engage in such activities as making collections, running experiments, investigating backyard artifacts, and asking questions endlessly. Providing an outlet to their wonderings is a vital part of teaching them to be lifelong learners. Allowing them to pursue interests can result in avocations or vocations that they may retain interest in throughout their lifetimes while giving them plenty of new knowledge, skills, and challenges in the present.

PROGRAM OPTIONS FOR ACCOMMODATING INDIVIDUAL INTERESTS

Dealing with individual interests within the regular classroom is an excellent way of assimilating the gifted and talented students into the mainstream while giving them an opportunity to be engaged in programming efforts that are meaningful to them. No doubt, many of the interests expressed by these students will, in fact, mirror those of other students in the class (particularly if cross-level grouping is a part of the program). With the gifted and talented students, though, you may witness a longer attention span, more insightful questions, avid pursuit of information, resistance to returning to other work, self-motivation, and direction of study beyond that which you see in the other students.

Programs within the Classroom

Guest Lecture Series.   When you are trying to respond to the interests of students, you very quickly learn that it is impossible for one person to know enough about each topic students pursue. Therefore, it becomes imperative that other resources are used to augment the knowledge and skills of the teacher. One way to accomplish this is through a guest lecture series. Not only does this relieve the pressure on the classroom teacher, but the hosting of guest speakers will be a way to expose the students to professionals in their fields of interest.

This type of program has two outcomes that can be especially useful for the gifted and talented students in the class. Most obvious is that this gives the students a greater opportunity to interact and learn from someone who is involved in an area of interest to them. Second, and equally important, it gives students (who might not be so interested in the topic) a chance to be exposed to new fields. Gifted and talented students are often quite sharply focused in the interests that they pursue. By incorporating a lecture series into the programming efforts, these students are acquainted with topics they might otherwise avoid. They may even find a new interest area.

Assembling a guest lecture series takes a good deal of preparation. To discover the types of lectures that would be of interest to the students, survey them through interest inventories (see Figure 7–1) or interviews. Also ask colleagues for suggestions. Be sure to contact possible presenters enough in advance that you have time to prepare both them and the students for the visit. The presenters will want to know about the purposes of the visit, the students with whom they will be working, and your expected outcomes for the visit. They may need to be reminded that with young students, the more active the presentation the better! Students should be at least slightly knowledgeable about the presenter and the topic and come prepared with questions they would like to have answered. These can even be given to the lecturers ahead of time to assist in their preparation.

Not only gifted and talented students should be involved in the lecture series. Any student who is interested in the advertised topic should be given the opportunity to attend. The teacher may wish to enhance the experience by inviting students from other grades or by having the students interview the guest for the class newspaper.

Interest Groups.   Establishing interest groups is another way to accommodate individual interests within the regular classroom (see Chapter 3). As diverse as student interests are, they always share many in common. Allowing a time to explore those interests is a way to expand the knowledge of the students and to assimilate the gifted and talented students into the whole group.

One way of accomplishing this is to set aside a time each week for the groups to meet. Community mentors can be brought in at that time to lead groups that are studying their areas of expertise. By surveying student interests (see Figure 7–1), groups can be designated and leaders found who know those interest areas. Meeting for thirty to sixty minutes a week should be sufficient, depending on the grade level and sophistication of the students.

Four groups of eight students each were organized in one fourth-

Figure 7-1   Sample Items from a Student Interest Inventory

Student Interest Inventory

Name _____   School _____

Grade _____   Date _____

- -

1. In your dreams, what two jobs would you like to have when you finish school?

   _____

   _____

2. After school, what three activities do you enjoy doing the most?

   _____

   _____

   _____

3. If you could invite any famous person to your home for dinner, who would you invite? _____

   Name another _____

4. List the two books you enjoyed reading the most.

   _____

   _____

   Why are these your favorites? _____

   _____

5. What are your favorite subjects in school? Which ones don't you like?

   Favorites   *Duds*

   1.   1.

   2.   2.

grade classroom after students were given interest inventories to determine their extracurricular activities and and areas about which they wanted to know more. When this information was compiled, the four groupings emerged, with some students taking their second or third choice of interest area. The groups to which they were assigned were Folk Dances of Greece, Experiments with Oxygen, Speaking French, and Word Processing on a Personal Computer. Students spent six weeks with their interest group for forty-five minutes each week. Community volunteers led the groups on dancing, French, and computers, while the teacher met with the group on oxygen. At the end of that time, students gave presentations about their areas of study and were then regrouped for the next round with newly enlisted community volunteers.

A less formal way to use interest groups in the classroom is to assemble the groups as an opportunity arises. For example, if a special exhibit on Hopi Indians is coming to the local historical museum, a group might be established who would like to visit the exhibit so that they could study the Indians in advance of going to the museum. Or, if a new book comes into the library on life in space, a group of interested students could be brought together to read and discuss that book.

This type of programming option gives students an opportunity to explore areas of interest with their classmates while gaining the extra benefit of being exposed to outside experts. They can learn new skills, interact with other students and adults, and perhaps develop new interests to investigate in the future.

Interest Centers.   A form of learning centers, interest centers can stimulate student interests and allow them the chance to explore topics they otherwise might not (see Chapter 6). Building predetermined skills is not as important in this type of center as exposing students to new ideas or new people. Gifted and talented students have a tendency to focus most of their time in one interest area, such as baseball, computers, fictional books, or bird nests. It is often a challenge to get them interested in anything new. Using interest centers in the classroom can be one avenue of new discovery.

For some teachers, interest centers are the only type of centers they use. Others will combine the use of interest and skill development centers as they rely on the centers approach more fully. Whatever works for an individual teacher is fine as long as it is a part of a multiple programming approach. Often found are interest centers that revolve around regularly rotated games and puzzles, current events, or books (see Figure 7-2). To augment the experience, students can develop their own activities or centers for other students to use.

Figure 7-2   Sample Activities from an Interest Center

Programs Outside the Classroom

Mentors.   Mentors are people with whom students study topics of interest in which the mentors have expertise. They can be a teacher, parent, or other community volunteer who is interested in working with students on a one-to-one basis in order to develop a student's knowledge in the area and a product from the experience. Generally, mentorships are for a given purpose and length of time, although some do develop into more extensive partnerships.

Mentors should be carefully chosen; willingness is not a sufficient criterion for selection. The mentors should be comfortable with the age of the student being placed and be able to convey their knowledge in a meaningful way. Usually placements occur after a student has expressed interest in such an arrangement or the teacher has deemed such a program to be of benefit to a particular student. The mechanics of establishing, maintaining, and monitoring such arrangements are complex enough that only one or two students are usually involved at any one time.

Gifted and talented students make particularly good candidates for this type of experience. Their baseline knowledge is often sufficient to require a mentor in order to go farther and learn the intricacies of their interest area. Talented violinists need to study with master teachers, and archeology buffs would greatly benefit from a chance to be involved with a local archeologist on a dig. These students also have the self-direction to continue through the experience in a manner that is of benefit to them.

Before embarking on a mentorship program, some guidelines should be considered that will make the program more likely to succeed:

1. Meet with the students and mentors to outline the purposes of the program and the timeline.

2. Have the parties concerned meet and discuss the past experiences the students have had in the interest area and what they would like to know more about.

3. Encourage the mentors and students to develop a plan for the experience and decide on an end product. This gives focus to the experience and will serve as an ending point for the activity.

4. Hold regular interviews with the students *and* the mentors to make sure that everything is progressing satisfactorily.

5. Give the students an opportunity to share their products with an appropriate audience and to become a mentor to other students with that interest.

6. Formally evaluate the students and decide if the mentors should be used in the future.

7. Thank the mentors for their time and talents.

Advanced Seminars.   Advanced seminars are yet another programming option that can be integral part of meeting the needs of the gifted students in the regular classroom. However, this type of program is generally held on a pullout basis and coordinated by a resource teacher or a staff member assigned to the program as part of the school day. Students are scheduled into the seminar either one class period a day or for a half a day a week. Cluster-group students or those of above average ability are brought together to study and discuss certain topics and to create projects of their own design related to those topics or interests.

Advanced seminars are used for a number of purposes and can fill many functions. One is to allow students a time during which they can work on independent studies or investigations on a regular basis. Another is to expose them to topical issues or current events in a seminar setting so that in-depth discussion can take place. Still another way in which advanced seminars have been used is to introduce students to topics that are new to them but have universal bearing on many areas of study, such as ethics or logic. Finally, this type of program has been used as a vehicle for monitoring students' progress and assisting the regular classroom teacher in curriculum compacting.

As you can see, the seminars can take on many different forms and have different types of expectations depending on the nature of the designed program. Regardless of the configuration or the way the time is spent, this program gives gifted and talented students an opportunity to meet together and explore topics of interest to them.

One adaptation of this programming approach can be seen in Renzulli's Revolving Door Model (Renzulli, Reis, and Smith, 1981). This is a program in which highly motivated students study topics that interest them. Students are identified from the talent pool when they exhibit a keen interest and desire to pursue a course of study through what is termed an *action information message*. These messages, which contain information about the nature of the students' interests, are sent to a resource room teacher who reviews them, interviews the students, and places students in the program, if deemed eligible, when there is a space available. When the students have completed their research, they are "revolved out" of the program until another one of their action information messages is accepted.

Some programs prefer to have students scheduled into the program on a permanent basis so that they do not have to deal with the flexible scheduling that is needed in a program such as the Revolving Door Model. In such instances, you often find a mixture of program activities. For example, the class may open with a current events seminar or a lesson in logic, which is followed by time for students to work on compacting contracts, interest centers, or independent projects.

National Programs.   There are a number of programs coordinated on a national and international basis that give students the opportunity to pursue interests beyond opportunities available in most schools. Three of these will be discussed here in order to present a picture of the types of programming options available in this category. They are: Future Problem Solving (FPS); Odyssey of the Mind (OM); and the Science Olympiad (SO).

Future Problem Solving was created by Torrance in 1974 as a means to expose students to futuristics through an adaptation of the creative problem-solving process (Parnes, 1977). Students work in teams and are guided by an instructor to solve problems that deal with life in the future. Its goals are to:

1. Acquaint students with future studies.
2. Develop creative and higher level thinking skills by using a six-step problem-solving method.
3. Acquaint teachers with the problem-solving method.
4. Help students develop abilities to deal with the unknown in the future.
5. Help students develop skills needed for teamwork.
6. Help students develop skills of organization and coherence through writing and verbal exercises.

Students meet to work on sample problems and learn the problem-solving technique. This study culminates in the Future Problem-Solving Bowl at the local level, which is often followed (for high-scoring teams) by state and national bowl participation. During the bowls, students are given problems to solve and are rated on each of the six problem solving steps. FPS is more than just a competition, however; it gives students problem-solving skills they can use in their studies across their lifetimes.

Odyssey of the Mind is also a national program with local, regional, and national competitions developed by Gourley and Micklus. As with FPS, students work with instructors to learn the techniques involved with creative problem solving. These are then brought to bear on problems that need to be solved (often through constructions or presentations). At the competitions, students are presented with "long-term" and "spontaneous" problems. The long-term problems are given to the students in advance so that they can research and prepare solutions which they then bring with them. One such problem involved the construction of a structure made from balsa wood and glue which could support a heavy object. Spontaneous problems are given to see how quickly the students can come up with innovative solutions to problems on the spot. These competitions are held in divisions ranging from elementary to high school students. Months of preparation are generally required along with teamwork and creative thinking.

The Science Olympiad (SO) is an academic interscholastic competition consisting of individual and team competitions in the sciences. Students are brought together for a number of events that revolve around the various areas of science. Some of these might include Biology Trivia, The Egg Drop (in which students construct a device to keep the egg from cracking), Science Bowl (patterned after Quiz Bowl), Paper Airplanes, and Computer Programming. During the competition day, students are also invited to participate in demonstrations and lectures in science. Although this is a competitive event, it does involve teamwork in many of the events.

Each of the programs described involves a competition. However, the value in the programs is not found in this aspect of the programs alone. Rather, students learn important inquiry, team work, and problem-solving skills as they prepare to test their abilities against competitors. The results of participation can be new knowledge, skills, resources, and friendships.

ASSEMBLING THE MOSAIC

The final pieces can now be added to the programming mosaic—the pieces that build programs accommodating individual student interests. Gifted and talented students tend to have interests that vary from their classmates. In order to develop appropriate programs for this population, these interests should be taken into account.

At this point in assembling the mosaic, it is desirable for the teacher to identify programming options that will allow flexible pacing, in-depth study, and interests to be accommodated (see Table 7-1). The multiple programming approach lends itself to this pursuit, as the teacher can identify program options from which the students, based on their profiles of ability, can take advantage. Not all students will be engaged in the same mix of programs; programs are tailored to individual abilities, needs, and interests. It is quite possible that the gifted and talented students will be involved with the regular programming a great deal of the time, spending a substantially smaller amount in the other programs. It is also likely that other classroom students will join the gifted and talented students in many of these programming efforts when their abilities, needs, and/or interests correspond to each other.

Shari is a fifth grader who is an avid reader. She is also interested in piano and has become quite accomplished at it. Most of her time outside of school is spent reading and practicing for her weekly piano lesson. In

Table 7-1   Program Combinations to Accommodate
Individual Interests

Grade Level	Programs
Second	Independent Studies
	Interest Centers
Fifth	Guest Lecture Series
	Independent Studies
	Mentorships
	Future Problem Solving
Seventh	Advanced Seminar
	Independent Studies
	Community Internships
	Science Olympiad

the classroom, she has also shown her ability in languages by scoring in the ninth stanine on achievement tests in reading comprehension, vocabulary, and word usage. Her math scores are in the seventh stanine, but she is still an above average mathematics student. Her fondest dream is to play with a symphony orchestra in Carnegie Hall after she attends Juilliard.

What type of programs should Shari be involved in during her school time? Obviously her reading ability far exceeds her classmates' abilities and will necessitate different provisions. Her musical ability is being nurtured outside of school, but could probably be further enhanced through the school music program. Among the appropriate programming configurations for Shari would be placing her in textbooks or a reading group in a higher grade (perhaps sixth) that is working at her reading level, along with the Junior Great Books program which meets once a week during reading time. Her propensity for language also makes her a prime candidate for the Conversational French class which meets after school once a week. The music teacher may also provide a piece of the mosaic by having Shari accompany the choirs during the Spring musical and the holiday concert. The rest of Shari's program would more closely align with the other fifth-grade students.

It is unlikely that another fifth-grade student would have the exact programming package as Shari's. Others may be involved in advanced materials, Junior Great Books, or the choir, but it is unlikely that others would have such an identical profile to Shari as to require the same provisions. However, other students will need program modifications of this type in order to be adequately served through their educational experiences. Building a programming mosaic will give teachers the flexibility to do so.

TEACHER'S RESPONSIBILITIES TO ACCOMMODATING INDIVIDUAL INTERESTS

The monitoring function is probably the most difficult, but most important, teacher responsibility in accommodating individual interests. Many of the programs in this area require students to work outside of the classroom or the regular curriculum, which requires teachers to devise ways to keep track of student progress so that problems can be averted and inappropriate placements corrected. Using management sheets, planning forms, regular conferences, and interviews can assist in this task. Student self-tracking and evaluation sheets can also give the teacher clues as to how the studies are progressing.

Finding meaningful experiences and qualified mentors is another major responsibility of the classroom teacher. In these programs, students profit most highly from being engaged in real-life experiences with people who can communicate their field and skills easily to children. Unfortunately, these kinds of people and experiences may not be readily available. Tapping the talents of other teachers, cultural institutions, community volunteers, and other students is one way to begin to develop a resource file of names and circumstances for student internships and mentorships.

Finally, it is critical for the teacher to identify meaningful outlets for the students' products from these programs. Art and science fairs, classroom newspapers, demonstrations, and parent nights are among the outlets teachers may consider. But do not stop there. Sending original writing into children's magazines, entering the Future Problem Solving Bowl, auditioning for student accompaniest with the local symphony, or giving a presentation on traffic patterns around the school to the local planning commission are all examples of outlets to student works with real implications. The experiences can give the students a glimpse of the future and of their own true talents.

STUDENTS' RESPONSIBILITIES TO ACCOMMODATING INDIVIDUAL INTERESTS

Gifted and talented students are often one-sided in their interests. They may be totally devoted to computers, immersed in finding out about outer space, or only interested in gymnastics. Getting them to broaden their horizons, take the risk of learning about new ideas and topics, and venture into worlds unknown to them can be a difficult task. But this is not solely the teacher's responsibility; the students must also share in the commitment to expand their interests. They do not have to abandon computers, space, or gymnastics—only be willing to take the responsibility of trying new experiences and broadening their interest base.

Second, the students involved in these programs must take the responsibility of being active learners. The types of experiences these programs provide require that students observe, question, probe, explore, and experiment. It is only the students who can do that. They must be informed what the programs will require, and then *they* must agree to give it all they have.

Part of being active learners is to take responsibility for planning their own studies, developing the necessary skills, and being a part of the monitoring process. This includes keeping journals up to date, taking notes on observations, completing evaluation forms, devising original products, and meeting regularly with supervising teachers. These actions are a reflection of the students' duty to take responsibility for their own learning.

Last, it is the students' responsibility to treat all their program involvements as important and worthwhile. One area of learning should not be short-changed for another. Independent investigations can be time and energy consuming, but this should not result in a lack of effort in mathematics, science, or other subjects. Involvement in the Junior Great Books Programs does not mean that students do not have to be concerned about their other reading assignments. Part of the learning that takes place is knowing how to balance time and responsibility. Multiple programming approaches to learning make this a necessity.

SUMMARY

The interests of students in a classroom vary greatly. The interests of gifted and talented students tend to be more advanced or of a different variety. Therefore, it becomes necessary for the classroom teacher to make programming options available that are flexible enough to allow students to investigate interests that are meaningful to them.

These programs can be installed in the classroom or in conjunction with special area teachers, community agencies, volunteers, or other members of the educational community. Even other students can serve as resources for students as they explore their interest areas. Being a part of the programming mosaic, the interests of students are given validity as an important component of the way students learn and the types of educational experiences from which they can profit.

ACTION STEPS

1. Review the current programs available in your school and district and list all that accommodate individual interests. Star any from which your students may profit.
2. Are there any programs that you would like to add to the list? Talk to other teachers to see what types of programs they know about, then implement one of your ideas.
3. Compile a complete list of programming options from your lists of flexible pacing programs, in-depth study programs, and individual interest programs. Circle the ten programming options in which you are most interested.
4. Review the student profiles of ability for students in the talent pool. Complete the process of matching the students to the programs from which they may benefit.
5. Investigate ways to schedule your classroom activities to accommodate students participating in these programs.
6. Choose a few students to begin the multiple programming approach. Add more students as you gain confidence and skill in managing the students.

REFERENCES YOU CAN USE

Cox, J., & Daniel, N. (1983). The role of the mentor. *G/C/T,* 29 (September–October), 54–61.

Karnes, F., & Collins, C. (1984). *Handbook of instructional resources and references for teaching the gifted* (2nd ed.). Boston: Allyn and Bacon.

Krulik, S., & Rudnick, J. (1984). *Sourcebook for teaching problem solving.* Boston: Allyn and Bacon.

Renzulli, J., & Reis, S. (1986). *Schoolwide enrichment model: Comprehensive plan for educational excellence.* Mansfield Center, CN: Creative Learning Press.

Thomas, J. (1975). *Learning centers: Opening up the classroom.* Boston: Holbrook Press.

PART THREE

Designing
the Curriculum

Whereas *programs* are the administrative configurations in which students are placed, *curriculum* refers to the manner in which they are taught, the content that is presented, and the resources that are used. In programs for the gifted, differentiated curriculum must be instituted in order to give these students an equal opportunity to develop their abilities. Maker (1982) lists four ways in which curriculum for the gifted can be modified: the content, process, product, and environmental aspects of curriculum. Since environment has been covered in Part One, the other three areas will be discussed in the following chapters.

In Chapter 8, the issue of differentiation of curriculum is discussed along with the ways teachers can select the modifications that fit with their ways of teaching. To make this more clear, sample curricular plans for various subject areas are presented which can serve as models for future curriculum development.

The ten models most common to programs for the gifted are presented in Chapter 9. For each, the model is described, its relationship to the ways in which curriculum can be modified is explored, and the appropriate use of the model is explained. Although these models do not represent all those meaningful for the gifted, they do give a sampling of what is available and how models can be used.

The last chapter of this section is composed of a number of case studies that present problems inherent in providing programs for the gifted in the regular classroom. The nature of the problems are described along with alternative solutions and the strategies actually used. Each case study is followed by a sample of lessons that respond to the various learning levels of students in a regular classroom.

Adhering to any one model or approach to instruction will not meet the needs of the students in that class. Rather, accomplished teachers know when various methods will work and under what conditions they should use different approaches to the subject matter at hand. The challenge for the regular classroom teachers who are dealing with a wide range of abilities is to deliver instruction in a way to which students at all levels can relate. This is where the *art* of teaching comes about.

8

Prescribing the Appropriate Curriculum

The meaning of the word *curriculum* is not always fully understood. It refers to the content, manner of presentation, materials, and processes used to instruct students in the classroom. The most frequent misunderstanding is how the *curriculum* differs from the *program* that is being mounted. The program is the administrative structure employed, whereas the curriculum is that which is taught and the manner in which it is taught.

The curriculum, or course of study, may or may not be written down in such a way that it represents a formal plan. At times, scope and sequence charts are available or curriculum guides have been prepared. At other times, teachers are free to develop their own curricular plans. It is important that the curricular plan not be left to chance or haphazard preparation. It should be built on a philosophy of how children learn and contain a pattern for the presentation of skills so that there is a prepared progression in student learning. The plan should also contain suggested resources and ways to present the content. Individual teachers can then take the plan and modify it to meet their own teaching style and the differing needs of their students.

DIFFERENTIATING CURRICULUM FOR THE GIFTED

Due to the unique needs and abilities of gifted and talented students, a separate consideration for these individuals is warranted when curriculum is being designed. Maker (1982) lists four areas in which the curriculum for the gifted may need modification from the norm: the content that is covered, the process or method of instruction, the products that are expected from the students, and the environment in which learning takes place. This chapter will look at the three areas that have not already been discussed (content, process/method, and product) in order to see how each applies in the case of gifted and talented students receiving appropriate curricular modifications in the regular classroom.

Modifying the Content of Curriculum

As we have seen, the gifted and talented students in a classroom may already have mastered the content of a particular unit or course of study before it is presented. Thus, they may be capable of going beyond the usual scope and sequence to more advanced skills and concepts. In order to facilitate student progress, curricular modifications must take place. This may mean making arrangements for more complex content, employing abstractions, arranging for more advanced materials, or finding alternative placements for the students so that they can take advantage of content modification through participation in a more advanced setting.

Programs such as fast-paced classes, cross-level grouping, independent studies, continuous progress curriculum, and curricular compacting can help make modifying curricular content more simple, but programmatic schema alone do not assure that appropriate curricular practice is taking place. *You must look beyond the program configuration to the instruction itself to determine if the students are involved in content that is appropriate to their abilities.*

A third-grade unit on the structure of the earth was modified by one teacher so that the content was differentiated for the students. The teacher was using such teaching techniques as whole group instruction, small group activities, an enrichment center on the unit, and demonstrations. It became obvious through the questions the students asked that some already knew the names of the layers in the earth and about the materials that composed those layers. Therefore, the teacher decided that some content modification was in order for those students, and created a small group for the study of earthquakes. This group met with the teacher while the other students were doing their small group activities. The earthquake group learned about why earthquakes occur and were assigned the task of finding out how the intensity of earthquakes is measured. Filmstrips, books, and charts were made available for their use in this project. After they found the answers to the questions, they were asked to design an activity to do with the rest of the class in order to instruct them in the information that they had learned. The outgrowth of this curricular modification was beyond the expected lecture and chart presentation. The students made a learning center for the class and arranged (with teacher assistance) for the students to visit the local university's seismology laboratory. In addition, two students pursued the idea further through an independent study on how scientists predict geological activity.

In another instance, a sixth-grade class was studying basic geometric shapes. As part of their study, students were to find shapes in the environment and make conjectures as to why particular shapes were used in those circumstances. They had little difficulty locating shapes, but justifying the use of the shapes was a far more difficult proposition. However, the investigation did lead three students to experiments using different shapes in design. After a number of toothpick and glue structures were made, the students were encouraged by the teacher to formalize their investigation by using the scientific method in their studies and recording their results in a journal format. Following their investigation, the results of their study were published in the school newspaper.

Both of these examples show how content modifications can be made. They can be as unobtrusive as asking questions that require students to think in abstract terms, or as obtrusive as setting up parallel lessons and conducting more than one course of study at the same time. Different circumstances call for different remedies. The key to successfully modifying the content of curriculum is to be flexible, on your guard to notice when it is needed, and equipped with access to a variety of resources for the students to use.

Modifying the Process/Method of Instruction

The process or method of presenting the content is the second way in which curricula can be differentiated for gifted and talented students. Such students often display unbridled curiosities, desires to probe subjects in depth, preferences to study on their own, capacity for disciplined investigation, and a capacity to think in ways that may differ from the rest of the class. These and other abilities, when coupled with the goals of preparing students to be independent and lifelong learners, may require that the teacher modifies the way in which content is presented and the way students conduct themselves in the classroom.

Again, there are programs that will enhance the teacher's ability to make these modifications without a great deal of disruption to the rest of the class. Among these are programs using high-level questioning techniques, simulations, contracting, mentors, Future Problem Solving, and Junior Great Books. But, as with content modifications, program structure alone is not sufficient to insure that proper curriculum is occurring. Changes in the way in which material is presented and the very roles of the teacher and students may also need to be adjusted.

There are many modifications to process that a teacher can make in order to assure that the needs of all the students in the classroom are being met. Among those most necessary for the gifted and talented students are: good questioning techniques requiring the use of the upper levels of thought to answer; allowing students to become involved in their learning through choosing content, flexible pacing, self-monitoring progress, and selecting resources; using both convergent and divergent activities to enhance students' abilities to solve problems; and group process activities to help students learn to work together in a cooperative fashion.

Again, flexibility is a key ingredient to successfully modifying the processes and methods of instruction. Using any one delivery system for instruction is not appropriate, whether it is the lecture method or self-discovery method of learning. Master teachers know when a particular strategy will be most beneficial in helping the students to grasp the content being studied. They also are in tune with which methods of instruction are the most beneficial to each of their students, as learning styles will differ. Thus, many different methods may be used at one time.

In the instance where kindergarten students were engaged in a unit on transportation, the teacher tried to vary the methods of instruction in order to accomodate the different students' instructional needs and abilities. This was apparent in that students were given choices throughout the unit as to which of the activities they engaged in and the types of products they made. A whole-group brainstorming activity began the unit, with students listing as many types of transportation as they could think of. This was followed by separating students into interest groups which proceeded to investigate three common types of transportation in depth. One group studied cars and their impact on the way we live. The other two groups had the same focus with trains and airplanes. Creative dramatics, student story telling, block construction, and interviews of family members were used to assemble information and relate it to the students in the other groups. At the end of the unit, students were again given a choice as to how their products would be prepared. The teacher presented the options of story writing, picture drawing or construction, and dramatic presentation or demonstration. Students were also allowed to suggest ideas of their own which were approved or modified by the teacher.

In another circumstance, the teacher of a fifth-grade class presented a unit on theater, particularly plays. The main focus of the unit was to have students understand how plays are constructed. Following a whole-group presentation, a number of different methods were used to reinforce the information. The teacher had the students review four plays and make a list of how their structures were alike and how they differed; cut a five-scene play into pieces, with each scene being a piece, and had the students assemble the play in the order in which they thought it was written and create a rationale for that order; and had students present short plays in which certain components were missing (props, staging directions, dialog), asking other students to determine what the missing parts were. Then, as a culminating experience, students were allowed to choose the activity in which they would like to participate: play writing, play critique and written review, or analysis of the work of one playwright in a form of the student's choice.

Perhaps the most difficult aspect of modifying the process or method of instruction is that it may require teachers to relinquish some of the control they maintain over the curriculum and students' activities. But by doing so, they open the door to student involvement and student-centered environments, resulting in students who are more involved with taking responsibility for their own learning. This type of differentiation will also require teachers to be more agile in the skills they use to instruct and more diligent about the monitoring of individual student progress.

Modifying the Products of Learning

The products of student learning are another area that may be differentiated for the gifted and talented students in the class. These students can use their abilities to explore topics in depth and to show creativity and perseverance in designing divergent products uniquely representative of the learning they have experienced. Although learning to write reports is an important skill for all students, there are other ways to present information in a summative way. All students should be encouraged to explore many avenues to product development and be creative in the ways they present their work.

Obviously, the skills involved with presenting divergent products are ones that should be developed by as many students in the classroom as possible. You might find, however, that the gifted and talented students are more able to develop products that are on a larger scale, more complex, or most closely related to the products generated in real-life circumstances.

From the previous scenarios, you can see that the teachers gave students options for their products and the chance to design their own. This has been a successful strategy in classrooms of kindergarten through college-level students. The students in those examples did such things as demonstrations, journals, newspaper articles, dramatics, constructions, interviews, and critiques to synthesize and present the knowledge that they had gained over the course of study. But the list of possible products extends far beyond that. The possibilities are limited only by the students' imaginations, resources, time available—and the teacher's patience!

Surprisingly enough, students often have to be taught how to create divergent products. They are far more comfortable with continuing what is known (written reports and pictures) and often resist delving into the unknown of mobile construction or filmstrip producing. However, experience shows that when students are encouraged and given the material and psychological support necessary, they quickly find the new methods of presentation fun and a learning experience in and of themselves. Students have been known to be quite competitive in their product generation, which sometimes calls for tempering by the teacher. But on the whole, the excitement and products generated make the challenges for both the students and teacher well worth the effort.

Finding outlets for student products is one of the greatest challenges faced by the teacher. During the course of the year, students should have products that are judged in real-life circumstances with true-to-life results. Science fairs, young authors' conferences, recitals, and exhibitions are among the vehicles used extensively. Beyond those, student investigations and products often indicate an outlet that is appropriate. For example, if a student is delving into the problems associated with Dutch elm disease, she may wish to prepare a proposal for presentation to the town council or create a foundation for fund raising to save the trees through spraying. A student who is interested in writing may wish to send a poem or short story to a magazine that publishes student work or perhaps publish such a magazine on his own. In both instances there are real-life audiences, real-life requirements in preparing the product, and real-life evaluation of that product.

CHOOSING MODIFICATIONS THAT ARE RIGHT FOR YOU

Installing modifications in content, process, and product in the classroom will require prior planning in order to be successful. It is the wise educator who begins on a conservative scale and escalates the changes as the students and the teacher become adept at the new procedures. As it is difficult for students to begin to make choices, to ask high-level questions, and to take responsibility for their learning at the onset, so is it difficult for teachers to relinquish total control over the classroom, to institute multiple programming options, and to make modifications to tried and true methods of instruction. The following guidelines should help make the transition easier.

1. Begin at a comfortable pace. Limit the scope by choosing one subject area or one group of students with which to begin. Gradually add more students and more subject areas to your programming mosaic as you feel comfortable. It would not be unusual for this process to take two to three school years to implement fully. So be patient and concentrate on the growth process. Do make a pact with yourself, however, to try at least one new approach per term. Designing a multiple-year plan will help you know in what direction you are going and help you keep track of the progress you have made (see Table 8-1).

2. Make a chart and list the programs you would like to institute

Table 8-1   Multiple-Year Plan for Curriculum Development and Modification

Year	Areas for Review
Year 1	1. Individualize the reading basal textbook. 2. Make question cards for books in class library. 3. Investigate Junior Great Books. 4. Review each unit as presented for modifying content, process, and products. 5. Review progress at end of year and develop detailed plan for Year 2.
Year 2	1. Individualize mathematics text. 2. Alter units to reflect needed modifications. 3. Continue work as needed in Language Arts. 4. Review and plan for Year 3.
Year 3	1. Concentrate on the science curriculum, making it more participatory.

and the curricular modifications that can be used with each one (see Table 8-2). Notice that most of the programs in the list can be modified in more than one way. For example, an independent study option will lend itself to curricular modifications in all three areas. Odyssey of the Mind is especially good for process and product modifications. This chart should help

Table 8-2   Relationship between Programming Options and Curricular Modifications

Program Option	Curricular Modification		
	Content	Process	Product
Fast-Paced Classes	x	x	x
Self-Instruction	x	x	x
Early Admission	x		
Contracting	x	x	x
Correspondence Courses	x	x	
Independent Studies	x	x	x
Simulations	x	x	x
Mentorships	x	x	x
Guest Lectures	x		
Junior Great Books	x	x	
Odyssey of the Mind		x	x

x = Compatibility between program option and curricular modification you coordinate your effort and demonstrate to you that it is not impossible to integrate programming options and curricular modifications.

3. Think about teaching style. How do teachers tend to interact with the students? What is the environment like in the classroom? What type of modifications are already being made for students of above average ability? Are there already modifications being made in content, process, and/or product? What do teachers do in their classroom of which they are most proud? What do the students seem to enjoy the most? Build the initial changes from the areas in which you excel; make them even better. Begin with the area in which you feel most confidence and expand into other areas. If a teacher is a whiz in language arts and has a particularly good unit on Caldecott winning books, that may be the place to start. Think of how you can enhance the unit even more to accommodate the needs of all the students in the class. Perhaps you could invite an author to talk with the students or demonstrate illustrating to the class, include options for the final project, or arrange for a student-sponsored book fair with the profits going to a special charity project of the students. By building on successes, you are more likely to have even greater success. Do not be content to work only within your comfort zone, however. Be bold and expand your efforts to areas in which you are less comfortable and build them into areas in which you can be proud.

4. Consider the resources you have at your disposal. Think about the materials that are already in the classroom, those in the storeroom and the basement at home, people who are available to assist you both in the school and the community, the cultural institutions in your area, companies that have school programs and instructional materials available, audio-visual devises, and even old class notes from your university classes. When you first start, rely on what you have at hand. As you expand your options, expand your resources at the same time, and open the doors to learning even farther. If you are interested in adding an art appreciation program to your programming mosaic and do not have a museum with an "Art Lady" program (volunteers who give art appreciation lectures in the classroom), you may be able to find a student or community person with an art history background who can do the job for you. Or, if you would like to investigate simulation gaming and have none available in your personal library, you may be able to order one through a computer software catalog, find one in the local library or media center, or make your own. Resource availability can make some techniques impossible to use, but there are plenty of others to take their place. Trusting your own ingenuity can often fill the gap that a lack of resources may make.

5. Give each option that you try an ample chance to develop. If you try one learning center and find that the students have trouble self-

directing their activities, it can be tempting to give up on that option all together. However, as was stated earlier, students have to learn such skills as how to make choices, budget their time, work with other students, and read directions carefully. The gifted and talented are no exception. Teachers also have be prepared to modify and experiment with their instructional techniques. This is not to say that everything you try will eventually work—only that sometimes it takes work to make things go the way we want them to.

6. Review your performance on a regular basis to see if you are moving in the right direction. Ask yourself these questions:

a. Are all students in this class working at levels commensurate with their abilities?

b. Do students have options from which they can choose some of their assignments?

c. Are the content, process, and products of instruction regularly being modified so that all students are involved in meaningful instruction?

d. Has a new strategy, program, or activity recently been tried with the students?

e. How well are the gifted and talented students integrated into the classroom activities? Have my attempts at providing appropriate instruction resulted in isolating them from the rest of the group?

f. Is the program more valid than it was prior to beginning the changes?

g. Am I happier? Are the students happier and more productive?

7. If you determine that a technique, program, or activity is not working out, try something else. Not all teachers will want to mount a guest lecture series. Remember: Your goal is to put together options in programming and curriculum that will form a balance for students in the areas of pacing, in-depth inquiry, content, methods of instruction, products, and student interests. An infinite number of configurations is possible.

8. Feel free to experiment. Educators are often afraid to try new things for fear that they will not work and they will look foolish. Discard those notions and have fun trying new techniques regardless of the anticipated outcome. How about staging a class debate, a make-your-own-sundae production line, or a class meeting to discuss problems that arise? What is the worse thing that can happen? It might not work, but there is always tomorrow and lots of other new experiences to explore. Being willing to experiment can bring excitement to the classroom, new vigor

to the teacher, and avid interests by the students about what is going to happen next. You may even want to set up half an hour a week as "Anything Goes Time," a time in which you try new ideas with the understanding of all involved that they are to give it a fair chance. You may end up enjoying it and it is good modeling for risk taking.

SAMPLE CURRICULAR PLANS

There are many ways to begin the process of curricular planning to insure that all students in the classroom are engaged in instruction that is suited to their abilities and needs. Content can be accelerated, compacted, enriched, and extended; processes can be open-ended, discovery-based, teacher-centered, and student-centered; and products can be conventional, unconventional, true to real life, simple, or complex. The variations and additions to this list are endless, but the task is really quite simple. Three sample lesson plans appear below to show the manner in which curriculum can be differentiated for the gifted and talented in the regular classroom.

Discovering the Decimal System

One of the basic monetary units taught in elementary schools deals with the decimal system. Usually there are a number of students who know little about the system and several who already have it mastered. It then becomes the teacher's task to differentiate the curriculum so that all of these students have a meaningful instructional experience rather than allowing some of the students to be involved in lessons about which they already know the content. In this case, the teacher chose to modify the content that was being taught in order to enrich the students' understanding of the decimal systems. This was done in a rather simple manner by having all of the students engaged in basically the same activities but with different frames of reference. One group studied the U.S. monetary system while the other students were told to choose the system of another country, which also uses a decimal base, for investigation. The curricular plan (see Table 8–3) shows the objectives, activities, and resources that were used for one segment of the unit.

Creative Story Composing

Creative writing is one subject area in which differentiation seems to occur naturally. Students who are able writers show their talents in the products they create, at times appearing to be unaffected by the assignment that is given. This should not be interpreted to suggest that teachers do not have to plan modifications for the gifted and talented writers,

Table 8-3   Plan for Differentiated Lesson on Decimal System

TOPIC: The Decimal System

OBJECTIVES:
1. The students will be able to assign the monetary value to each coin presented.
2. The students will know that the decimal system is based on units of ten.

ACTIVITIES:
1. Administer pretest and determine if any students already have mastery of concepts.
2. Students who do not will meet in group for instruction on the value of U.S. coins and the decimal equivalent of each.
3. Students who have mastered content will choose another country that has a decimal-based monetary system, study the value of each coin and its decimal equivalent, and report their results in a small group meeting with the teacher.
4. Students will show their knowledge through successfully using the monetary system (U.S. or foreign) in the class store.

RESOURCES:
1. Mathematics textbooks and library books.
2. Filmstrip/Video on coins of the world.

---

for that is not the case! It is vital to their growth that they be given the opportunity to do so. This can be accomplished in a fairly unobtrusive way. The lesson plan shown (see Table 8-4) differentiates for the gifted and talented writing students through the open-ended process that is used. The primary resource used is the book, *The Silver Pony* by Lynd Ward (1973). This classic book tells the story of a little boy who lives on a farm and discovers a magical silver pony. When his father does not believe that the pony exists, the pony and the boy run away to have adventures throughout the world and return to the farm at the end of the story. What makes this book uniquely suited to the lesson is that there are no words in the story, only pictures, and the pictures are displayed on the right-hand pages only, leaving white space on the left-hand side for story composing (in the imagination or on the paper). Thus, the students can write the story at their own writing levels with as much dialog, embellishment, phraseology, and figurative language as they desire, using the pictures for inspiration. No special grouping, resources, or instructions are needed in order to give the students a chance to write at their individual levels.

Table 8-4   Plan for Differentiated Lesson in Creative Writing

---

TOPIC: Story writing

OBJECTIVE:
1. Students will write a story using dialog between at least two characters.

ACTIVITIES:
1. The book *The Silver Pony* will be shown to the students.
2. Students will volunteer to tell the story for the first chapter, including dialog between the father and the boy.
3. The students will choose one chapter for which to write the story and include dialog between two characters. All chapters will have at least one writer so that the entire story will be told.
4. The composite story will be read and critiqued by the class.

RESOURCE:
Lynd Ward, *The Silver Pony* (Boston: Houghton Mifflin Company, 1973).

Drawing a Still Life

Arranging instruction so that students can grow at their own rates in the arts is also an important matter to consider. This lesson (see Table 8-5) focuses on the discipline of drawing, with a still life as the subject. In

Table 8-5   Plan for Differentiated Lesson in Drawing

TOPIC: Drawing a still life

OBJECTIVE:
1. Students will draw a still life, including shadowing and gradations of color.

ACTIVITIES:
1. The still life will be composed by two of the students from a variety of objects made available by the instructor.
2. The technique of shading will be reviewed.
3. Students will choose their own perspective for drawing and will then do so.
4. Advanced students will limit their color selection to one.
5. Drawings will be displayed and critiqued.

RESOURCES:
1. Objects for the still life.
2. Books on still life.
3. Paper and crayons.

---

this case, the teacher has designated the subject, the materials, and the products that are to be used. However, the lesson is differentiated for the more talented art students and has been done in an intriguing way. The challenge has been made greater for these students by *limiting* the materials that they can use. They sit in the same studio, draw the same still life under the same lighting, for the same amount of time, but they use only one color of crayon to do so. Requiring this limitation forces the students to seek alternative ways of showing gradations of color and shading in their composition. Therefore, they are working on techniques that are more advanced than those techniques being used by the other students, and are essentially receiving accelerated content in the same setting as the rest of the class. Again, this is an example of a lesson that has been differentiated for student abilities without special assignments, resources, or settings for some of the students. Although such alterations in the curriculum are sometimes needed in meeting the curricular needs of the gifted students in the regular classroom, this is not always the case and much can be done to provide suitable curriculum within that setting.

STUDENT OUTCOMES
FROM APPROPRIATE CURRICULUM

Differentiating curriculum so that students receive meaningful instruction extends beyond presenting more and different information. The intellectual and emotional health of students is affected by the manner in which curriculum is implemented. Appropriate curriculum contributes to students' feelings of accomplishment, vitality, and growth, whereas inappropriate curriculum can lead to potential difficulties.

When students are involved in learning new skills and content rather than information they already know, they may be more active learners and less bored with their schooling. The challenge of learning new information and skills keeps the gifted and talented interested in school as they see its relevancy to their lives. It can also help deter later problems such as underachievement and dropping out of school altogether.

Appropriate curricular experiences can also give students the tools to continue to learn on their own. By exposing the students to processes, information, and resources that are diverse and suited to their needs and interests, they may find doors opening for them in their own mind and lead to new areas of interest and exploration.

SUMMARY

Because of the various abilities and needs of the students in a classroom, a single curricular plan may not be sufficient to instruct them appropriately. With the gifted and talented students, there are at least four factors (Maker, 1982) that may need to be modified in order to provide these students with instruction that is suited to them. These areas are the environment in which instruction takes place, the content of that instruction, the process or method of the instruction, and the products that are the results of the students' learning. By so doing, the students can continue as active learners in an environment that nurtures growth and development of new skills and abilities.

ACTION STEPS

1. Consider how curriculum decisions are currently being made. Do you have a curriculum guide, teachers' manuals, or scope and sequence charts? If so, familiarize yourself with their content, if you have not already done so.
2. What curricular modifications are already being made in regular classrooms? Are these adequate for the needs of your students? If not, choose one modification to make tomorrow.
3. Design a plan for differentiated curriculum building for the next year. What areas are the strength of the curriculum? Begin here and then extend to areas that are less strong.
4. At the end of the first year, assess your progress and develop a multiple-year plan for programming and curricular development for dealing with multiple student abilities.
5. Meet with the school's curriculum committee and arrange for materials and inservice presentations to assist you and the staff in this activity.

REFERENCES YOU CAN USE

Gallagher, J. (1985). *Teaching the gifted child* (3rd. ed.). Boston: Allyn and Bacon.

Maker, J. (1982). *Curriculum development for the gifted.* Rockville, MD: Aspen Systems Corporation.

Ostrander, S., & Schroeder, L. (1979). *Superlearning.* New York: Dell Publishing Company.

Swassing, R. (Ed.). (1985). *Teaching gifted children and adolescents.* Columbus, OH: Merrill Publishing Company.

VanTassel-Baska, J. (1986). *Handbook on curriculum for the gifted.* Evanston, IL: Center for Talent Development.

9

Models for
Developing Curriculum

There have been many models proposed upon which curriculum for gifted and talented students can be based. Some of these models have been designed with the gifted students specifically in mind; others have been adopted for the skills they develop or the processes they employ. This chapter will describe examples of both and will provide information about the appropriate use of each model with gifted and talented students. These are not, however, the only curricular models that correspond to the needs of gifted students. Rather, they represent the types of models that teachers should consider using as bases for designing their curricula.

The models chosen were selected based on a number of factors. First, each builds skills that are vital to gifted students and enhances the students' ability to meet objectives. Next, these models can be used with students of varying abilities and will not result in accomplished students being segregated from the rest of the class. The last criteria for selection was that the models be easily employed. Those presented in this chapter are easily understood and assimilated into the current curriculum and can be used to enrich or supplant that which is currently taking place.

ROLE OF MODELS
IN PLANNING CURRICULUM

Models for curriculum development should be used in such a way that curricular decision making is enhanced by using the models for determining the content of instruction and the methods for delivering that content. Models rarely dictate the content or delivery system, but they do provide a framework for making those selections. By presenting the model, the author is proposing a manner in which curriculum can be determined. However, it is an accomplished teacher who can look at the model and determine which part or parts will work in his or her teaching situation.

It is inappropriate to use models blindly and in such a way that the responsibility for decision making is relinquished by the teacher. Teachers should select models that will work for them, fitting their methods and philosophy of teaching. You cannot assume that by following a model for curriculum development that the students in the classroom are receiving a valid program. It is how the model is used that determines its effectiveness, not its mere use.

In addition, it is unlikely that one model will serve all the curricular needs a teacher will have. It is more likely that a number of models will be needed in order to meet the needs of the students effectively. The most beneficial use of curricular models comes when teachers have a working knowledge of many and use them when a situation calls for a particular approach. Knowing what to use and when to use it is a sign of an accomplished instructor.

The next section will describe ten models for instructing gifted students and their cohorts. This chapter describes how these models can be used in combination through subject area case studies. Again, keep in mind that these models may be appropriate for a number of students in the class who are not designated as gifted. However, this does not necessarily weaken their benefit to the gifted. As long as they contribute in a positive manner to the skills and abilities of the students, their use is warranted.

BLOOM'S TAXONOMY OF OBJECTIVES FOR THE COGNITIVE DOMAIN

Most programs for the gifted use the *Taxonomy of Educational Objectives: Cognitive Domain* (Bloom, 1956), or "Bloom's Taxonomy," for a major part of the curricular decision making. This model, which presents six levels of thinking skills, was intended to be used as a basis for classifying educational objectives. It has surpassed this original intent, however, and is now seen as a means of planning and evaluating student activities in such a way that students can develop their cognitive abilities more fully.

The greatest use of the *Taxonomy* has been in the area classified as the higher level thinking skills. These skills are frequently mentioned in discussions of differentiating curriculum for the gifted, and "Bloom's Taxonomy" has been the standard reference point. Yet it has application possibilities beyond this and can be used in the classroom without a great deal of expense or alteration in current procedures or materials.

The Model

As mentioned, Bloom's Taxonomy is composed of six levels of cognitive behaviors: knowledge, comprehension, application, analysis, synthesis, and evaluation (see Table 9-1). The *knowledge* level deals with the students' abilities to remember, or memory. *Comprehension* is the ability to recall information and use it as presented. It does not involve using the information in new or different circumstances. Translation, interpretation, and extrapolation are considered comprehension skills. At level three, *application*, students should be able to use information in a new way or under new circumstances. This is a more complex skill than comprehending in that a student must not only understand the information in its original context but be able to use it in a new or different way, demonstrating the development of a principle or abstraction. *Analysis,*

Table 9-1   Bloom's Taxonomy of Cognitive Objectives

Level	Skills	Sample Questions/Activities
Knowledge	Recall Memorize	What is the chemical symbol for water? How many keys are on a piano?
Comprehension	Translate Relate Interpret	Convert zero degrees Fahrenheit to Celsius. Retell *Goldilocks* in your own words.
Application	Apply Demonstrate Use known in new situation	If John has six apples and Judy has two, how many do they have together?
Analysis	Dissect Categorize Classify	Chart the weather for the month of April. What items from this list go together?
Synthesis	Assemble Generate Create new from known	Write a new ending to this story. Design a class logo.
Evaluation	Judge Decide Recommend	How could we improve the class newspaper? What did you do well in class today?

the fourth level, involves the ability to separate items into their components in order to see the relationships of the parts and how they correspond. This is frequently cited as the beginning of the higher level thinking skills. Putting together parts in order to make a new whole is called *synthesis*. This fifth level of the *Taxonomy* involves the students' creativity in that it requires students to recombine known pieces of information or materials into structures previously unknown. The final level, *evaluation*, is also the last of the three "higher thinking" levels. It involves the ability to make value judgments for decision making on an internal (consistency, logic, accuracy) or external basis (compared to other works, theories, or principles established in a field).

For the gifted students in the classroom, this model provides the framework for developing curricula that use thinking skills beyond memorization and recall. The real world requires students to be able to use information in settings other than school and to be able to make judgments about their actions. Therefore, these skills should also be built as part of a curricular package.

The "higher level thinking skills" (analysis, synthesis, evaluation) are part of the cognitive abilities that all students should develop. They are not the private domain of the gifted. It may well be the case, however, that gifted students will have more time available to work at this level, as they are particularly adept at memorization and comprehension skills. Whereas all students in the class can profit from dealing with the entire *Taxonomy*, the *proportion* of time spent on the higher or lower level skills may differ depending on the students' capacity to use their cognitive abilities.

Relationship to Content, Process, Product, and Environmental Modifications

Bloom's Taxonomy primarily provides a means through which the *processes* of instruction are modified. By its use, teachers give students the opportunity to extend their thinking processes in new areas. For example, students are asked not only to add 10 + 5 on a math facts sheet (knowledge/comprehension), but must also be able to enter a grocery store and pay fifteen cents for a ten-cent and five-cent piece of candy (application) or decide how they would most like to spend the fifteen cents (evaluation).

It is interesting to observe students who learn the *Taxonomy* as *content*. They soon learn to recognize the manner in which they are thinking, the levels at which the questions they are asking fall, and the nature of the activities in which they are engaged. When they begin this classification, not only do they participate in an analysis level activity, but they also tend to find it a challenge to work more often in the higher levels.

They begin to ask better questions and attempt to function as fully as possible.

Appropriate Uses of Bloom's *Taxonomy*

The original intent of the people who assembled this taxonomy of cognitive skills was to introduce a classification system so that members of the educational community could discuss the skills involved in cognition and develop student objectives in this area. This remains a viable use of the *Taxonomy*. However, there are other uses that may be equally as serviceable in the development of curriculum.

Perhaps the most far-reaching use of this model is as a means of developing and evaluating the questions that teachers ask the students in their classes. Most questions are of the recall (knowledge) and understanding (comprehension) variety, thus, they are not very challenging to the gifted students. By developing skill in asking questions at each level of the *Taxonomy*, teachers challenge their students to use more cognitive ability and to develop their use of higher level thinking skills. Students need practice and opportunities to learn to do so in an effective manner. An interesting outgrowth of the teacher learning to ask better questions is that students also seem to develop their abilities in this area. Keeping notecards with questions at each level of the *Taxonomy* in books read to students is a good method with which to begin developing question-asking skills. After practicing for a while, it will become second nature. But, to make sure that a variety of levels are being used, tape record a lesson during class and classify the questions according to the levels of the *Taxonomy*.

In addition to asking good questions, Bloom's Taxonomy can be used to develop activities and to write test items. Activities can be generated that use different levels of the *Taxonomy* and are used in learning centers, lessons, as extra work, or as assignments for in or out of class. The key to making activities is to include a number of levels in each activity or a balance of levels throughout a group of activities. Then, when assessing student proficiency, remember to give them an opportunity to show their abilities to think beyond the knowledge and comprehension levels. Since new skills are being built, they should be measured through such means as essay questions, demonstrations, and projects.

The *Taxonomy of Education Objectives: Cognitive Domain* is a relatively simple model to adopt and great benefits are possible for those who use it. It gives the students in the classroom a chance to develop and use their thinking skills and it provides the teachers with a method to differentiate instruction without segregating students. Teachers need only to vary the amount of time students spend on the different levels, allowing those who master content at the lower levels of the *Taxonomy* quickly to spend more time in the higher thinking skill levels. In this way, all students are receiving appropriate instruction within one framework.

CLARK'S INTEGRATIVE EDUCATION MODEL

The *Integrative Education Model* (Clark, 1986) is based on the growing brain/mind research of the last decade. It has as its focal point the fully functioning mind of the individual and seeks to help students use all their abilities in their attempts at learning. To do so, the model combines the use of students' thinking, feeling, sensing, and intuiting skills and brings them to bear on the academic and nonacademic areas of schooling.

The strength of this model is in its integrated approach to learning. It recognizes students as fully functioning human beings who have interacting systems that influence performance. This view is very pragmatic in that it is certainly a recognized fact that the way a student feels will influence the way she or he thinks; the opposite is also true. Clark extends this reality into a model for building curriculum that is humane in its approach to learning and child-centered in its intent.

The Model

The *Integrative Education Model* is shown by a circle divided into four quadrants (see Figure 9-1). These parts each represent a function of the brain which interacts and supports the other functions when students are learning. These four functions are: the thinking function (cognitive); the feeling or emotional function (affective); the physical function (sensing); and the intuitive function (insightful, creative). The broken lines that separate the functions symbolize the manner in which the functions work together.

Clark (1986) describes the four quadrants in the following ways. The *cognitive function* "includes the analytic, problem solving, sequential, evaluative specialization of the left cortical hemisphere of the brain as well as the more spatially oriented, gestalt specialization of the right cortical hemisphere" (p. 27). The *affective function* "is expressed in emotions and feelings . . . (providing) the gateway to enhance or limit higher cognitive function" (p. 27). The *physical function* "involves movement, physical encoding, sight, hearing, smell, taste, and touch . . . (determining) how we perceive reality" (p. 28). And the *intuitive function* "is the sense of total understanding, of directly and immediately gaining a concept in its whole, living existence, and is in part the result of a high level of synthesis of all the brain functions" (p. 29).

Clark relates expected results of using the model as follows:

By use of the Integrative Education Model and strategies incorporating this construct, students can expect to make impressive gains in areas of cogni-

Figure 9-1   Clark's Integrative Education Model

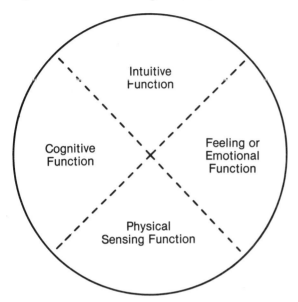

Source: B. Clark, *Optimizing Learning* (Columbus, Ohio: Merrill Publishing Company, 1986), p. 27. Copyright 1986 by Merrill Publishing Company. Reprinted by permission of the publisher.

tion, self concept, and social-emotional development. Among the cognitive gains will be accelerated learning, higher levels of retention and recall, and high interest in content. They can also improve self-esteem, find pleasure in learning, and improve interpersonal relations and teacher-student rapport (p. 31).

There are seven key components upon which the *Integrative Model* is built. Although Clark states that not all are absolutely necessary in every instance in which the model is being used, she does caution that the use of all seven will result in the most effective use of the model. The components are:

1. Responsive learning environment
2. Relaxation and tension reduction
3. Movement and physical encoding
4. Empowering language and behavior
5. Choice and perceived control
6. Complex and challenging cognitive activity
7. Intuition and integration

From the curricular point of view, then, the *Integrative Model* builds learning experiences to enhance students' abilities in each of the seven key component areas. This integration of skills and brain functions is what leads to the fully functioning student. By recognizing the impact of the parts on the whole, the model optimizes the learning environment and the students' chances of succeeding within that setting.

Relationship to Content, Process, Product, and Environmental Modifications

The *Integrative Education Model* influences curricular modifications for gifted students in all four of these areas. The *content* of learning is expanded to include the typical subject areas along with such topics as relaxation, tension reduction, use of empowering language, and tapping into one's intuition. This is a broader agenda than most curricula outline and it extends into some areas rarely addressed in schools.

Processes of learning are also dealt with in this model through the emphasis on techniques to use the mind more fully. Most school programs deal primarily with the cognitive functions of the brain, whereas this model looks at the importance of the feelings, senses, and creativity of the students and the manner in which all four functions of the brain affect the learning processes.

The redefinition of the *products* of learning is another facet of the model that lends itself to differentiating curriculum for the gifted. Products of learning are not only papers, projects, mobiles, and reports, but also self-management, self-esteem, independent learning, and higher mental processing. These outcomes are extremely compatible with the goals we set for the gifted students.

Finally, the learning *environment* is recognized as a central part of the learning experience. The model integrates the environment into the total educational schema and acknowledges its impact on the learning processes of the students. Conditions are established to encourage success and feelings of self-worth through a student-centered approach to learning.

Appropriate Uses of the *Integrated Education Model*

The *Integrated Education Model* is easily adaptable to whole-class use. Certainly the model is appropriate for use with all students in the regular classroom. It does, however, benefit the gifted and talented students in some very direct ways.

First, it presents information in an integrated fashion, corresponding to the way many gifted students think. By allowing them to use all their abilities, gifted and talented students are given the opportunity to develop more than just their cognitive abilities, resulting in more well-rounded students and human beings.

Next, by incorporating the relaxation and tension-reducing techniques, the model equips the gifted with strategies to deal with their natural tendency to be perfectionists and stressed. Children learn better when they are not under stressful conditions (Albrecht, 1979); they also tend to be more creative when they are relaxed. For the gifted, developing these abilities as students can be the beginning of successful stress management across their lifetimes.

A third use of the model is in the area of self-management. Clark includes the areas of empowering language and behavior and making choices as a central part of the model. By giving students the opportunity to develop these skills, they can take greater control of their own learning and develop the basic skills required to be life-long learners. Regardless of how good the teachers of the gifted and talented are, it will always be necessary for these students to have the capability of finding and digesting information on their own. This model allows students to be the people responsible for their own learning—a responsibility that they actually have had all along.

Finally, the model recognizes the need for complex and challenging activity as a way to keep students thriving in the learning environment. This is often a problem for gifted students in the regular classroom. Adopting this model involves commitment to educating the whole child and dealing with all students in terms of their individual abilities. Thus, gifted students are given the opportunity to learn at their own pace and in a way that is meaningful to them.

DEBONO'S CoRT THINKING MODEL

The *CoRT Thinking Model*, designed by DeBono (1986), is a system through which thinking is directly taught as a skill. This direct teaching of thinking has gained great acceptance over the past five years and has been the basis for developing curriculum for the gifted even longer. It has finally been recognized by educators that the skills involved with thinking go beyond the memorization and recall of facts and that students need to develop this ability in order to use information in ways that will aid their cognitive and affective processes.

The Model

CoRT Thinking Lessons have been developed in such a way that they can be used at all grade levels and with all students in the class. Since all students are in need of thinking skills, DeBono has developed a system in which they can all participate. It is broken down into three segments: basic skills training, creative thinking, and critical and interactive thinking. Lessons in the basic skills training area are developed by teaching students seven thinking operations. They are PMI, or plus, minus, interesting (treatment of ideas); CAF, or consider all facts (factors involved); C&S, or consequences and sequel (focus on the consequences); AGO, or aims, goals, objectives (focus on the purpose); FIP, or first important priorities (focus on priorities); APC, or alternatives, possibilities, choices (focus on alternatives); and OPV, or other people's views (other people involved).

DeBono (1986) describes the operations in basic skills training in this way. "(PMI) has you make an effort to find the good points (P = Plus), the bad points (M = Minus) and the interesting points (I = Interesting) about an idea" (p. 9). CAF is an operation through which students "consider all the facts in a situation. . . . (A) lesson can be taught in terms of: the factors affecting oneself . . . other people . . . (or) society in general" (p. 13). During C&S, students look "ahead to see the consequences of some action, plan, decision, rule, invention, etc." (p. 20). AGO "introduce(s) and emphasize(s) the idea of purpose (behind actions) . . . as distinct from reaction(s)" (p. 23). FIP "is the crystallization of the process of picking out the most important ideas, factors, objectives, consequences, etc. . . . (and) is a judgment situation (in which) there are no absolute answers" (p. 29). APC is "the process of deliberately trying to find alternatives" (p. 32) while OPV is "the process of looking at other people's viewpoints so that the process can be used consciously and deliberately" (p. 40).

Lessons in each of these areas are designed to last for thirty-five minutes and are conducted once a week. Each skill is covered in one session with the total program (sixty lessons) lasting approximately two years. The structure of the lesson is divided into five activities. An "introduction" is given to the lesson by the teacher (or facilitator), followed by "practice" problems, available on skill cards, which are worked on in groups. The "process" section of the lesson involves a class discussion on an aspect of thinking that is the subject of the lesson. This is followed by a time in which "five basic 'principles' concerning the subject of the lesson" (p. 46) are given to the groups for their examination and comment. Finally, "projects" can be developed in order to give students further practice in the thinking skill.

Although the program is available commercially, the only resources that are needed are the students' minds and imaginations. They are given ways to structure their thoughts and methods through which their newly developed thinking skills can be used in new situations.

Relationship to Content, Process, Product, and Environmental Modifications

The *CoRT Thinking Model* is primarily a means to differentiate the *processes* of instruction. Students are taught ways to use their cognitive abilities more fully and to problem solve. DeBono's purpose is to develop those abilities and to enhance creative thinking abilities at the same time. However, by learning the system and the ways of organizing thinking, the program also becomes a way to modify the *content* of instruction. The new strategies and ways to organize their thoughts give students new direction for developing their cognitive functions.

Appropriate Uses of the CoRT Thinking Model

The *CoRT Thinking Model* has been developed for all students to use. Therefore, it can be integrated easily into the regular classroom structure. Students of greater ability can simply work on problems of greater complexity as they learn the skill lesson for the week.

It cannot be assumed that the brighter students will already know how to use these operations or have the skills needed to think in creative or critical ways. In many cases they may only *appear* to have the skills due to their ability to verbalize in seemingly sophisticated ways. Curricular models that teach the skills involved with critical and creative thinking provide the opportunity for the teacher to assess which skills the students may be lacking and a process through which the skills can be mastered and used.

GALLAGHER'S MODEL FOR CONTENT MODIFICATION

The *Model for Content Modification* (Gallagher, 1985) is a four-faceted approach to differentiating the content of instruction for the gifted. Although it is usually quite clear that some students in a classroom have mastered the content of a lesson or a unit before the others, some teachers do not know how to differentiate instruction in such a way that these students can be involved in the lesson with content that is challenging for them.

The *Model for Content Modification* gives the teacher a framework upon which the differentiation can occur in a way that is compatible with the traits of gifted students. This model not only provides a schema for content changes, it also neatly fits the academic needs that these students typically have.

The Model

The *Model for Content Modification* includes four ways in which the content of a lesson can be altered to fit the needs of the gifted students in the class. These are: content acceleration, content enrichment, content sophistication, and content novelty (see Table 9-2). Although each modification can stand separately, Gallagher points out that many curricular variations will include more than one category.

Content acceleration is based on the philosophy that gifted students should be given work that is at their ability level, even if it is two to three years advanced, so that they can begin the process of coping with complex ideas. Gifted students are recognizable in that they learn more quickly than most students; therefore, they are more likely to need accelerated content. Using this strategy, a fourth grader might use a sixth-grade text or a seventh grader might be enrolled in the high school algebra course.

Content enrichment is accomplished through elaborating on the regular content in such a way that the students study the same basic concepts but in ways that differ from the other students. This more firmly establishes the fundamental concepts in the students' minds while exposing them to different avenues to attain knowledge and giving them the opportunity to study a topic in depth. For example, a third-grade science class was studying a unit on nutrition. It became obvious in the first days of the unit that a cadre of students were already familiar with the basic food groups and would not gain new information by making the "Basic Four"

Table 9-2   Gallagher's Model for Content Modification

Strategy	Corresponding Characteristics of Gifted Students
Content Acceleration	Learns rapidly Knows great amounts of information
Content Enrichment	Wide-ranging interests Capable of learning in greater depth
Content Sophistication	Greater ability to make generalizations and relationships Early ability to conceptualize
Content Novelty	Unusual curiosity Variety of Interests Persistence

collage with the rest of the students. Therefore, the teacher gave an alternative assignment, asking the small group to keep a three-day diary of all that they ate and to do an analysis of the extent to which their diets met the basic requirements of good nutrition. In this way, all the students were involved in the content of the unit, but from different points of view.

Content sophistication is described by Gallagher (1985) as a strategy "to provide material that will allow the gifted student to see larger systems of ideas and concepts related to the basic content for the course" (p. 104). This is achieved through exposing students to more complex information and helping them to see generalizations and associations to larger concepts or abstractions. Gifted students are more adept at these skills than their classmates and this type of modification encourages them to use that ability. A fifth-grade teacher was using this strategy in a social studies unit on conflict. The gifted students in the class took an alternative route to studying this topic when they were given scenarios of six different international wars and were asked to note any similarities among the conflicts. After they completed that part of the assignment, they were asked to speculate on the nature of conflict, if it is inevitable, and how it can be avoided.

Content novelty involves introducing students to content that they would not ordinarily have the opportunity to study. This strategy is particularly useful to gifted students in that it provides a chance for them to study areas in which only they may be interested or topics that are so different that they suit only the advanced career and academic directions of these students. Some of this variation comes naturally as students select courses of study in high school and college. However, it can be made available earlier through such programs as mentorships, mini-courses, or independent studies.

Relationship to Content, Process, Product, and Environmental Modifications

This model focuses primarily on the area of *content*. However, it is compatible with other models that emphasize the other areas. Combining this model with Bloom's Taxonomy or within the *Integrative Education Model* segment of cognition would certainly be appropriate. All four content modifications listed in the model are necessary in order to deal with gifted children in the regular classroom. The modifications provide a means to include meaningful content for instruction and an avenue to respond to the unique learning characteristics of the gifted.

Appropriate Uses of the *Model for Content Modification*

The versatility of this model is a major asset and a primary reason why it has been included as part of this discussion. The model can be used at any grade level and in any subject area in order to give students the chance to study content that is appropriate to their abilities and needs. By integrating the four strategies for modifying curriculum, the teacher can be assured that the students within the class are engaged in meaningful studies.

Gifted students complain long and hard about being "forced" to do work that they already know or that they learned before the rest of the class. This situation can lead to problems with students acting out, not completing seemingly easy work, developing poor attitudes toward school, and experiencing an inability to learn new information since the strategies to do so have not been developed. Students have the right to be involved with content that is challenging to them; this model provides a mechanism to assure that such content is available.

Again, this is a model that can be used with other models in order to provide an integrated and balanced curriculum for the students. Content is just one part of the alterations that may have to be made for the gifted students in the classroom. By joining this approach with others of your choice, the students can reap the benefits of a curriculum that is flexible enough to correspond with their requirements for sound academic preparation.

KRATHWOHL'S TAXONOMY OF OBJECTIVES FOR THE AFFECTIVE DOMAIN

The *Taxonomy of Educational Objectives: Affective Domain* (Krathwohl, Bloom, and Masia, 1964) was developed by essentially the same educators who were responsible for the *Taxonomy of Educational Objectives: Cognitive Domain*. The basic purposes and procedures were also the same, except they were now applied to the affective, or feeling, domain of intelligence. As with Bloom's Taxonomy, Krathwohl's is a set of skills that students can develop pertaining to the way they feel. These skills are appropriate for students of all ages and can be interspersed throughout the curriculum.

The taxonomies do *not* reflect an order of importance; greater value should not be placed on one level as opposed to another. Rather, all are essential skills for students to develop fully as they will need to use them all as part of healthy emotional growth. However, the skills do require more complex abilities as they ascend to the higher levels and may take more time and effort to develop.

The Model

Krathwohl's *Affective Taxonomy* is composed of five levels: receiving, willingness to respond, valuing, organizing a value system, and characterization by a values complex (see Table 9-3). These five levels represent the affective skills needed to use the cognitive taxonomy successfully. Functioning with the six cognitive levels is necessary to use the affective skills. Thus, the taxonomies are not mutually exclusive as affective and cognitive skills do affect one another. As in the *Integrative Education*

Table 9-3   Krathwohl's Taxonomy of Affective Objectives

Level	Skills	Sample Questions/Activites
Receiving	Sensing Awareness	Ask students to demonstrate three emotions. Read a scary book.
Responding	Compliance Enjoyment Interests	Develop a list of class rules with students. Play the "Grand Canyon Suite" and ask students to describe how they feel.
Valuing	Accepting Acting consistently Convincing	Ask students to tell how they would respond to a moral dilemma. Place "I Believe" statements written by the students on the board.
Organizing	Systematizing Synthesizing Adapting Accommodating	If Joe invited you to a party on the same day you had promised your younger brother you would take him to a movie, which would you do? Why?
Characterization	Internalizing Developed life philosophy	Role play a situation in which students must demonstrate their values. Discuss ethics as it relates to schools, law, and medicine.

Model, the two areas work together and interact with one another, making each somewhat dependent on the other.

Receiving, level one, is the ability to sense feelings. At this level, students are simply aware of their emotions and can exhibit them at one of three sublevels: awareness, willingness to receive, and controlled or selected attention. These three sublevels (Maker, 1982) indicate that students can be passive in their use of the "receiving" skill (as in awareness) or active (as in controlled or selected attention).

Responding is the next level of the *Affective Taxonomy.* At this level, students are aware of things in their environment (receiving) and are interested enough to "respond" in some manner and possibly find enjoyment in that response. Three sublevels are also found in this category, with passive to active response patterns. They are: acquiescence in responding (complying), willingness to respond, and satisfaction in response.

Valuing, level three, implies that a student has found worth in an object or emotion and has placed some value on it. To be functioning at this level, a student must show consistency in his or her valuing such that it is apparent that a value system exists. Again, three sublevels are listed: acceptance of a value, preference for a value, and commitment to a value. Thus, valuing can be found in varying degrees with some being more of the tolerating variety (acceptance of a value) and others being actively campaigning for converts to a value system (commitment).

Level four, *organization,* represents the level at which values are internalized and systematized into value systems or value complexes. This may require prioritizing certain values and accommodating one to another so that there is a consistency of behavior based on the system. The two sublevels in this category are conceptualization of a value and organization of a value system.

The final level, *characterization by a value or value complex,* is the highest level of the *Affective Taxonomy.* In it, values have been translated into behaviors, and the underlying value systems that the students have developed will determine the manner in which they act. Two sublevels are found in which students begin to experience conditions of trust, respect, appreciation, and affection. They are: developing a generalized set of values and characterization (behavior based on a life's philosophy).

The five levels described, then, make up the *Taxonomy of Objectives for the Affective Domain.* It is apparent that the levels are hierarchical in that in order to proceed from one to the next, the students must build skills from the bottom to the top. However, the lower skills are as important as the higher skills and should be given attention, for it is upon that base that the higher level skills are built.

Relationship to Content, Process, Product, and Environmental Modifications

As with Bloom's Taxonomy, the *Taxonomy of Educational Objectives for the Affective Domain* is mainly a model through which the content and processes of instruction can be modified. This taxonomy can be viewed as *content* and taught to the students as a means of explaining behavior and assisting their understanding of themselves and the teacher's goals for them. Students who are taught the taxonomy seem to enjoy knowing the steps and identifying them as behaviors occur. Although student interest in the taxonomy will vary between students, the gifted will most likely show more interest in how it was developed and the ways in which it can be used.

The *process* modifications indicated by the model are applicable to all the students in a classroom, for all should be in the process of developing beliefs and belief systems upon which to base their behavior. School curriculum is a part of the manner in which students learn about values, whether it is taught directly or not. Therefore, teachers may as well construct their lessons for the greatest benefit by attempting to give students the opportunities to develop these abilities in an environment where it is safe to do so. This requires that teachers develop lessons and activities that cultivate the entire spectrum of the taxonomy in such a way that it will be balanced with upper as well as lower level skills.

Appropriate Uses of Krathwohl's *Affective Taxonomy*

Gifted students are very sensitive to their own belief systems and those of other people. They tend to hold strong beliefs at an early age and will tenaciously direct their behavior based on what they believe. Thus, they seem to be ready to develop the higher level skills represented in the taxonomy at an earlier age and in greater degree than the rest of the students.

Teachers may find that gifted students are able to spend a larger proportion of their time in upper level skills, since their abilities to work at the lower levels may be more highly developed. A caution should be mentioned, however. There are many gifted students who seem to hold belief systems but who cannot tell you why they believe the way they do or substantiate their behaviors beyond a slogan or a phrase. These students may, in fact, not function at the Organization or Characterization levels at all. They may merely have the verbal ability that allows them to appear to be at that level, while it is simply their rhetoric that is advanced.

The *Affective Taxonomy,* then, can be used as a means to develop activities that are balanced in such a way that students can develop skills at all the levels. Or it can be used as a vehicle for challenging students to develop their value systems and evaluate them as they progress. Gifted students have a tendency to question and probe their feelings as well as their cognitive abilities. By working from this taxonomy, teachers can assure that the students have a framework from which to grow.

PARNES' CREATIVE PROBLEM-SOLVING MODEL

The goal of many programs for gifted and talented students is to develop the creative abilities of students. Most educators recognize the importance of creative thinking abilities and understand the need to develop these skills in students. Certainly the skills that will be required of today's students, when they enter the working world, will include creative problem-solving skills to an even greater extent than now. Therefore, schools must be in the business of enhancing these skills through curricular models that affect the creative aspects of the intellect.

Parnes' *Creative Problem-Solving Model* (Parnes, 1977) is one model that provides a schema through which students can generate new ideas and learn a process for resolving problems. What distinguishes this model even further is its method for generating many ideas, withholding judgments while developing alternatives, and then evaluating alternatives through the establishment of criteria. Hopefully, by teaching students to use such a model, they will be better prepared to solve problems on their own.

The Model

The *Creative Problem-Solving Model* is a five-step process for finding problems and generating solutions to problems. From the start, Parnes shows that finding problems can be as demanding on the creative abilities as finding solutions. This is an important concept for students to understand and for which to have strategies available to respond.

The first step in the model is *fact-finding.* During fact-finding, students are presented with a scenario or a problem in an unclear form called the "mess." Since most problems are not totally clear, this step has students determine what is already known about the "mess" and gather additional information about the "mess" with which they have been presented.

In step two, *problem-finding,* they embark on the task of determining what the problems are in the "mess." This is accomplished through identifying many possible problems as seen from various viewpoints and then narrowing these down to a few major problems. They are then asked to choose one problem with which to proceed through the remaining steps and to state the problem in such a way that it can be investigated. The standard prefix used for questions at this level is "In what ways might I . . ." (IWWMI).

Idea-finding is the third step in the *Creative Problem-Solving Model.* At this time, students brainstorm as many solutions to their problems as they can. The goal of this step is to generate a vast number of solutions from as many points of view as possible. The standard rules of brainstorming (quantity over quality, defer judgment, hitchhike on others' ideas) are employed.

Solution-finding follows in which the students identify their most likely solutions to the problem and develop criteria (money, time, human resources needed, etc.) upon which to judge these solutions. Students then develop a grid, including the solutions and the criteria, and try to rate each solution objectively on the criteria that they have developed. The solution with the greatest likelihood of succeeding is taken to the final step.

The last step, *acceptance-finding,* engages students in an often forgotten step in problem-solving schemas. That is, after students have found solutions, they must create a plan for getting others to accept that solution. This step has students develop a plan for getting their ideas accepted and investigate the manner in which their audience will react. In this way, they take the problem-solving model into a plan-of-action stage.

Relationship to Content, Process, Product, and Environmental Modifications

The *Creative Problem-Solving Model* is primarily a strategy that can impact gifted students through modifying the *processes* of learning. However, it also has relevance to the areas of *content, product,* and *environment.* The model uses *processes* that require students to develop new skills in thinking more flexibly and fluently, using their originality, suspending their judgments for the sake of generating more ideas, and developing and using criteria for decision making. These processes can be generalized beyond this model into other problem-solving and independent learning situations.

The *content* modifications for the gifted come in the form of the model itself. Gifted students are problem solvers by nature. They love to answer trivia questions, solve riddles, and master puzzles. This model, when taught as content, can give them an additional plan to use in solving their everyday problems, ranging from disagreements on the playground to identifying a topic for a term paper.

The modifications for the gifted in the *products* and *environmental* areas are also apparent. By using the model, students are more likely to develop divergent products than if conventional formats are used. Additionally, in order to use the model successfully, students must be in an environment that accepts divergence, "messes," and outrageous thinking. Thus, the environment should be more open to exploration and asking questions—both being environmental conditions in which learning can thrive.

Appropriate Uses of the *Creative Problem-Solving Model*

There are a number of ways to use this model in order to enhance the learning of gifted students. Its use need not be confined solely to those students, however, and can be very successful with a wide range of abilities. One of the distinct advantages of using this model in the regular classroom setting is its capability to be meaningful for students of many ability and achievement levels.

As stated above, this model gives students a method of problem finding and problem solving. Having a schema to follow can help them attack problems, find their component parts, develop lists of possible solutions, choose those most viable, and then develop strategies to find acceptance for their solutions within a framework that encourages cooperation and understanding of others. Also, it is quite likely that gifted students will some day be in career situations where innovation and problem solving are needed. By exposing them early to the process, they can develop lifelong skills that will serve them well.

The *Creative Problem-Solving Model* is similar to the *Future Problem-Solving Model* used in the FPS competition bowls. This bowl gives students an outlet where they use their creative abilities to their maximum. Being involved in such programs is inspiring for many gifted students, and it gives them the chance to work together in team situations.

The *Creative Problem-Solving Model* can also be adapted to the content of most grade levels. Scientific problems, moral dilemmas, unanswered social studies questions, or problems in the lunchroom can all be tackled. By using the model throughout the curriculum as well as part of the curriculum, the teacher can show students how to generalize the skills to problems in many areas.

RENZULLI'S ENRICHMENT TRIAD MODEL

The *Enrichment Triad Model* (Renzulli, 1977) is another plan for program and curriculum development that is frequently used in programs including gifted students. In fact, Renzulli claims that by using this type of model, not only are the students being well served, but the program itself becomes valid, as it is qualitatively different from other programming efforts that are less suited to the gifted.

Although the model (see Figure 9-2) appears to be quite simple, it encompasses numerous skill-building opportunities, gives teachers a method for dealing with the rate and depth of learning issues and interest differences displayed by the gifted, and is tailored to exposing students to experiences they might otherwise miss. Thus, it will not come as a surprise that some programs for the gifted are based solely on this model, and a great number of other programs use it at least part of the time.

Figure 9-2   Renzulli's Enrichment Triad Model

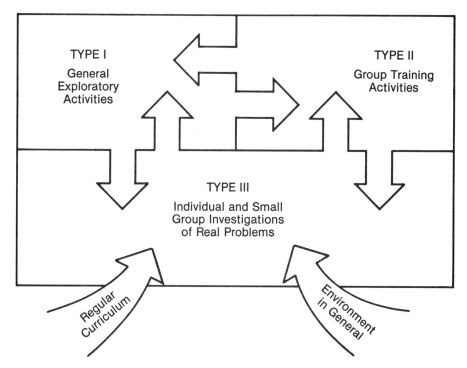

Source: J. Renzulli, *The Enrichment Triad Model* (Mansfield Center, Conn.: Creative Learning Press, 1977), p. 14. Reprinted with permission by Creative Learning Press, copyright © 1977.

The Model

From the name alone, it is apparent that the *Enrichment Triad Model* is designed to be used for enrichment purposes. Renzulli (1977) defines enrichment as "experiences or activities that are above and beyond the so called "regular curriculum" (pp. 13–14). The model uses three types of enrichment activities in order to provide appropriate programs for gifted students: *General Exploratory Activities, Group Training Activities, and Individual and Small Group Investigations of Real-World Problems.* It is Renzulli's position that the first two types of enrichment are beneficial to all students, whereas the third type, individual and small group investigations of real-world problems, is most appropriately used with gifted and talented students.

General Exploratory Activities, or Type I activities, are described by Renzulli (1977) as "those experiences and activities that are designed to bring the learner into touch with the kinds of topics or areas of study in which he or she may have a sincere interest" (p. 17). These activities can be in such forms as field trips, guest speakers, interviews, publications, learning centers, or films. They are intended to expose students to different areas of interest that they might like to pursue in greater depth in the future. These activities also give the students a chance to experience new things and may broaden their interest base (an important outcome for many gifted students).

Group Training Activities, or Type II activities, consist of "methods, materials, and instructional techniques that are mainly concerned with the development of thinking and feeling processes" (Renzulli, 1977, p. 24). The use of the taxonomies of educational objectives (Bloom, 1956; Krathwohl, 1964), Parnes' *Creative Problem-Solving Model,* and independent studies are among the types of process formats that can be used in this category, making them not only compatible with the *Enrichment Triad Model,* but actually an integral part of the model. Among the skills Renzulli recommends for this block are:

Brainstorming	Elaboration	Observation
Hypothesizing	Classifying	Values
Originality	Analysis	Synthesis
Evaluation	Flexibility	Fluency

The ultimate purpose of this level for gifted students is to build the process skills needed to continue to the next level. Through general exploratory activities they discover topical areas of interest; through group training activities they develop the means to do the explorations.

Individual and Small Group Investigations of Real Problems, or Type

III activities, is the final segment of this model and builds on the information and skills developed in the other two areas. In this type of enrichment activity the students become *investigators* of real problems or topics and employ standard methods of inquiry to arrive at solutions. Thus, they go beyond the standard independent study format and actually take on the role of the professional in the field in which they are studying. A student who is interested in plants would take on the persona of a horticulturist or botanist and proceed through the investigation in that manner. A study of the stars would employ the same techniques, responsibilities, and products as an astronomer would employ. The complexity of these tasks and the perseverance needed to design and carry out such investigations are what make this type of activity particularly suited to gifted students.

Relationship to Content, Process, Product, and Environmental Modifications

The *Enrichment Triad Model* is best suited to modify curriculum through *processes* and *products* of learning. Type II activities are based mostly on process-building formats and may include the use of many of the standard models for instructing process skills. The use of these activities gives the students in the class a chance to learn how to learn and methods for making the most of their cognitive and affective capabilities.

Products of learning can also be impacted by this model in that they take on a different scope and dimension when students are engaged in true Type III activities. The accountability and public nature of the products force students to develop them as fully as possible and they are evaluated in real-world terms. This level of accountability and scrutiny places Type III activities in a different class from reports or conventional independent study products, thereby making the activities suited to the gifted.

Appropriate Uses of Renzulli's *Enrichment Triad Model*

As stated earlier, the *Enrichment Triad Model* can be used in the regular classroom as well as in special programs for gifted students. It has been successfully used as a means through which curriculum can be extended beyond the normal scope and sequence of skills. All students can engage in the Type I and Type II activities and profit from these experiences. When the more able students are dealing with Type III activities, the rest of the class can be doing more traditional independent study projects. In this way, the students still remain part of the class activities; only the expectations for and products of their activities differ.

When students have the skill to deal with Type III activities, the teacher may want to institute a provision in their learning contracts through which they can apply to do this type of activity. This can be managed through the use of a formal research proposal that outlines the problem, the questions to be investigated, possible resources, and planned products of the investigation. Fully prepared and well-thought out proposals can be accepted for study. Depending on the arrangements made with the teacher, students can then use their extra time, study halls, after school hours, or formal lesson time to work on their studies.

Type I and Type II activities can be easily integrated into the curriculum of the classroom; however, Type III activities require additional types of responsibilities that may limit their use to certain times or fewer students. They are demanding on students' and teacher's time and resources as they take regular monitoring and follow-up. Therefore, it may be wise to allow only one or two students at a time to take on a study of this magnitude and responsibility. Other students may follow when the procedures and resources are more fully known.

SUCHMAN'S INQUIRY DEVELOPMENT MODEL

One of the primary objectives upon which curricula for gifted students is based is the development of independent learning skills. Teaching students how to inquire in a formalized manner is one approach that can be used to develop this skill. There are many models available that can be used to train inquiry skills; Suchman's *Inquiry Development Model* is presented here due to its easily understood and adaptable methods.

When using an inquiry approach to learning, students are trained in the process of observing separate phenomena, noting their similarities and differences, determining what is important in the observations, and discovering the underlying principles or generalizations that tie them together. This training can give the students the necessary tools to continue inductive thinking and explorations in other less contrived situations.

The Model

The *Inquiry Development Model* (see Figure 9-3) is composed of a four-step process through which students develop and test hypotheses about how events, things, or phenomena interrelate. The four steps are: *data collection, data organization, hypothesizing,* and *hypothesis testing.* Prior to beginning the steps in the model, students are presented with a "dis-

Figure 9-3   Suchman's Inquiry Development Model

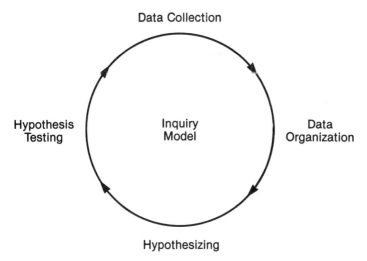

Data Collection

Hypothesis
Testing

Inquiry
Model

Data
Organization

Hypothesizing

Source: B. Clark, *Growing Up Gifted* (Columbus, Ohio: Merrill Publishing Company, 1983), p. 226. Copyright 1983 by Merrill Publishing Company. Reprinted by permission of the publisher.

crepant" or "dissonant" event by the teacher. This event breaks the students' preconceived notions of the outcomes and leads them to wonder about the nature of what they observed. They begin their *data collection* by asking the teacher questions that can be answered by "yes" or "no" or by gathering additional information through books, interviews, or additional observations. These data are reviewed and analyzed during a debriefing session in the *data organization* stage in order to determine what is relevant and what additional pieces of information are needed. If more information is needed, students can return to data collecting; if not, they can proceed to *hypothesizing*. At this point, students develop a theory that explains the nature of what they observed. They then test their hypotheses in the last stage of the model, *hypothesis testing*. If a hypothesis does not prove to be true, the students return to previous steps in order to develop a new theory for testing. During these final two stages, the teacher does not answer the students' questions with "yes" and/or "no" responses. To do so could lead students to premature closure and lack of true understanding. Clark (1983) lists the following rules for inquiry:

1. Students must ask questions that can be answered yes or no.
2. Students, when recognized by the facilitator, may ask questions until they wish to yield. They indicate this by declaring that they "pass."
3. The facilitator does not answer statements of theories or questions at-

tempting to gain approval for a theory (whether the facilitator accepts the theory or not).

4. Any student may test a theory at any time.

5. During inquiry, students are not allowed to discuss among themselves unless they call for a conference. This may be done at any time.

6. Inquirers may consult resources in the room at any time (p. 244).

One classic inquiry session begins with the teacher showing students two cups half filled with a clear liquid. Into the first glass the teacher drops an ice cube, then repeats the procedure with the second glass. The first ice cube floats, whereas the second ice cube sinks. Students must discover why the ice cubes did not respond in the same way to being dropped in the liquid.

Relationship to Content, Process, Product, and Environmental Modifications

The *Inquiry Development Model* is particularly suited for modifying the *processes* of the curriculum and the *environment* in which learning takes place. Inquiry is a method for solving problems and drawing conclusions that are based in process skills. Students learn to observe critically, ask probing questions, suspend their judgments, evaluate data, and develop hypotheses. The process of delivering content, then, is modified by establishing these process-based skills as basic tools of independent learning.

Inquiry also requires an *environment* in which exploration can take place freely. Students must feel free to ask questions, seek multiple resources, and see themselves as resourceful thinkers. An environment that is totally teacher-directed and tightly controlled through fear or intimidation will not successfully breed inquiring minds. Environments that do allow this type of discovery will be enlivened as students use the techniques and gain confidence in their abilities to develop and test hypotheses.

Appropriate Uses of Suchman's *Inquiry Development Model*

The *Inquiry Development Model* can be used throughout the content areas of a curriculum. Although it is easily suited to science and topics that deal with scientific methods, it can also be used in areas such as language arts, social studies, and the arts. By using the model in this way, students will see that inductive reasoning and discovery are vital parts of generating new information in all fields.

The use of the model can reap unusual rewards for gifted and talented students through its developing of another method of gaining information and answering questions. Gifted students are likely more able to use multiple means of problem solving and knowledge production, and the use of inquiry methods can further enhance this ability. At the same time, it can introduce intrigue and mystery into learning as the seemingly unexplainable becomes explained. Inquiry learning is fun for the gifted because it is a challenge. This model brings amusement into the classroom and lays a foundation for serious exploration of the unknown in innovative and creative ways.

TREFFINGER'S MODEL FOR ENCOURAGING CREATIVE LEARNING

Creativity is one of the abilities that most programs for gifted students wish to enhance. In order to do so, however, more than just creativity training is necessary. Rather, students should be exposed to classrooms in which creativity is acknowledged and nurtured throughout the day and in all facets of classroom life. Having thirty minutes a day set aside for "Creativity Time" will not result in students who are able to use their creative abilities. More comprehensive approaches must be taken in order to truly help students develop this ability.

Treffinger's *Model for Encouraging Creative Learning* (see Figure 9-4) is one of the few models that confronts this problem head on and offers practical recommendations on how to achieve the needed integration. By incorporating both cognitive and affective skills across the various levels of the model, Treffinger points out their interrelationship and interdependency when encouraging creative learning.

The Model

Treffinger's *Model for Encouraging Creative Learning* (Treffinger, 1986) is a three-level configuration that begins with basic elements and progresses to more complex functions of creative thinking. As in the *Enrichment Triad Model* (Renzulli, 1977), the student is involved in skill-building activities in the first two levels which are brought to bear on real-life problems in the last. The model is composed of the following steps: *Basic Tools, Practice with Process,* and *Working with Real Problems.*

Level I, *Basic Tools,* includes the skills of divergent thinking drawn from the work of Guilford (1967). Their development will allow students not only to be flexible and fluent in their thinking but also to be willing to express innovative thinking to others.

Practice with Process, Level II, provides the students with a chance to apply the skills learned in Level I in practice situations. Strategies

Figure 9-4   Treffinger's Model for Encouraging Creative Learning

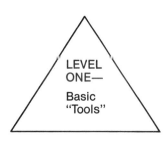

● Find ways to incorporate thinking skills into existing course content.

LEVEL ONE— Basic "Tools"

Brainstorming
Attribute listing
Idea checklists
Morphological analysis
"What if..." or "Just Suppose..." questions
Forced relationships
Analogies
Judging relevant data
Making inferences
Comparing/Contrasting
Evaluating statements/Conclusions

● Provide opportunities for students to practice problem solving methods.

LEVEL TWO— Practice with the Process

Case studies
Simulations/Games
Role playing
Contrived problems
Future study—scenarios/problem solving
Group work on sample problems within class (problems drawn from literature)

● Opportunities for work on real problems

LEVEL THREE— Working with Real Problems

Personal, school, community concerns
Resource group for outside clients
Service club activities or projects
Work with local civic/fraternal groups
Independent study using CPS methods
Term papers, "Senior Honors" papers
Project for publication, presentation at meetings or conferences

Source: D. Treffinger, *Thinking Skills and Problem Solving* (Honeoye, N.Y.: Center for Creative Learning, 1986). Reprinted with permission by Center for Creative Learning, copyright © 1986.

such as role playing, simulations, and case studies are employed for this purpose. Becoming adept at creative thinking requires that students have the skill to perform such functions as analysis, evaluation, imagining, and fantasizing beyond their classroom assignments.

Working with Real Problems, Level III, applies the skills learned in the first two levels to real-world challenges. As with Type III activities in the *Enrichment Triad Model,* students use their abilities in ways that have meaning in their lives. Thus, students not only learn the skills involved in creative thinking, but also how to apply this information to their lives. Unfortunately, this application step is missing in many curricular plans, leaving students with skills they do not know how to use everyday.

Relationship to Content, Process, Product, and Environmental Modifications

The *Model for Encouraging Creative Learning* is most effective when it is adapted for use throughout the curriculum. Therefore, it is a vehicle for all four types of modifications for the gifted and talented students in a classroom. However, it has its greatest strength in the areas of *process* and *product* modification.

Both cognitive and affective processes are developed in the model, ranging in level of complexity. Students who more quickly master the skills in Level I or Level II can proceed to Level III activities, applying what they know to new and different problems or circumstances in their lives. This practice should result in students learning a wide range of skills and being able to use them when needed.

Products of learning also take on a new dimension. The products of learning under this schema are not just the development of new skills but using the skills in real-life challenges. Thus, the products of learning are the problems solved as well as the learning of problem-solving processes. By using all three levels of the model, students build skills in using their creative abilities and finding outlets for expressing creativity throughout their lives.

Appropriate Uses of the *Model for Encouraging Creative Learning*

Perhaps the greatest contribution the *Model for Encouraging Creative Learning* makes to curriculum development for the gifted and talented is in the way it shows a progression of skills beyond just the basics. This model graphically shows that there is learning beyond the more simplistic components of creative thought that should take place. For the gifted students, particularly those who are more creatively inclined, mastering the Level I and Level II skills may come more quickly than to the rest of the class. For these students, the proportion of time and energy spent at the lower levels may be minimized. All of the students in the class can be involved in the activities of the model, but some will have the ability to progress beyond the rest into the application stages.

Additionally, the model should be used throughout the classroom curricula. Creative thinking is a part of all the disciplines taught in schools. Advances in professions are made through the creative process. Therefore, the model can be incorporated into every facet of school life, from conflict resolution to scientific theory building. Students will see their ability to use creativity in their lives and will be given the opportunity to develop their abilities in an environment that encourages and allows their use.

WILLIAMS' MODEL FOR IMPLEMENTING COGNITIVE-AFFECTIVE BEHAVIORS IN THE CLASSROOM

Another curriculum model that is useful in planning instruction in the area of creativity is Williams' (1978) *Model for Implementing Cognitive-Affective Behaviors in the Classroom.* This model is also based on the premise that creative thinking should be encouraged throughout the curriculum and students should develop the capability to think creatively in all their endeavors. It combines cognitive and affective skills in creativity development with the traditional content areas taught in school.

The Model

The *Model for Implementing Cognitive-Affective Behaviors in the Classroom* (see Figure 9-5) is a three-dimensional representation of how curriculum, teaching strategies, and student behaviors interact to enhance thinking. One segment from each dimension is chosen and then combined with the segments from the other two dimensions in order to design activities for the students. These dimensions are: curriculum (subject matter content), teacher behavior (strategies or modes of teaching), and pupil behaviors (both cognitive and affective).

Dimension 1, *Curriculum,* is composed of six subject areas typically taught at most grade levels: art, music, science, social studies, arithmetic, and language. Although these are the content areas pictured in the model, others can be substituted.

Teacher behaviors, Dimension 2, lists a sample of teaching strategies and modes of teaching that are found in the content areas listed in Dimension 1. Among the teacher behaviors listed in the model are: paradoxes, organized random search, evaluate situations, and creative writing skill. The eighteen behaviors listed in the model should not be considered exhaustive of the potential strategies that can be used; they are simply a representation.

Dimension 3, *Pupil behaviors,* includes eight skills, four in both the cognitive and affective domains. These behaviors (fluent thinking, flexible thinking, original thinking, elaborative thinking, curiosity, risk taking, complexity, and imagination) draw heavily on creative thinking

Figure 9-5 Williams' Model for Implementing Cognitive-Affective Behaviors in the Classroom

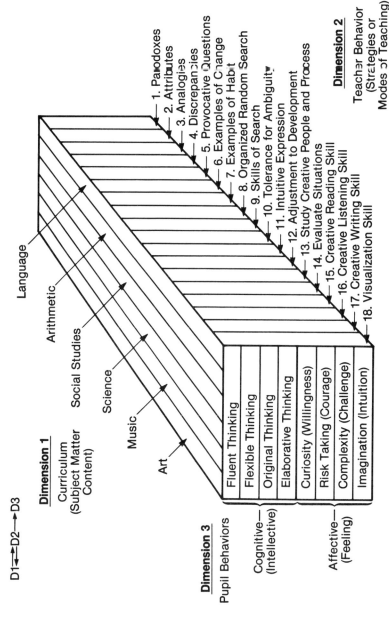

Source: F. Williams, Classroom Ideas for Encouraging Thinking and Feeling (Buffalo: N.Y.: D.O.K. Publishers, 1970), p. ii. Reprinted by permission by D.O.K. Publishers, Inc., copyright © 1970.

skills. Addressing the students' cognitive and affective domains allows them to develop a desire and an ability to use their skills.

When using the model, then, the teacher selects one aspect of each dimension upon which to develop an activity. For example, a lesson could be built around the areas of language (Dimension 1), creative writing skill (Dimension 2), and risk taking (Dimension 3) in which the students are asked to write a story with these directions: "You are the lone survivor of a shipwreck. You find yourself floating alone on the ocean in a life raft with provisions for two days. What do you do?" Students then use their skills from Dimension 3 in a situation determined by the aspects of Dimensions 1 and 2 chosen for the activity.

Relationship to Content, Process, Product, and Environmental Modifications

Williams' *Model for Implementing Cognitive-Affective Behaviors in the Classroom* primarily deals with the *processes* of learning. *Content, product,* and *environment* are not ignored; however, they are not the major point of emphasis. *Process* development, particularly as it relates to the development of creative thinking abilities, is quite strong. The listing of student behaviors in Dimension 3 contains the skills most frequently noted when discussing the development of creative thinking. When modifying curriculum for the gifted, these skills should be developed as the bases for further creative uses of the mind.

For *content* and *product* modifications, combining this model with others, such as the *Enrichment Triad Model,* the *Model for Content Modification, Integrated Education Model,* and the *Model for Encouraging Creative Learning,* can lead to a more comprehensive curricular package for the gifted and talented.

Environmental modifications to the curriculum can also be made compatible with this model. It is based on student needs and can generate a student-centered environment. In addition, one of its purposes is to develop independent thinking in students. It can do this when implemented in the way in which it is intended.

Appropriate Uses of the *Model for Implementing Cognitive-Affective Behaviors in the Classroom*

As stated earlier, the *Model for Implementing Cognitive-Affective Behaviors in the Classroom* does not form a comprehensive base for modifying curriculum for gifted and talented students. It does, however, provide a piece of the curriculum development puzzle in the area of processes of learning. When used in conjunction with other models, it can make a significant contribution to infusing creative thinking throughout the curriculum.

The model also lends itself to the development of individualized programs in creative thinking abilities. The components of Dimension 3 can be used for assessing the extent to which students can use these abilities. The assessment information can then be put into student profiles of ability and used to prescribe curriculum to develop the areas of weaknesses through building on the strengths.

The plan for curriculum development outlined by Williams can be used in the classroom with students of wide-ranging ability. It is not for use with gifted students only. Therefore, the teacher can use the model without the risk of segregating the gifted students or disenfranchising the others. The gifted students may be engaged in more complex activities or those that combine the use of many of the skills listed. The combinations are endless and can lead to a large variety of experiences.

Finally, the model can be used as a gauge for teachers who wish to present a balanced approach to creative thinking. By building a profile of the types of activities that they use and questions that they ask, teachers can determine the extent to which their classrooms give students an opportunity to develop creative thinking abilities fully.

USING MODELS TO ADAPT CURRICULUM FOR THE GIFTED AND TALENTED

In many cases, teachers are bound to the basal textbooks and scope and sequence charts that have been adopted by the school district when planning the curricula for their students. Although this may hamper the attempts to bring appropriate experiences to the students, it does not preclude them. By integrating the required components with the new approaches, a blending can occur that will lead to better educational opportunities for the students.

Begin this process by determining the answers to two questions: What parts of the current curriculum are necessary or worthwhile to keep as part of the new system? and What am I trying to accomplish for the students and myself through a curricular plan? Once you have the answers to these questions you can begin to plot the course you will take to bring responsive curriculum to your students.

One useful way to proceed is to focus on one subject area at the start. Through experience or with assistance from a Teachers' Manual, begin to list the major points or themes for the lessons taught. Once these have been identified, begin to look at how they can be taught to the students. Will some of the students already have mastery of the concepts? Will some type of differentiation be necessary for the students to be learning at their instructional levels? If so, determine a method of instruction that will take individual differences into account and allow students to engage in meaningful work.

Different types of themes for lessons will call for alternative approaches to the task. Knowing when to use a model and which one or combination to use is essential to good instruction. Bringing meaningful curricular practice into the classroom does not necessarily mean that all old practices must be discarded. The changes that should be made must correspond to the gaps in the way the curriculum fits the individual needs of the students and the instructor. Consequently, different variations in delivery will be needed for different circumstances, teachers, and students. The next chapter explores case studies of how some teachers solved curricular problems by blending their current practices and constraints with new ideas and approaches.

SUMMARY

There are many models for developing curriculum that have benefits for gifted and talented students in regular classroom settings. Those presented in this chapter are among the many that can make positive contributions to the education of this population. However, they are not the only models that can do so. The work of such notable theorists as Guilford (1967), Taba (1962), Bruner (1960), and Kohlberg (1966) also have a place when developing curricular packages. These models have different strengths and weaknesses when being used with the gifted. In order to provide a comprehensive curriculum, combining the models or using them only for certain purposes will be necessary. It is in knowing what model (or part of a model) to use and when that makes instruction most successful.

ACTION STEPS

1. Review your list of modifications that are made in regular classrooms. What areas were weak (process modification, product modification)? Choose one area of modifying curriculum in which to begin strengthening the offerings.

2. When you have decided where to start, choose one or two models that emphasize that area. Use them as your basis for curricular change.

3. Create a plan to expand the changes to other areas of instruction. Be practical and realize that such changes cannot be made quickly.

4. Design a grid to evaluate your curriculum. Write the types of characteristics in your ideal curriculum across the top. On the side list the methods and materials you are using. Then check where these intersect so that you have a graphic representation of the balance in your curriculum.

REFERENCES YOU CAN USE

Clark, B. (1986). *Optimizing learning: The integrative education model in the classroom.* Columbus, OH: Merrill Publishing Company.

Davis, G., & Rimm, S. (1985). *Education of the gifted and talented.* Englewood Cliffs, NJ: Prentice-Hall.

Maker, J. (1982). *Teaching models in education of the gifted.* Rockville, MD: Aspen Systems Corporation.

Renzulli, J. (Ed.). (1986). *Systems and models for developing programs for the gifted and talented.* Mansfield Center, CN: Creative Learning Press.

Williams, F. (1970). *Classroom ideas for encouraging thinking and feeling* (2nd ed.). Buffalo, NY: D.O.K. Publishers.

10

Putting It All Together: Case Studies

It should be very apparent by now that there are a great number of factors that educators can consider when deciding on the programs and curricula to use with gifted children in the regular classroom. One point should be remembered at all times: *there are many possible approaches that are correct.* Creating learning experiences that are based on the abilities, needs, and interests of the students will lead to programming that is exciting and appropriate for these students.

Five case studies will be described in this chapter. They represent the most common challenges that gifted and talented students in the regular classroom present to their teachers. Mathematics, language arts, science, social studies, and art are the content areas upon which these scenarios are based. Each case has the problem listed, the modifications made in the program(s) and curricula, and sample lessons. These case studies provide examples of how to combine and implement the provisions that have already been discussed in such a way that students will profit and teachers will have manageable classrooms.

CASE STUDY: MATHEMATICS

Setting

Mrs. Arnold teaches a split fourth/fifth grade in a suburban school district that prides itself on having an outstanding continuous progress curriculum in both reading and mathematics. Within her elementary school (K–5), there are two classes and a split class at each grade level, making about sixty-five students per level. The fourth/fifth split was instituted for two reasons: to ease overcrowding in the other two classrooms and to provide a configuration that would allow telescoping.

Problem

Even though the students in Mrs. Arnold's class have been involved in continuous progress curriculum, some of the most mathematically talented students were reaching the end of the materials available to the school. When fifth-grade materials were completed, there were no additional provisions made for the advanced students. They were usually placed in supplemental fifth-grade materials from other publishing companies for enrichment. Both the parents and the students were unhappy with this situation and demanded that the students be allowed to continue to develop their mathematical abilities beyond the skills presented through the fifth-grade materials.

This problem is unique to the students with exceptional talent. Their abilities to grasp information quickly and to comprehend concepts beyond their classmates can result in their progressing rapidly through the mathematics materials to the point where they actually run out! This is exacerbated when school policies limit the materials and course offerings for students based on their grade level assignments or schools. Policies that allow students to progress only one grade level above their assigned level or that limit teachers to using only basal textbooks at the grade level they teach can impede the progress that students are often able and anxious to achieve.

In this instance, the highly defensible program of continuous progress curriculum was fatally flawed by not adhering to the intentions of the program—continuous progress. In this case, it was "continue to progress until you reach the end of the elementary (fifth grade) materials." For the majority of students, this approach works quite well. For those students gifted in mathematics, however, trouble can arise as early as third or fourth grade. In such a situation, then, how do you modify the circumstances in order to produce a sound mathematics program that responds to children with high-level skill?

Possible Solutions

A number of remedies to this dilemma are possible. Although the problem is primarily in the area of programming, there are also curricular considerations to be made. Here are three possible solutions to the programming side of the issue.

1. Institute a true continuous progress curriculum in which students *are* able to proceed at their own rates and to work with materials they can comprehend. This would require opening up the ceiling on materials and allowing the teachers to use resources beyond the fifth-grade level. In this way, students have access to meaningful materials and re-

main in the regular classroom at the same time. Coordination with the middle school teachers is vital to program success.

2. Allow those students who exhaust the available elementary materials to take their mathematics classes at the middle school. This would require compatible scheduling and transporting the students to the other location, but it results in students being engaged in mathematics at their own ability levels.

3. Institute alternative mathematics classes for these students in order to enrich their understanding of the discipline. Courses in logic, computer designs, or mathematics in music are but three possible alternatives to enhance the standard curricular offerings. The drawback to this approach is in finding the number of students suited for the enrichment program in order to justify the expense and time of the offerings.

Mrs. Arnold's Solution

Mrs. Arnold quickly realized that she was dealing with an administrative problem. She was functioning under policies that were impeding her ability to provide adequate mathematics programs for her students gifted in mathematics. Therefore, she brought her problem and the parents' concerns to the attention of her building administrator. Together, along with the school system's curriculum committee and the Assistant Superintendent for Instruction, they devised the following modifications in the mathematics program in the elementary grades.

It was determined by this group that there were two unnegotiable components to any plan that they would conceive: these students had to be allowed access to materials at their ability level and this had to be done within the home school setting. Such young students would not be allowed to attend the middle school for class. Therefore, the school system invested in higher level materials for all of the elementary schools and made plans for including these materials in the continuous progress schema. The committee was enlightened enough about the needs of gifted and talented students, however, to understand that acceleration is not the only way to enhance mathematical ability. In order to provide enriching experiences, mini-courses were instituted once a week in which students studied various facets of mathematics as an integral part of their mathematics instruction.

The mathematics program for the elementary grades was thus composed of two basic provisions: the continuous progress curriculum as the base upon which the mathematics skills were built and assessed, and the mini-courses in which students could extend these skills into new areas.

Dealing with this issue intrigued the curriculum committee to the extent that they issued recommendations as to how the curriculum should be instituted for the gifted. They followed Gallagher's *Model for Content Modifications* (1985) and suggested that teachers think in terms of content acceleration, content enrichment, content sophistication, and content novelty when planning curricula for these students in mathematics. They felt that this model was compatible with their current programming efforts and could serve to guide future curriculum development.

Content acceleration and content sophistication were achieved with the assistance of the continuous progress curriculum. Students were a part of an ongoing diagnostic-prescriptive approach by virtue of their participation in continuous progress. These data were useful in prescribing curriculum and curriculum compacting which led to content at the appropriate level. Although self-instruction is a primary part of this approach, small group instruction and contracts were suggested as ways to instruct new skills, monitor student progress, and assess student success.

Content novelty and content enrichment were initiated through the mini-course series. During the first year, Mrs. Arnold combined forces with the other fourth- and fifth-grade teachers to plan a one-year series of courses. The students were taught by the current teaching staff; one teacher was freed by grouping the other students among the other four teachers. The teacher with computing expertise planned and conducted a course on using coordinates on a computer to design pictures. A second course in the metric system was taught by another teacher for ten weeks, while a third class in logic was developed and taught by yet another teacher well versed in that area.

MATHEMATICS LESSONS THAT CHALLENGE

One of the attributes consistently found in gifted students is their interest in solving problems. The activities listed in this section are designed to pique their interest and challenge their minds to find solutions to puzzles.

Mazes

Present the students with a series of mazes that become progressively more difficult. When students have shown their ability to anticipate and successfully complete mazes, challenge them by having them design their own mazes, which can be laminated and shared with the class.

Word Puzzles—Using Logical Reasoning Power

Problem: Ann, Ben, Carlos, and Dina like different types of books: humor, mystery, sports, and adventure. One of Ann's classmates in the group likes mystery books best. Carlos and Dina do not like adventure

Figure 10-1   Word Puzzles Diagram

	Ann	Ben	Carlos	Dina
Humor				NO
Mystery	NO			
Sports		YES		
Adventure			NO	NO

Source: P. O'Daffer, "Problem Solving Tips for Teachers," *Arithmetic Teacher 21*(6) (1985): 62. Reprinted with permission by National Council of Teachers of Mathematics. Copyright © 1985.

books. Ben's favorite type of book is sports. Dina did like humor books but has changed her favorite. What is Dina's favorite book?*

To solve this problem, use a chart to organize the data given in the problem (see Figure 10-1). Then use the information given and logical reasoning to extend the chart.

Flow Charting

Ask students to complete the flow chart in Figure 10-2, reminding them of the purpose of a flow chart and the significance of the various shapes used in the charting process. After they have successfully mastered their use, have them devise flow charts for other purposes that their classmates can solve.

Tac-Tic-Toe, Chinese Version

A variation of the perennial favorite strategy game of Tic-Tac-Toe is outlined by Krulik and Rudnick (1980). They describe the game as follows:

This game is played on the surface shown in [Figure 10-3a]. Players use four chips, each player having a different color. Starting position is as shown in [Figure 10-3a]. Each player may move only his or her own chips. A move involves placing one of one's own pieces into an adjacent, vacant cell, following the lines on the board. There is no jumping and no capturing. The player

*Problem by Phares G. O'Daffer (1985), *Arithmetic Teacher 32*(6), p. 62. Reprinted by permission by National Council of Teachers of Mathematics. Copyright© 1985 by NCTM.

Figure 10-2   Flow Chart

Fill in column *B* on the table by following the steps in the flowchart.

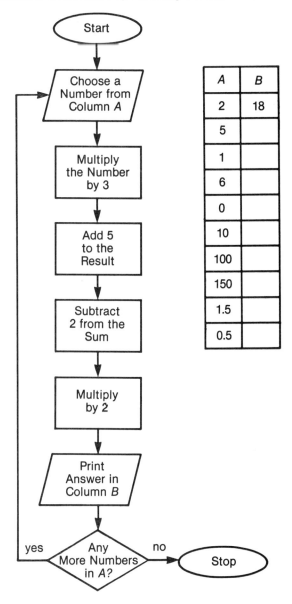

Source: G. Immerzeel and M. Thomas, *Ideas from the Arithmetic Teacher* (Reston, Va.: National Council of Teachers of Mathematics, 1982), p. 77. Reprinted with permission by National Council of Teachers of Mathematics. Copyright © 1982.

Figure 10-3   (A) Starting Position for Tac-Tic-Toe, Chinese Version; (B) A Winning Position and a Nonwinning Position

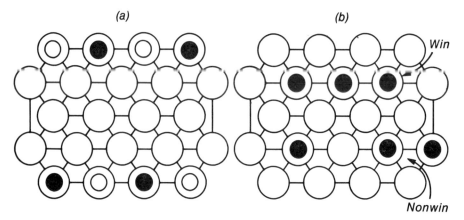

Source: S. Krulick and J. Rudnick, *Problem Solving: A Handbook for Teachers* (Boston: Allyn and Bacon, Inc., 1980), p. 71. Reprinted with permission by Allyn and Bacon, Inc., Copyright© 1980.

who places three of his or her pieces in the same straight line, with no vacant spaces intervening and none of the opponent's pieces intervening, is the winner.

Cube Puzzle

Students are asked to study the three sides of one cube (shown in Figure 10-4) and to answer the following questions based on those pictures:

1. What letter is opposite B?
2. What letter is opposite C?

Figure 10-4   Cube Puzzle

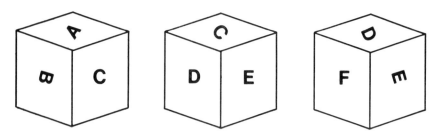

Source: Adapted from G. Clifford, R. Heger, and S. Sebree, *The World of the Gifted* (Toledo, Ohio: Toledo Public Schools, 1974), p. 37.

3. What letter is opposite E?
4. What letter is opposite D?
5. What letter is opposite F?
6. What letter is opposite A?
7. How long did it take you to complete this puzzle?

This puzzle is found in *The World of the Gifted* (Clifford, Heger, & Sebree, 1974) published by the Toledo Public Schools.

CASE STUDY: LANGUAGE ARTS

Setting

Mr. Klein teaches third graders in a self-contained classroom in a rural school district. Due to the small enrollment, there is only one class per grade level and the next closest elementary school is ten miles away. The schools within the district are self-sufficient and autonomous in the way they operate. This independence has spilled over to the teaching staff and has resulted in little cooperation or sharing of ideas and resources. In addition, there is no program for gifted and talented students sponsored by the district and grade skipping is not allowed.

Problem

Among the thirty students in Mr. Klein's classroom are four with exceptional talent in the area of language arts. They have the capability to read fifth- and sixth-grade books, write exceptionally well, and are advanced in spelling and dictionary skills. Up until this time, they have been limited to using grade-level texts despite the fact that they are also reading library books of far greater difficulty.

Mr. Klein's efforts to work with the fourth- and fifth-grade teachers have not been successful. He first tried to place these students in higher level classrooms for their language arts, but this idea was rebuffed by both the teachers and the administration. His second idea was to regroup the students so that there would be 1/2, 3/4, and 5/6 grade groupings with two teachers team teaching the students in their assigned classes. This, too, was not acceptable to his colleagues who preferred to run their own classrooms without the interference from other teachers.

What he was left with, then, were his own devices and talents. Providing for the multiple abilities in his classroom would be a task Mr. Klein would have to tackle on his own. Although he had expressed a desire to approach this problem with the assistance of others, he did recognize the advantages of working by himself. He would have total control of the situation and could make all the decisions. But he was bothered by the clear underlying sentiment that each grade level had its own resources and books, and that other teachers should not infringe on that territory by using those materials. If he did, he risked the wrath of the rest of the teaching staff.

How could Mr. Klein provide a sufficiently advanced language arts program for the gifted students in his classroom without stepping on the toes of the other teachers? How could he give these students an advanced curriculum without using materials that had been earmarked for the fourth, fifth, and sixth grades?

Mr. Klein's problems are in no way confined to rural settings. Teachers everywhere have faced similar awkward situations in which they have had to risk alienating their colleagues in order to service the students in their classroom. The job of responding to multiple abilities is far easier when there are cooperative efforts toward this goal; in actuality, this is not always possible. At this point, then, what choices are available?

Possible Solutions

There are numerous ways in which Mr. Klein can respond to this situation. The four listed below are among those that will help the children. A fifth solution, forgetting the students' needs and providing only grade-level work, is dismissed since it is irresponsible and totally unacceptable.

1. Bolster the enrichment activities in the classroom so that students are making full use of the skills they have already developed. If you cannot employ acceleration of any type, then enriching the environment is a tactic that can fill that gap. This might include developing special programs like *Junior Great Books* and *Philosophy for Children* in which the students may participate. Keeping above-grade-level books in the classroom library, playing challenging spelling games, and learning a foreign language are activities that can enhance students' learning without stepping over the boundaries informally established by the teaching staff.

2. Recruit other people from outside of the school setting to help you. Students from the high school "Growth and Development" class, Future Teachers of America club members, parents, senior citizens, or retired teachers may be available to work with students in small groups or to conduct special activities for which the teacher does not have time. They can be the group leaders for *Junior Great Books*, help students write and produce a slide tape presentation on their community, read stories to the students, or lead an adventure through the nature trail in order to identify the flora on the school grounds.

3. Develop before- and after-school programming options. These programs seem to be less threatening to other staff members because they are often not well publicized and are usually of an enriching nature. Future Problem Solving, Odyssey of the Mind, French, and a young authors' club are among the types of activities that can be initiated. Students profit from involvement in these activities and they are beyond the scope of most curricula in the language arts. Since this is a rural setting, the students may have trouble getting to school early or leaving at times other than that prescribed by the bus schedule. In this instance, special transportation arrangements may need to be made or students may crave such experiences to the extent that they will be willing to use their lunch and recess times in order to participate.

4. The last solution is the most drastic and risky of the four presented here. That is, risk the wrath of the other teachers and give the students the materials that are at their ability levels. Obviously, in order to assure one's job is not in jeopardy, this should be done with the full knowledge and support of the building administrator. The materials given the students under these circumstances can be either the actual materials for the higher grades or books that are parallel in scope and sequence but from another publisher. One should not enter into this approach without being fully aware of possible consequences: (1) The students may be placed in an even more precarious circumstance when they enter the fourth or fifth grade; (2) The students may well have to reuse the exact textbooks they used in the third grade unless the building administrator steps in and requires that the students be given appropriately challenging materials; and (3) Mr. Klein may be ostrasized by his colleagues and informal sanctions may be imposed upon him.

Mr. Klein's Solution

After much soul searching, Mr. Klein decided that he would have to put the students' needs above his own relationship with colleagues and set upon a course to develop programs and curricula that would allow the students in his class to work at their ability levels. This did require changing his approach to teaching somewhat and an acceptance of the fact that he would be without assistance from the other teachers. However, he was determined that the students would have an appropriate educational experience while in his room and that he would do his best to make that experience such that students would not be penalized in the years that followed.

Mr. Klein chose Clark's (1986) *Integrative Education Model* as the basis for making decisions about the curricular efforts. In particular, he focused on the integration of the cognitive, affective, physical, and intuitive functions and did a quick analysis of how his previous techniques balanced in terms of those areas. Next, he decided to pay extra attention to three of the seven key components of the model and to begin his modifications, which were: a responsive learning environment, student choice and perceived control, and complex and challenging cognitive activity. Finally, since his ultimate goal was to develop all seven components in each subject area, he decided to start with those three in the area of language arts.

The initial changes that were made took time to develop before they were introduced to the students. A contracting system was devised in which all the students in the classroom would contract for at least part of their language arts time block. To support this approach, Mr. Klein also prepared management sheets (see Figure 10-5) for each of the text-

Figure 10-5   Sample Management Sheet for Reading Book

Name: _____

A Second Look

Vocabulary Page	Number	Score	Read	Workbook Page	Number	Score
1	5		Pages 6–11	2	8	
				3	10	
				4	6	
				5	10	
6	6		Pages 12–25	7	20	
				8	11	
				9	12	
				10	6	
11	6		Pages 28–33	12	8	
				13	12	

books that he had chosen to use (those in the advanced level were from different publishers).

A schedule for student conferences was established in which each student had one ten- to fifteen-minute conference a week, on the same day each week. These conferences were meant to give students the opportunity to have input on their language arts programs while giving the teacher a chance to monitor their progress in a formalized fashion. During this time, workbook pages were checked, students were asked comprehension questions about the stories they had read during the week, and some oral reading was done. The time was also spent determining the schedule the students would keep for spelling, any writing they would like to do on their own, and the library books that they would like to read. This was an ambitious schedule for both the students and Mr. Klein.

Reading was handled by combining the contracting with management sheets, conferences, and skill groups. Students met together only when they were in skill groups (composed through diagnostic-prescriptive testing) and when Mr. Klein or one of the students was reading library books aloud to the rest of the class. The students gifted in reading were encouraged to read more than the minimum two stories per week and were given books at their skill levels. In addition, once a week during language arts time they participated with a volunteer in a Junior Great Books seminar.

In spelling, students were assigned a minimum of one workbook lesson a week and did the work in a prescribed manner. They wrote each spelling word on a sheet of paper which was then placed in the students' work folder and collected by Mr. Klein. Then they completed the workbook pages that corresponded to that lesson. Students were free at that point to take their spelling tests (when they felt prepared) by going to the listening center and playing the taped spelling test for their list of words. The tests were then corrected by Mr. Klein who either gave the student permission to proceed to the next lesson or prescribed a remedial loop to develop mastery of the word list. Most students completed one lesson per week, but the students adept in spelling often completed two or three and completed more than one spelling workbook during the school year.

Writing and language/English were handled as whole-group activities for the most part. Therefore, Mr. Klein had to develop lessons and activities that could be meaningful to all the students at one time. Writing was part of everyday life as students kept daily journals of their thoughts, feelings, and accomplishments in addition to formal writing lessons. Since most students were at similar skill levels in language/English, most lessons were whole-group activities; assignments allowed students to develop their ideas to the extent that they were capable. Interspersed throughout the day and on signs on the classroom walls were conversational French words and phrases. Students were encouraged to speak French throughout the day along with their usual English responses.

The changes that Mr. Klein made in his classroom were of benefit to the students and minimally infringing on the rest of the faculty. The principal did agree to see that the students were protected and he committed himself to trying to make changes at the other grade levels. Mr. Klein felt comfortable in that he was conducting a student-centered classroom in which learning was the greatest concern and students were allowed to make decisions, develop independent learning skills and strong self-concepts, and engage in challenging activities.

LANGUAGE ARTS LESSONS THAT CHALLENGE

The most commonly recognized attributes of gifted and talented students are their abilities to manipulate symbols and use language to express themselves. They tend to read earlier, talk more, and continually express themselves to all who will lend an ear. However, this ability to communicate can lag behind their ability to reason and create, a condition that can lead to great frustration. Therefore, many of the activities that are appropriate for these students go beyond skill development and extend into the areas of self-expression, developing intuitive skills, and being patient with oneself.

Cookbook Writing

In this activity, students (nursery–2) compile a cookbook of their favorite recipes from home. The children dictate or write the recipes and then the teacher types these into a cookbook for distribution. Here are some of the recipes from students at Gateway Nursery School in Toledo, Ohio.

The Best Pizza
Recipe provided by Aimee, age 4

Ingredients:

12 ft. frozen pizza	4 circles pizza meat
Green pepper	1 pack of cheese
2 packs of sauce	

Directions:
Take frozen pizza out of the frigerdator. Put on the green pepper. Put on the cheese. Put on the meat. Pour on the sauce. Bake it at 60 degrees for

1 hour. Take it out and say, "Ralph, your pizza's ready. Aimee, do you want some pizza?"

Best Hot Dogs and Macaroni and Cheese
Recipe provided by Darnelle, age 5

Ingredients:

9 hot dogs	10 cups of milk
1 box of cheese	1 box of Kraft macaroni & cheese

Directions:
Roast the hot dogs for 10 hours at 6 degrees. Stir ingredients together and cook on a high flame for one hour. I set the table and sometimes, I serve the food. Mom can't have any cause she's on a diet.

In Other Words

On a worksheet (see Figure 10-6) list descriptions that can be said in another way by using two rhyming words. Have students write in their responses and compose additional examples for the other students to solve.

Complete the Mystery

There are many books on the market that have mystery stories in which students have to generate a solution to the mystery. One such book is *5-Minute Mysteries* (Avallone, 1978), published by Scholastic Book Services. In this book students are given a clue and a description of the mystery. They then must write their solutions. The author also has written solutions for each mystery to which students can compare their responses. Have the students decide which solution they like the best and compile a class book of mysteries and solutions.

Mistakes Are Great

Mistakes Are Great (Zadra and Moawad, 1986) is one book in a series published by Creative Education that are designed to elicit students' feelings and encourage them to be comfortable with themselves. This particular book discusses making mistakes and the fact that all people do. The authors write, "The truth is, everyone makes mistakes. But here's a beautiful fact that may surprise you: If you look back through history, you will discover that the people who made the *most* mistakes are usually the same people we admire!" (p. 7). Have students read the book to them-

Figure 10-6   "In Other Words" Worksheet

In Other Words

Name: _____

****

Write the two rhyming words that mean the same as the following phrases:

1. Pastel beverage *Pink Drink* _____

2. Extra fur _____

3. Cheerful father _____

4. Laughable rabbit _____

5. Solitary rock _____

6. Skinny horse _____

7. Bee lying down _____

8. Hog dance _____

9. Burning place _____

Now write some of your own:

_____

_____

_____

---

selves or read it aloud, enjoying the humor buried within situations in which mistakes have been made. Then have the students recount through role-play, write, or discuss mistakes they have made. Provide an opportunity in which they can discuss how they feel and how they ought to feel when they do make a mistake. Although all students in the classroom can participate in this activity, it is well suited to the gifted and talented because they often avoid risking making mistakes in order to preserve the appearance of being perfect.

Chocolate-Covered Idioms

Teaching idioms usually happens between the fourth and sixth grades, but the subject can be taught to students in younger grades as well. Gwynne has written a series of books composed of idioms that students find delightful. Two are: *The King Who Reigned* (1970) and *A Chocolate Moose for Dinner* (1976). These books contain familiar sayings that should not be interpreted in their literal sense. For example, one idiom is "It is raining cats and dogs." Obviously, the animals are not truly falling from the sky, but the description of the rain (if taken literally) would seem to indicate that they are. Gwynne presents these idioms with pictures showing the literal translation of the phrase. "Mom says she has a frog in her throat" is accompanied by a picture showing a woman looking in a mirror examining her throat that has a frog emerging from it. "Daddy says he plays the piano by ear" is shown with a picture of a man with his head lying on the keyboard. Children take great delight at these representations and quickly see the humor in idioms. As an activity, after reading the book(s), have the students write their own idioms on one side of a paper and then illustrate the idiom in its literal sense on the other. Have students guess the idiom from the picture. The gifted and talented will most likely generate ideas that are more complex than the other students, allowing them to profit from the activity without having it altered in some way.

Stories with Holes

The book, *Stories with Holes*, is a compendium of stories in which solutions are not readily apparent. One reads: "The man was afraid to go home, because the man with the mask was there."*

The students, having heard the story, are to determine what happened. They can do this by asking questions of a group leader that can be answered "yes" or "no," or they can simply write responses to the puzzle. What about the masked man? The man with the mask was a catcher in a baseball game; the other man was a base-runner.

CASE STUDY: SCIENCE
Setting

The sixth-grade science program at a large urban middle school was fortunate to have a science major, Mrs. Howard, teaching the five sections. Students were placed by the school counselors into sections calibrated by

*Reprinted with permission by Nathan Levy. Copyright© Nathan Levy Associates, Inc., P.O. Box 1199, Hightstown, NJ.

difficulty. Two sections were considered "Basic Science" and were geared to students who needed remediation in the subject. "Earth Science" was taught to another two sections of students who could handle a more rigorous science curriculum. For the students adept at science, "Advanced Science" was taught in order to allow acceleration and enrichment opportunities for these budding scientists.

Problem

Advanced Science was made up of the top twenty-five science students in the sixth grade. They were carefully selected through an evaluation of their previous grades in science, achievement tests, science projects, and an interview in which the program was described. Mrs. Howard soon found out, however, that they were not a homogeneous group and that there was a range of ability in science represented among the students.

One student, in particular, caught Mrs. Howard's eye—Benjamin Hyatt. He was so far advanced from even this select group that his abilities were hard to miss. He had consistently earned first place in the district-wide science fairs and had even been invited to exhibit his work at the local university. While at the university fair, he was recruited by the admissions staff to be a part of a Saturday program for students of exceptional scientific talent held on campus. His participation in the program had given him many new insights into the subject area and left him even more dedicated to pursuing a career as a nuclear biologist.

Mrs. Howard was well aware that she had a sticky situation on her hands. How could she provide a learning environment for a highly gifted science student like Ben without ignoring the needs of the other advanced students and totally abandoning the curriculum established for the sixth-grade Advanced Science class?

Possible Solutions

In all curricular areas there are going to be times when a student is so highly talented in that area that the general operating rules do not work. In this case, more radical remedies were called for since the student was far advanced from the rest of the class. Four options were considered as reasonable alternatives for Ben.

1. He could enroll in the science sequence at the local high school while he was still taking his other classes at the middle school. This would put him on a track that would give him at least two high school science courses while still in middle school, and would give him the opportunity to take the Advanced Placement science courses in Chemistry and Physics during his freshman and sophomore years. Since these two years of high school level science would complete his graduation requirement, he

could then take university level science courses in his junior and senior years.

2. The next alternative that was considered is more of an enrichment experience. It involved the possibility of enrolling Ben in the high school internship program. This program matches students of high ability to scientists in the community and allows the students to work along with the professional for at least one academic term. This internship was flexible in its timing, so Ben would be able to go after school, on weekends, or during his science and lunch hours.

3. Since it was not clear if transportation would be available for Ben to participate in the internship program, a mentorship opportunity was considered as another option. In this alternative, he would be teamed with a volunteer teacher or person from the community in order to pursue his study of science. He had expressed an interest in furthering his research in a more vigorous fashion and it was felt by Mrs. Howard that this endeavor would be enhanced by the association with a mentor.

4. The last option considered was to keep Ben in the classroom, have him work with the rest of the class on the regular Advanced Science curriculum, but to give him alternative assignments as part of his studies. This could include being a tutor to the other students, serving as lab assistant, doing independent projects, or Type III (Renzulli, 1977) activities. Mrs. Howard was concerned, however, that such an approach, although enriching for some students, would not begin to be challenging for Ben. It would merely fill his time until he reached the seventh grade.

Mrs. Howard's Solution

The first step Mrs. Howard took was one often forgotten when making decision about students—she sat down and talked with Ben about what he wanted to accomplish during the academic year. He expressed an interest in being a part of what the rest of the class would be doing for he knew Mrs. Howard's reputation of basing her science on an *Inquiry Model* (Suchman, 1975). But he also told Mrs. Howard that he wanted to be a real scientist, not just a student of science.

Taking this information and her instincts into account, Mrs. Howard decided to make a temporary plan that would combine two of the approaches listed among her options. Ben and she would evaluate the success of the approach at the end of the first term in order to determine if it was sufficiently challenging to him. If it was not, changes would be made at that time. In this plan, Ben was part of the regular class activities for four days a week and participated in an internship on the fifth day.

During class, he was given the opportunity to work on independent research and be the teacher's lab assistant so that he could become more familiar with the equipment used in scientific inquiry. He even developed some inquiry-based lessons, on his own, which he presented to the class. He was clearly above the rest of the students in his knowledge and scientific technique, but he still was an emerging adolescent and found comfort in being a part of this group.

His internship was with a chemist at a local research and development company. During his association with this company, he was able to observe the chemists at work, learn the basic rules of dealing with chemicals, familiarize himself with some chemicals, and run controlled experiments under the guidance of the chief chemist. He recorded his work by keeping a journal and reported regularly to Mrs. Howard and his classmates on what he had learned.

SCIENCE LESSONS THAT CHALLENGE

There seems to be a tendency not to get serious about science before students are at least in the upper elementary grades. Gifted students, with their natural curiosity and desire for knowledge, investigate the field, either formally or informally, at ages far younger than twelve. Inquiring is one of the behaviors they do best! They always want to know how things work or from where things come. Exposing them to activities dealing with science can start as early as they express an interest in knowing. Below are some examples of the types of experiences from which students gifted in science can profit.

Animal Fact/Animal Fable

Many gifted students find their first fascination with science through observing nature and animals. Seymour Simon (1979) has written a book titled *Animal Fact/Animal Fable* in which he asks the reader to decide if certain statements about animals are "Fact or Fable." For example, he states, "Bats are blind—Fact or Fable?" and "Crickets tell the temperature with their chirps—Fact or Fable?" The reader can make a conjecture about the statement while looking at a picture illustrating it and then read the truth on the following page. Augment the activity further by having students write their own "Fact or Fables" for a class book. Do not limit yourself to animals; have the students explore other areas in this manner as well.

Space Suit Designer

This activity can be part of a unit on space or as an "extra time" activity. A number of educational materials for students about space and space travel are available from NASA. One of the brochures describes how and from what materials spacesuits are made and the functions they serve. Staple this brochure inside a filing folder and write directions on the outside of the folder. Have students read the article, write down the major points about design, composition, and function. Then have them add to that list the requirements they would have for a spacesuit and ask them to develop their own design for the garment. For those students who wish to actually construct a spacesuit, make paper grocery bags, plastic bags, scissors, and other materials available for their use. Have a spacesuit fashion show in which the astronauts describe the special features that make their suits unique.

Fad Diets and Nutrition

Throughout the elementary grades, students study the area of nutrition. However, as they reach their teenage years, many students begin to practice poor eating habits and may eventually develop eating disorders. Anorexia and bulimia are becoming increasingly more prevalent and seem to affect young girls the most. Fad dieting and nutrition are topics that are meaningful to students as they begin to worry about their appearances and being attractive to the other gender.

This activity builds on the knowledge students have about proper eating habits and the skills they have acquired about research and analysis. Students identify five fad diets that they have read about or they develop their own. Have them compare the nutritional value of each to the guidelines established by the United States Food and Drug Administration or the American Heart Association. How do these compare? What improvements can they make in the fad diets? How many of their classmates actually maintain healthy diets? This research can become the foundation for a class presentation of a film strip that can be shown to other students.

Class Journal of Research

Students of all ages enjoy conducting research experiments. While they are learning the techniques involved in conducting research they can also become familiar with the manner in which research findings are disseminated. As as integral part of the inquiry process, have students keep a journal on their investigations, including their hypotheses, observations, and results. These can be formally written as scientific journals. (Have some on hand from which students can model their own reports.) Students can then submit their research papers to a class editorial board who is responsible for publishing an end-of-the-year journal of the finest research papers and experiments.

CASE STUDY: SOCIAL STUDIES

Setting

The second-grade classroom of Mr. Brian Roberts is one of three self-contained classrooms in a K–6 elementary school. For the most part, the teacher-pupil ratio is about 1 to 32 with few aides or paraprofessionals. Most of the teachers adhere to the state-determined minimum time guidelines for each subject matter. Second-grade social studies is to be taught not less than ninety minutes per week. Mr. Roberts allots that amount of time every Thursday and uses the social studies series adopted by the school district as the source for curricular decision making.

Problem

Mr. Roberts is also the teacher of the gifted cluster group at the second-grade level. Among his thirty students are the five top students in the grade. The other students in the class were randomly assigned and represented the full range of ability in the school. Although special provisions were made for these students in reading, language arts, and mathematics, he decided to keep social studies and science as whole-group activities. In this way he could involve the cluster students as part of the classroom group and make them feel less segregated from the whole.

Although Mr. Roberts's intentions were good, one problem continually arose that was causing both him and the students distress. At the end of the lessons, he was being approached by cluster students saying, "I want to know more!" His social studies plans did include enriching activities such as field trips, guest speakers, investigations, and simulations, but these did not seem to satisfy the students' need for more in-depth study.

Mr. Roberts's challenge was quite clear. He wanted to enact a procedure through which students, and particularly the cluster students, could get involved in in-depth investigations of topics that interested them in social studies. Ninety minutes a week, however, did not leave much time. How could Mr. Roberts present the basic social studies lessons and still give students time to work on projects they wished to pursue?

Possible Solutions

As seen in the other case studies, there are always a number of possible solutions to a problem dealing with delivering services to gifted and talented students in the regular classroom. This problem is not an exception to that rule. Here are a few ways to deal with this problem.

1. Organize the structure of the social studies lessons around Renzulli's *Enrichment Triad Model* (1977). This does not necessitate a change in curriculum, only in the delivery to some degree. The content remains that which is specified by the adopted textbook, but the manner in which the class is organized and the activities that are presented are Triad-based. Students are involved with Type I—General Exploratory Activities (field trips, speakers, books, filmstrips), Type II—Group Training Activities (questioning skills, higher level thinking skills, independent studies), and (for the cluster students and other students who have the necessary skills) Type III—Individual and Small Group Investigations of Real Problems. Using this model, students learn the content *and* how it relates to the rest of the world.

2. Institute an independent research program for the class in which students can submit proposals for the research studies they would like to do as part of their social studies curriculum. These proposals should be formalized documents in which students specify what the topic of the investigation will be, how they intend to get information on the topic, how long they anticipate it will take, and what type of product they plan as a culminating activity. Mr. Roberts could then review the proposals alone or in conjunction with a review panel composed of classroom students and grant aid and resources to the proposals that were complete and worthy of intensive study. Students are free to work on their research during and after school hours when they have extra time or when time is allotted by Mr. Roberts.

3. Curriculum compacting is another way to gain extra time for students to pursue topics in depth. This requires Mr. Roberts to formalize procedures through which students can demonstrate the social studies skills they have already mastered so that they do not have to participate in those parts of the lesson(s) and will have time free for alternative activities. This technique requires that teachers admit that students may already know some of what is to be taught and can profit to a greater extent from activities that may not be teacher directed. Curriculum compacting can be used in tandem with either of the other solutions offered for this problem. Its main advantage is that it creates the time needed for students to do meaningful investigations or independent studies.

Mr. Roberts's Solution

The solution that made the most sense to Mr. Roberts was to structure his curriculum around the techniques of curriculum compacting and the *Enrichment Triad Model*. In that way, the cluster group students would still be an integral part of the curriculum in this subject area (which was his original intent) and *all* the students would benefit from the opportunity to answer the questions inherent in their "I want to know more" statements.

As a first step for a unit in social studies, Mr. Roberts compiled a list of the major knowledge and skill areas that students should gain from the unit. This was easily drawn from his teacher's manual and past experiences in teaching the units. He then prepared and administered an assessment to the students and drew a class profile of skills and knowledge already attained that were integral to the unit. From this profile, he was able to draw a plan for the unit, involving students in the lectures and class discussions they needed. The rest of the time was devoted to individual and small-group investigations and independent studies.

Type I and Type II activities were considered appropriate for all the students. During the course of the social studies unit, students were exposed to many new ideas and activities and were expected to develop process skills such as independent investigation techniques, problem-solving skills, higher level thinking skills, and flexible thinking. At this grade level, most of these skills were yet to be sufficiently developed, so Mr. Roberts found that most students ended up participating in most of the unit's activities.

Type III activities were an exception. Mr. Roberts found that Renzulli's position was accurate. The cluster group students *were* the most prepared and most capable of completing true Type III investigations. Although with such young students these were of a smaller scale, they nonetheless met the requirements to be Type IIIs. The other classroom students found plenty of challenge in conducting more typical independent studies involving social studies issues and concepts. Since most students were involved in some type of independent investigation, the fact that the cluster students' studies were of a more in-depth nature was not a concern to their classmates.

At the end of the first year operating under this structure, Mr. Roberts did his own assessment of its success. He was pleased to find out that most of the students did learn the content and skills he had outlined at the beginning of the year and had developed their independent investigative skills beyond those that they had initially. The cluster group students reported feeling comfortable in the classroom and challenged by the activities in which they engaged. They did express a desire to share more fully the products of their investigations with their classmates, so Mr. Roberts made a mental note to find ways to disseminate their work more widely next year. As for Mr. Roberts himself, he found the year in social studies to be exhausting of his energy and classroom resources. The demands of stressing independent studies was quite taxing on him, yet exhilarating at the same time. He decided to keep the approach, but to find some assistance for its management. Media specialists, parents, and older students were all considered as potential assistants for the upcoming year.

SOCIAL STUDIES LESSONS
THAT CHALLENGE

The interdisciplinary nature of social studies makes it naturally interesting to gifted and talented students. They see relationships, generalizations, and overriding concepts more readily than do their peers. Yet they also have a tendency to be less adept at skills that allow those ideas to be processed than they are in their understanding of the concepts. Activities that challenge gifted and talented students, then, are those that teach new content and also instruct the cognitive and affective skills needed to use the information creatively and effectively.

Meeting of the Minds

Meeting of the Minds was a television show developed by Steve Allen which ran for a number of years on the Public Broadcasting Station. The show depicted the conversations that historical figures might have had, showing each of their perspectives on issues that are relevant today. Have the students choose two historical and one contemporary or three historical figures from different eras as the basis of a television show script that they will write, giving the characters' views on contemporary issues. Enact the show for the class and have students discuss whether or not they feel the script accurately portrays the anticipated views of the characters.

Campaigns

The political process is no more evident than in the campaigns that are conducted to influence public opinion. These can be for political offices, advertising, or changing points of view through lobbying efforts. Choose one of these areas and have students research and conduct a campaign designed to influence the opinions of their classmates. This could be a campaign for classroom officer, official classroom pet, or most delicious dessert. Students can select roles (manager, publicist, spokesperson, artist) to play in the campaign or these can be assigned by the teacher. After the campaign is over, a vote can be taken and a discussion of the campaign techniques used should ensue. Plans for future campaigns can be outlined in a debriefing session, noting changes students would like to make in order to have more successful campaigns.

Dipsey-Doodles

Dipsey-Doodles are "What if . . ." statements from which students project what would be different if historical events had happened in another way. They must draw on their knowledge of such social science areas as history, sociology, psychology, economy, and anthropology to answer the questions in an informed manner. Here are some Dipsey-Doodles with which to begin:

> What if the Confederacy had won the Civil War?
>
> What if everyone on earth was the same race?
>
> What if electricity was never discovered?
>
> What if the sun rose in the south and set in the north?

Transitions

Change and transition are basic themes for many social studies units; one example is death. Gifted students are very interested in death and want to talk about the topic. The book, *The Tenth Good Thing About Barney* (Viorst, 1971), tells the story of a boy whose cat, Barney, has died. His parents suggest that he think of ten good things about Barney to recite at the cat's funeral. In so doing, he learns to cope with the death of his pet. Students can discuss the loss of their pets, the good things about them, and become familiar with the stages of death and dying.

Yesterday and Today

The theme of change can also be investigated through looking at similarities and differences between life today and yesteryear. Give students the opportunity to read such books as *Caddie Woodlawn* (Brink, 1935) and *Little House in a Big Woods* (Wilder, 1932), interview older generations of their families, and peruse historical archives to find the answer to the following questions: In what ways are things today like they were one hundred years ago? In what ways are they different? How do you anticipate things will be different in the future?

CASE STUDY: ARTS

Setting

Traditionally, the music program at Elizabeth Lake Elementary School was composed of vocal music classes one day a week for each classroom. There were no string, orchestra, or band programs, holiday shows, or special choruses or choirs. As it was, with budgetary cutbacks, the music department felt lucky to have the personnel to conduct classes for each school classroom in the district. However, with the community's economy improving, the Assistant Superintendent for Instruction decided that it was time to revitalize the music program and hired three new full-time instructors. This gave all the teachers of music a chance to rearrange their schedules in order to provide additional services to their schools.

Problem

Margaret Joyce was a veteran vocal music teacher with fifteen years' seniority in the school system and five years at Elizabeth Lake School. She knew the students, faculty, community, and administrators well due to her ongoing assignment at that school. From this association, she also knew that the music program was inadequate and was just touching the surface of what could be done with the talented students in the school.

With the license to expand the music program and her own expertise in vocal music, Ms. Joyce decided to begin with what she knew best and develop a vocal music program in which special talent could be more fully developed. It was her opinion that the basic vocal music needs of most of the students were satisfied by the weekly class. However, there were students at every grade level (K–6) who showed exceptional talent and could benefit from additional music instruction and performance.

Her problem was to decide how to deliver the service in a way that was comprehensive enough to be meaningful to the students, and, at the same time, not involve a great deal of student time away from the regular classroom. Any plan was to be approved by the Director of Music and the school's principal.

Possible Solutions

It is difficult to reconstruct building class schedules in order to accommodate new programs. Particularly when programs are in the art, music, or physical education, resistance can be met from those who do not see these subjects as integral to schooling. For the minority who hold that position, there is a majority who do not. Therefore, with cooperation of the entire school, a new schedule, including advanced classes in music, could be generated including all or part of the following solutions.

1. Special classes are the most common way to meet the needs of talented students in music. These are often in the form of a special choir, string ensemble, or concert band. Holding special classes for the advanced students allows them to progress more rapidly and to feel the sensations of being a musician. These classes, however, do not have to be confined to accelerating the development of technique. Music enrichment

classes such as composition, Medieval music, or the music of Franz
Schubert could also benefit advanced students a great deal. Special
classes can be held before or after school or during school time. It is best
to use school time since these students are usually involved in many other
activities, including private lessons, after school.

2. Mentorships are another solution to providing advanced instruction for gifted musicians. As in other areas, music students can profit
from an association with community members or teachers who are musicians in their own right. From these people, students can learn advanced
technique, dedication, and a love of music that they may not have time
to develop in weekly classes with their peers. Mentorship programs can
also be conducted before, after, or during school hours. In fact, this is
the path taken by most serious musicians, except their association with
professionals are not arranged by the school.

3. Another solution to this problem comes through focusing on the
products of the music program. It has been well established that one way
to challenge talented students is to involve them in products with real-
life consequences. This can also be true in music. By arranging for performances, holiday concerts, and talent exhibitions, students can find motivation to excel at higher levels. With evaluation of their work coming
from consumers rather than the teacher, they can also see the way people
relate to music and interpret it from their own points of view.

Ms. Joyce's Solution

Recognizing that her problem was one of scheduling, Ms. Joyce decided
to tackle her dilemma from a total school approach. She knew that students at all grade levels could qualify for advanced instruction in music
but that it would be difficult to free them from class at the same time.
So, with the cooperation of the school principal, the Director of Music,
and the other faculty members, she proceeded to implement the following
plan.

Ms. Joyce kept the basic schedule intact and continued to meet with
each class one day a week for an hour. With these classes, she used the
steps in Treffinger's *Model for Creative Learning* (1985): basic tools, practice with process, and working with real problems. This part of her schedule consumed all but her two preparation periods per week and two additional hours (which she had previously used for travel between schools).
Those two hours happened to fall the last period on both Tuesday and
Friday afternoons. In the Tuesday slot, she instituted an all-school honors
choir for the top twenty vocal students in the school. The Friday period
coincided with the school-wide special class schedule in which six-week
courses were offered in enrichment areas for which students enrolled

based on their interests. Ms. Joyce decided to offer a series of music courses during the year and convinced the instructor of the computer course to purchase software for composing music and also offer that as a special class.

The advanced music students then had the opportunity to engage in three hours of music a week, certainly a great amount of time considering many of them also took private lessons in voice or an instrument. To enhance the program even more, two special performances a year were held—a holiday concert and an end-of-the-year "gala musical extravaganza." Students prepared for these during their music periods and the advanced students rehearsed special selections during their honors choir time.

The program was successful to the extent that the students and parents requested that the school board consider beginning an elementary and middle school orchestra program. In the year that followed Ms. Joyce's attempt at providing a vocal music program for advanced students, an orchestra *and* band program were also begun.

ARTS LESSONS THAT CHALLENGE

The same basic principles for differentiating curriculum for gifted and talented students also apply in the disciplines of the arts. Visual and performing arts areas have students demonstrating a variety of skill levels. The more able students in these areas need instruction and opportunities at their levels of ability. The following are a few examples of lessons in the arts that challenge the talented.

Historical Mural

Every school and/or community has a history. Bringing that history to the attention of the students in the school can be accomplished through many approaches. One is to acquaint students with the art form of murals and to ask those adept at drawing and painting to submit sketches for a mural or a segment of a mural depicting the history of the school and/or community. The best sketches can then be assembled into a plan and the mural can be painted by students under the supervision of a muralist or the art teacher.

"Is It Real or Is It Memorex?"

Voice control is a goal for which vocal musicians strive. One challenging and fun activity is to have students develop imitations of musical instruments using only their voices. After the students have developed their imitations, have them present them to the rest of the class and see if the other students can guess the instrument being imitated. The quicker the recognition, the better the imitation.

Scoring a Soundtrack

Students who enjoy composing will be challenged by the rigor of fitting a musical composition to a piece of film, video tape, or a series of pictures. Stage a film festival in which the students present their soundtracks with the film or pictures. For variety and comparison purposes, have a group of students each use the same footage as the basis of their compositions, then see how their interpretations differ.

Monet Magic

Some of the most famous paintings created by Monet are part of his series of pictures depicting the Notre Dame Cathedral at different times of day. The paintings, although using the same composition and subject matter, look quite different since each has been painted at a different time of day. Have the students study this series of paintings by Monet and choose a subject of their own to depict at different times of day. Discuss in what areas of design the views will differ. Display the series together.

SUMMARY

Differentiating programs and curricula in order to meet the needs of gifted and talented students in the regular classroom setting can be accomplished in all subject areas. The guidelines for doing so, however, remain the same: providing students with opportunities to learn at their own rates, in the depth at which they are capable, and in areas of interest that are vital to each subject area. At the same time, arranging the circumstances of instruction so that students can take responsibility for their learning and develop their knowledge base and skills as independent learners should also be integral to the programs developed. These factors can and should be incorporated throughout the curriculum. In this way, students will see how the various disciplines and skills that they study interrelate.

PART FOUR

Maintaining the Programs

A great deal of energy is often expended in mounting programming options for gifted students, yet program organizers often forget that program maintenance is an even tougher task. Losing programs after about three years of operation is not an uncommon phenomenon. There are many factors that lead to this state; a few are discussed in this section along with ways to avoid the pitfalls common to providing programs for this population.

One way to keep programs strong is to understand that gifted students *do* have problems; they are not perfect. Among the problems discussed in Chapter 11 are underachievement, arrogance, and unwillingness to be cooperative. The special problems faced by gifted girls are also presented along with ways to minimize them.

Another way to strengthen programs for the gifted is to seek and maintain cooperation among educators and parents. Each has a role in developing and maintaining the types of programs that benefit students. Actively nurturing these relationships is essential to program continuance, and tips on doing so are also presented in Chapter 11.

Program evaluation is a third factor in keeping programs healthy and responsive to the needs of children. Chapter 11 ends with a discussion of the importance of program evaluation and the types of questions that should be answered in order to gauge program success.

Chapter 12 deals with providing full programming packages for the gifted and talented students and is predicated on the fact the regular classroom placements will not be appropriate for many of them. They are a necessary part of the programming mosaic and vital to the success of student placements. However, highly gifted students rarely have a place in regular classroom environments. They have trouble flourishing and the teachers in those situations are often stretched beyond their capabilities in trying to give them what they need. Programs outside the regular classroom will be needed and should be available as an option for these students.

Recognizing the limits of program options will strengthen the programs as a whole. When one configuration is used to address the needs of all gifted students, it is destined to fail because it cannot withstand the pressure of trying to meet the needs of all the students. Avoiding the dangers central to maintaining programs for the gifted will enhance present programs and increase the likelihood that they will become permanent parts of the school offerings.

11

Troubleshooting

The most effective way to assure that programs for gifted and talented students flourish and grow is to anticipate problems and use preplanning efforts to hedge against future trouble. In order to do so, prior understanding of potential problem spots is helpful so that strategies to lessen their impact or avoid them altogether can be determined. This chapter will discuss problems common to programs for the gifted and will suggest some possible solutions. The areas that are discussed include: students with problems, dealing with other educators and parents, attaining administrative cooperation, and program evaluation.

STUDENTS WITH PROBLEMS

When gifted and talented students have negative attitudes toward school, themselves, or others around them, trouble can ensue for both the students and the programs in which they participate. Therefore, it is important to understand from where these attitudes emerge and what (if anything) can be done about them. Three attitude problems common to gifted and talented students are evidenced by underachievement, arrogance, and an unwillingness to cooperate. Gifted girls also face certain challenges that may cause problems for them and those around them. These are discussed below along with comments about how each is seen behaviorally, possible reasons for the behaviors, and potential remedies for the behaviors.

Underachievement

Many people believe that the phrase *gifted underachievers* is a contradiction in terms. They base their belief on the position that gifted students must act in a gifted manner. Although most gifted and talented students do display their abilities at one time or another, there are students who cannot or choose not to, for some reason, and therefore perform at levels that are below their capabilities. Ironically, they may even be underachieving while performing at seemingly high levels. For example, a student gifted in the interpretation of literature may be receiving As in English without truly using her talents to the fullest.

More frequently, however, underachievement is seen in students about whom teachers or parents remark, "I know he can do much better than this. He has the ability—he just isn't using it!" For these students, the tragic path to underachievement may have begun in the early elementary grades. Slowly, but steadily, behaviors begin to arise that indicate the students are not performing up to their ability levels for one reason or another. Whitmore (1980) lists the following telltale behaviors among the characteristics of gifted underachievers in her book *Giftedness, Conflict, and Underachievement*:

1. Consistently incomplete schoolwork;
2. Vast gap between qualitative level of oral and written work;
3. Test phobic, poor test results;
4. Low self-esteem and unhealthy self-concept producing: difficulties coping emotionally; lack of self-confidence; and inferiority feelings;
5. An autonomous spirit;
6. Inability to work constructively in groups;
7. Tendency to continually set goals and standards too high;
8. Not motivated by usual devices;
9. Lack of academic initiative (as defined by schools); and
10. Distractability (p. 88).

There has been much speculation as to why gifted students do underachieve. One theory proposes that by underachieving the gifted students never actually display their abilities and, therefore, any judgments made of their performances have no meaning since those performances were not at the students' true ability level. In this way, the gifted and talented students feel they can avoid failure or meaningful criticism since they have not shown their true ability.

Other possible causes of underachievement (Whitmore, 1985) include:

1. Lack of motivation due to inappropriate restrictions in their learning environments or conflicts between learning styles and instructional styles;
2. Values conflict between student and program or student's cultural values and program;

3. Lack of environmental nurturance of intellectual potential at home or at school;

4. Developmental delays or chronically bad health;

5. Specific disabilities such as learning disabilities, cerebral dysfunction, neurological impairments, etc; and

6. Specific or general academic skill deficits in subject matters such as reading, math, or higher level thinking skills (p. 1).

What can be done for these students? Whitmore (1985) suggests five factors that should be considered in order to help chronically underachieving gifted students have profitable school experiences. They are:

1. The teacher must accept the fact that the student is gifted, does not want to underachieve or fail, has low self-esteem, and needs to develop constructive coping skills and self-understanding;

2. The curriculum must be challenging, personally meaningful, and rewarding to the gifted underachiever;

3. The instruction must require minimal memorization and drill/practice activity and provide maximal opportunity for inquiry, scientific investigation, and creative production;

4. The peer group must include at least a few other gifted students, possibly other underachievers, who may become special friends; and

5. Special services should be provided as needed for handicapped students, for those in need of remedial instruction, or for group counseling (p. 2).

Arrogance

Some gifted and talented students have been accused by their peers of being arrogant and snobbish. Students complain that the gifted students feel they are better than the other students and that they try to inflict their will on others. Although this is not true of most gifted and talented students, some do show these traits and can lose friends by doing so.

Being involved in a program for the gifted and/or talented can change the way students think about themselves. At times, they do begin to believe that they are special and different from the other students in the classroom. Whereas they are different, they are not better than their classmates. Steps should be taken at the onset of such behavior in order to minimize the damage to the students' relationships and to give the students a true sense of their abilities. This can be accomplished by taking the following steps:

1. Treat all students in the classroom equally; each child is special. By pointing out the unique qualities of each student, they will

begin to see the talents that they all have. The gifted students will see that persons of all abilities and talents are valued and valuable.

2. Avoid making an example of the gifted students. Be sure that all the students in the class receive praise for the special accomplishments they make.

3. Give the gifted students a chance to interact with one another. When they work and talk together they soon discover that there are other people like themselves in the world and some of those people have even more ability than they do. This helps to give the gifted students a more accurate sense of their own abilities.

4. Talk to the gifted students directly about their abilities and what the meaning and responsibility of that giftedness is. At times, the appearance of arrogance is a shield against rejection and ridicule by peers. Help students learn the skills needed to deal with the other students in the class.

Unwillingness to Cooperate

Although most gifted and talented students enjoy school and are very cooperative with their teachers and classmates, it is not unusual to come upon students who are not. Comments like, "This work is too babyish" or "I already know how to do this, so why do I have to do it again?" have been heard by more than one teacher.

Why do such seemingly talented students become obstinate? Sometimes they have good reason for such objections. Not all gifted students are willing to conform to the rules of the classroom when they include doing all that the teacher wishes whether it is appropriate to the students' abilities or not. Under such circumstances they may object to constantly doing work that they already know how to do. At other times, however, you may see students who are in challenging environments with plenty of opportunity to flourish and they still are uncooperative with the teachers and students in the class. Such students may have more serious problems in dealing with competition, making friends, and perfectionism. They may feel that their work will be tarnished if other students have a hand in it and will prefer to work alone rather than risking cooperating with others.

Under the most extreme situations, the teacher may have to request assistance from a counselor or psychologist to develop a method of dealing with these students. However, preventive steps can also be taken to minimize the chance that such behavior will become manifest. These include:

1. Provide learning experiences that are at the students' ability and achievement levels so that they are challenged and stimulated in their work.

2. Encourage cooperation through small group work or cooperative games in which students must work together to win and minimize the competitive nature of the classroom experiences. Some competition is fine, but it should be kept in balance.

3. Use contingency contracting in the most extreme cases. In this technique, students work toward privileges and goals by agreeing (in the contract) to do certain tasks. For example, a student can contract for twenty minutes of free time alone, for successfully engaging in the skill group meetings for the week, and so on.

4. Uncooperative behaviors may be indicating deeper problems. Make counseling services available for students who continue to be uncooperative despite appropriate programming and direct intervention.

Gifted Girls

Gifted girls face a unique set of challenges across their lifetimes that may lead to problems at home, school, or with their friends. Educators who have been involved with programs for the gifted and talented often comment that there are many female candidates for such programs when program selection is done in the early grades, but that the numbers decrease substantially when procedures for selection come in the middle school or junior high school years. How can this be? Do gifted girls disappear or do they exhibit behaviors (intentionally or unintentionally) that preclude their selection? Most likely, the answer is the latter.

Although circumstances are improving, some gifted girls find that societal expectations still may lead to conditions in schools that do not encourage their progress. Some gifted girls report being discouraged from taking classes in the mathematics and science disciplines that will prepare them for more advanced work in their later years. Parents may also have different levels of expectation for achievement and careers for their male and female children. This translates into the children having different expectations for themselves, which can affect the choices they make about their education.

Puberty and early adolescence also seem to be a factor in the performance levels and behaviors of gifted girls. As they become more socially aware, they often find there is pressure to become "more like everyone else," which is translated as being less smart. So they begin to take the classes that their less able friends do or to show less concern about grades and achievement than what the boys think of them.

All of these factors, and certainly others, result in such conditions as (1) very few females in advanced mathematics classes (and fewer who actually flourish); (2) high-level science courses with mostly male members; and (3) women still underrepresented in such careers as computer science, hard sciences, and mathematics. Although the past decade has seen a substantial increase in the number of women doctors, lawyers, and MBAs, more progress can be made to assure that the trend continues and that gifted females are given equal access and opportunity to develop their abilities. Among the steps that can be taken are the following:

1. Acquaint school counselors and academic staff with the special needs of gifted female students so that they can more carefully guide them in their course and college selections or through support groups.
2. Expose gifted girls to successful gifted women from whom they can learn about the challenges they will face across their lifetimes and the strategies for surviving relatively unscathed.
3. Make an extra effort to find qualified gifted girls for special programs at the middle school and junior high school levels. After they have been placed, provide support services to them (counseling, tutoring, etc.) so they will be successful in the program.
4. Provide activities that will give the girls an advantage of excelling without being in competition with the boys.

DEALING WITH OTHER EDUCATORS AND PARENTS

When providing programs for gifted and talented students in the regular classroom, problems can arise when dealing with educators and students' parents. Constructing adequate programs for the gifted necessarily means that other educators may have to make adjustments in their instruction. It is very likely that the students will have knowledge of the skills taught at higher grade levels and may have completed the materials designated for those classes. The teachers, then, are going to have students coming into their classes who already know the skills and the materials that they have typically offered. Therefore, they will either have to make adjustments and accommodations or put the students through the destructive process of going through the same materials again. To avoid such trauma to the students and conflict with the rest of the faculty, it is wise to seek cooperation from colleagues, parents, and administrators at the onset of efforts to provide instruction that is appropriate for all the students in the classroom.

Areas for Cooperation Among Educators

Whon a oohool or oohool diotrict hao a gcncral atmoophere and histoi y of cooperation, instituting provisions for the gifted and talented is a far easier task than when cooperation is at a minimum. In either instance, however, there are three primary facets in which cooperation is advised: program planning, curriculum articulation, and staffing.

Program planning efforts for these students, even when confined to regular classroom placements, will be most successful when they have the endorsement and cooperation of other faculty members. Mounting programs that include such techniques as cluster grouping, multiaged classes, telescoping, or continuous progress curriculum cannot be adequately accomplished without the assistance of other teachers. They are needed to help in planning, sharing materials, joining in developing and teaching certain groups of students, and in endorsing the program. There is no room for misguided jealousies or subversion of programming efforts. It is easy to untrack programs of this type. Cooperation and student-centered decision making can help keep programs on the track to successful implementation and a long life.

Articulating curriculum across grade and building levels is another area that demands cooperative efforts within individual schools and the district as a whole. Full-scale comprehensive programming and curricular efforts must be based on a scope and sequence of skills across years. By developing such a scope and sequence, the progression of skills and activities can be outlined in such a way that the students' programs and skill development does not become haphazard and gaps in knowledge and skills do not develop. Obviously, building such a document requires cooperation between faculty members. Implementing the document also requires cooperative efforts between teachers and administrators in the individual buildings.

Staffing is the third area in which cooperation is vital to program success. More flexibility and less territorialism are two goals that need to be achieved before cooperation can begin to take place. When implementing programs that are responsive to student needs, teachers begin to make staffing decisions based on what will enhance the learning of the students. This may mean working with groups of students in new ways or taking on an additional number of students so that another teacher can be free to work with other groups of students. Changing old patterns of interaction is often necessary along with opening mutual resource banks to support the new grouping patterns. Another common staffing problem is found when cluster grouping is instituted. Some teachers do not like to have all the gifted students in one classroom because they feel that they are losing their "good" students and their "sparkplugs." Hopefully, they can be convinced that it is to the students' benefit to be in contact with other gifted students and that they are better served under this configuration.

Building Cooperative Ventures

Beginning the process of building cooperative ventures should start by a meeting with the administrator in charge of the building(s) immediately involved in the program. The support of this individual is vital to the program's success and he or she can be of great assistance in developing cooperative efforts among faculty or plotting a strategy through which cooperation can be gained.

One step that can be taken to build cooperative teaching efforts is to talk with the school curriculum committee. Most schools have building-level curriculum committees composed of faculty and administrative representatives to whom proposals for program modification can be presented. This group is in the position of endorsing the plan, helping to promote it to their colleagues, and finding ways to implement the plan in the best possible way. Circumventing this group is a real mistake; such an oversight can lead to the appearance of unwillingness to cooperate on the part of the program organizers and certain program demise.

In the absence of a curriculum committee, or after the committee has endorsed the plan, the teachers at the same grade level and the contiguous grades should meet to discuss the impact that the proposed programming will have on their teaching. Granted, a program can be mounted in isolation from other faculty members, but this should be seen as a course taken only as the last resort. People attending this meeting might discuss such matters as grouping patterns, sharing and organizing resources, using above-level textbooks, and curricular articulation.

When Cooperation Is Not Possible

In the absence of any success in gaining cooperation, two possible avenues exist. One is for the administrator to step in and require that the programming efforts take place. Although this type of intervention is sure to make as many problems as it solves, it is sometimes the only way to assure that some semblance of appropriate programs is available for the students. Generally, the cooperation level in this instance is marginal, but it may be enough to maintain the program.

When that remedy does not work or if the administrator is unable or unwilling to do so, then the classroom teacher is faced with a difficult decision. Should she or he proceed with the plans and curricular changes for the program? Or in what way can the plans be altered in order to make them more palatable to the rest of the faculty? These are tough questions to answer because they may have unpleasant consequences. The teacher who does decide to proceed and provide programming and curricular opportunities at the students' ability and achievement levels will be comforted by knowing that the students are involved in meaningful and challenging learning experiences.

Parents and Their Roles

The roles that parents of gifted and talented students play are often forgotten in the confusion of trying to implement and maintain programs for their children. They do represent a powerful force whose energy and influence can be harnessed to bring stability to the programming efforts. Parents are the students' first teachers and they often have great insight into their children and their needs. They are also highly invested in assuring that their children get the best educational opportunities possible. For teachers of the gifted and program planners, a great ally can be found in these people.

It is also noteworthy to remember that parents of gifted children are among the constituents to whom the Board of Education members are accountable. Therefore, parents have power to influence policy generation through their votes and their lobbying efforts. To have informed advocates among this group will be a definite asset to programs for the gifted.

How can educators build alliances with parents in order to strengthen programs for the children? The answers are many, but communication leads the list. Perhaps the largest number of complaints arise when parents are not consistently informed about what their children are doing in the programs. The students are not the best conduit for information about school activities, as most parents know, and they cannot be expected to relay information regularly or accurately. Provisions must be made through which parents receive information about the programs as a whole and the individual progress of their children. This may need to come through a variety of forms. The most widely used procedures are newsletters, parents' nights, individual progress reports (as part of or apart from regular report cards), parent group meetings, conferences, and program visitations. How you communicate with the parents is secondary to the fact that it is done on a regular basis both in writing and in person.

Establishing parent groups can facilitate communication between parents and program personnel, but can also serve other purposes that will strengthen the program. Group meetings allow the parents to get to know one another, talk about common problems and interests, and often come to the realization that their children are like many others in the program. Like their children, parents of the gifted often feel that their problems in raising their children are unique to their households. They find comfort in the fact that many of the behaviors they find unusual are actually quite like other children of similar ability. These group meetings are almost like therapy sessions for the parents. Parents who are involved become stronger supporters of programming efforts as they begin to have a greater investment in the program and see the necessity for differential programming.

Generating informed advocates is another function that group meetings can serve. By having speakers, exhibitions, or roundtable discussions as part of group meetings, parents can learn about the nature of giftedness and the special needs that their students have. By doing so, they will increase their parenting skills and their knowledge about giftedness, making them more prepared to be effective advocates when dealing with Boards of Education and state legislatures.

Informed parents are also contributing members to class activities and committees dealing with programs for the gifted. They can serve as mentors, teacher aides, internship sponsors, or leaders for *Junior Great Books*, as the need arises. As they gain skill and insight, they may also be used in committee work to give parental input into program planning and placement decisions.

There is a commonly held belief that all parents think their children are gifted. Although this may be true in a broad interpretation of the word *gifted*, it is rarely the case that parents want their children in situations in which they will not succeed. Not all parents want their children in programs for the gifted; not all parents want the responsibility inherent in having a gifted child. For all those parents accused of being pushy parents there are far more who have their child's interest in mind more than their own. Rather than avoiding dealing with them, it is best to engage their help in implementing and promoting programs for their children in a positive manner.

ADMINISTRATIVE PARTICIPATION

One of the most certain ways to insure program maintenance and minimize problem situations in programs for the gifted and talented is to engage building and district administrators actively in the program planning and implementation activities. It is clear from the research on what makes schools effective (Edmonds, 1979) that strong leadership, especially from building principals, is a critical factor in mounting successful programs for children. Without their endorsement and active support, program maintenance is practically impossible for it is they who make decisions about budgets, staffing, resource allocation, and scheduling.

Role of the Building Principals

Building principals are central to the process of initiating and maintaining programs for the gifted and talented. They set the tone for the school and they can help establish student-centered environments through their decisions, policies, and expectations. They are pivotal to program success because they can allow or block the accommodations necessary for this type of programming to occur.

Dealing with staffing decisions is one of the most important roles that principals play in programs for these students. They can determine such matters as which staff member teaches the class with the cluster group, where split-grade classes will occur, how the staff will be arranged so that one teacher will have the last period free to work with a special class in mathematics, or how the art teacher's time can be arranged so that an advanced art class can meet. Their willingness to make such modifications and their understanding of the merit in doing so cannot be replaced through other techniques or allegiances. Principals are also the people who must intervene when some staff members are not cooperative and are harming programming efforts. At these times, it is the building principals who must persuade the staff members to change their approaches or they must make arrangements for the teachers to work at a school more compatible to their teaching styles (or not at all). These two areas of administrative prerogative, staffing placements and dealing with problem teachers, put the building principal in a central decision-making role.

Listening to parental concerns about programs is another role that principals play in maintaining programs for the gifted. Parent complaints about programs, teachers, or other requests pertinent to the program are best referred to the principal for consideration. The principal can then take the appropriate action. At times this may mean making a placement for a student in the classroom of a requested teacher, urging a teacher to allow students to work at the reading levels that are appropriate, or defending a teacher's instructional techniques to objecting parents. It is important to the health of a program to know what the administrative concerns are and for the principal to make those areas clear to the staff. The principal should be in the position to listen to parents, to try to the extent appropriate to accommodate their wishes, and to protect their teachers from unfounded accusations or unreasonable demands.

It is the building administrator who sets the budget for the school and thus has an impact on programming efforts. Through the budget process, decisions can be made that will allow the financing of out-of-level texts for the students, team entrance fees for competitions, or an Author in Residence program. Although programs for these students do not require high budgetary line items, some pecuniary consideration is helpful and the lack of such consideration can be crippling.

Putting a priority on the exhibition of student learning is a fourth role that building principals play in programs for the gifted and talented. By sponsoring or supporting such events as science fairs, musicals, Future Problem Solving bowls, recitals, talent shows, and Shakespeare festivals, the principal sends a clear message that products are important and that talents should be enjoyed. It is the preparation for and participation in the events that is critical and should be emphasized, not the competitive side of such activities. Students see the principals as people of stature; hosting such events can be sufficient motivation for the students to try their best to produce top-notch products.

Role of the District-Wide Administrators

Central office administrators are also in the position of making or breaking programs for the gifted and talented. Their authority and power to recommend and implement Board of Education policy places them in the center of the decision-making process. Therefore, it is important to understand what their roles should be and the types of situations with which they should deal.

The most important role of district-wide administrators in providing programs for this population is found in their influence on policy decisions. They are in the position of recommending to the Board of Education that they adopt a policy that makes programs of this type possible and, perhaps, mandatory. Policies dealing with the issues faced by gifted and talented students, such as early entrance, early graduation, concurrent enrollment, and acceleration, are set at the central office level. Buttressing these policies with standing committees of the Board or district-wide teachers' committees will further strengthen program planning. Having people in these positions who are sympathetic to the plight of gifted and talented students can greatly assist in the struggle to institute and maintain programs.

Providing professional development opportunities for the staff is another major role of district-wide administrators that affects programs for the gifted. When plans for professional development are being made, it helps the program to have meetings that deal with building the skills needed to serve this population effectively. These sessions may be at the knowledge, skill development, or awareness level, for most districts have personnel in each group. Bringing in experts in such areas as classroom management, asking good questions, *Philosophy for Children, Talents Unlimited*, and underachievement can enhance programming efforts for the gifted while giving the participants added information that will also assist in their work with other students.

Hiring a coordinator for programs for the gifted and talented is a third role that central administrators can adopt. Certainly, having a person in charge of coordinating and building the programs is a great asset in program development and maintenance. The position gives instant importance and credibility to the programs and provides the teachers involved in the program with assistance in such matters as working out problems, scheduling, and obtaining resources. A coordinator can provide the vision of "what can be" so that the program can continue to grow and flourish in ways that benefit students with special needs.

Giving students recognition for work well done is another area in which district-wide administrators can become involved. Many schools are extending beyond honor roles to other means of rewarding excellence. Issuing academic letters is one activity that is gaining in popularity. Students, like athletes, who display exceptional ability in the academic areas of school life are eligible for varsity letters which were previously reserved for athletes alone. This token of recognition is an important statement to the students; that is, that academic excellence is valued in the same light as athletic prowess. Other programs of this type extend extra privileges to students, hold special outings, and display student accomplishments in such a way that students know that these are important and are valued by the school district.

Finally, sponsoring programs for these students is a role that district-wide administrators can play. Testing for early admission, mounting an honors program, sponsoring the Art Lady program, and conducting an all-district choir are just a few of the options available. By holding all-district events, students of high ability can come together to study and work in an environment that gives them the opportunity to be with other students of similar ability, whereas the building-based programs make it possible for students to receive appropriate programs within their home school setting. A combination of both types of programs will serve the students the best because they can choose the programs that are the most advantageous to them.

PROGRAM EVALUATION

Evaluating the success of programming efforts is a step in program maintenance that is often overlooked. It is vital to the ongoing strength of a program to determine on a regular basis the extent to which the program is achieving its goals. Evaluations can be conducted formally or informally, depending on the resources at hand. The important thing is to be sure that evaluation data are being collected. In this way the effect that the program is having on the students can be documented and the information can be used to make decisions about what changes need to be made.

There are any number of questions that can be asked during a program evaluation. Historically, most evaluations of programs for the gifted and talented have focused on whether or not the students enjoyed the program and if the parents thought the program was successful. This type of information is important, but it is not sufficient for the purposes of maintaining and building strong programs. Program organizers should extend their investigations of program success to include some measures of student change. This student-change data should document the ways and extent to which students are different due to their participation in the program. If these changes are positive, a clear notion of program effects will emerge that will support the continuation of the programming activities. When changes are negative, steps must be taken to make the program more responsive to students' needs.

Callahan (1985) lists eight purposes for program evaluation. They are:

1. Documentation of the need for a program;

2. Documentation of the case for a particular approach;

3. Documentation of the feasibility of a program;

4. Documentation of program implementation;

5. Identification of program strengths and weaknesses;

6. Provision of data for in-progress revisions of the program;

7. Documentation of the results or impacts of the program; and

8. Explanation and description of the program to interested and uninformed audiences (p. 1).

The purpose for which the evaluation is conducted will determine the types of data that are collected.

For a comprehensive evaluation process, nine steps should be taken over the course of the study. These are:

1. Prepare a description of the program about which all program planners agree.

2. Identify the program goals and objectives and write these down as part of the program description.

3. Write evaluation questions that reflect your major concerns or priorities for evaluation.

4. Develop an evaluation design that details when and from whom information will be gathered.
5. Select or design and administer the instrumentation.
6. Collect the data.
7. Analyze the data using methods that are appropriate to the questions and understandable by your audience.
8. Prepare and report the results to the necessary audience(s).
9. Prepare a plan for ongoing evaluation.

The instruments used to gather data can be of a wide variety. They need only to be accurate and effective in gathering the information needed for your questions (Parke and Buescher, 1982). Commonly used instruments include questionnaires and surveys, norm-referenced and criterion-referenced tests, sociograms, product scales, observations, journals or diaries, case studies, and interviews (see Figures 11-1, 11-2, and 11-3). When selecting instruments, it is best to use more than one instrument to measure each question and to question more than one constituent.

One classroom teacher was concerned that the students in her cluster group were not interacting sufficiently with the other students in the class. In order to investigate whether or not this perception was accurate, she decided to gather data pertinent to the question, "To what extent are the cluster group students interacting with students who are not in the cluster?" Three types of instruments were used in the study—a sociogram, observation of student interaction patterns, and a self-concept scale to see the extent to which all the students in the class felt good about themselves. The data were then submitted to a panel, composed of the school principal, the psychologist, and the classroom teacher, for analysis. After careful study, they determined that a problem was emerging but that it was not at a critical state. Students were beginning to break into two separate groups but they still felt positively about themselves and one another. The classroom teacher began to make alterations in the way the cluster students worked so that the segregation was minimized.

Program evaluation is an integral part of troubleshooting in programs for the gifted and talented. When done on an ongoing basis it can detect problems before they get out of hand as well as provide a data base upon which decisions about the program can be made. It is difficult for the classroom teacher to mount an evaluation that is comprehensive and ongoing. To make the process easier, central office or local university personnel may be available to assist. The use of extant data is also a viable and time-saving technique.

Figure 11-1   Sample Page from the Student Product Assessment Form

1. EARLY STATEMENT OF PURPOSE

Is the purpose (theme, thesis, research question) readily apparent in the early stages of the student's product? In other words, did the student define the topic or problem in such a manner that a clear understanding about the nature of the product emerges shortly after a review of the material?

For example, in a research project dealing with skunks of northwestern Connecticut completed by a first grade student, the overall purpose and scope of the product are readily apparent after reading the introductory paragraphs.

5	4	3	2	1	NA
To a great extent		Somewhat		To a limited extent	

2. PROBLEM FOCUSING

Did the student focus or clearly define the topic so that it represents a relatively specific problem within a larger area of study?

For example, a study of "Drama in Elizabethan England" would be more focused that "A Study of Drama."

5	4	3	2	1	NA
To a great extent		Somewhat		To a limited extent	

3. LEVEL OF RESOURCES

Is there evidence that the student used resource materials or equipment that are more advanced, technical, or complex than materials ordinarily used by students at this age/grade level?

(continued)

Figure 11-1   (*Continued*)

For example, a sixth grade student utilizes a nearby university library to locate information about the history of clowns in the twelfth through sixteenth century in the major European countries.

5	4	3	2	1	NA
To a great extent		Somewhat		To a limited extent	

4. DIVERSITY OF RESOURCES

Has the student made an effort to use several different types of resource materials in the development of the product? Has the student used any of the following information sources in addition to the standard use of encyclopedias: textbooks, record/statistic books, biographics, how-to-do-it books, periodicals, films and filmstrips, letters, phone calls, personal interviews, surveys or polls, catalogs and/or others?

For example, a fourth grade student interested in the weapons and vehicles used in World War II reads several adult-level books on this subject which included biographies, autobiographies, periodicals, and record books. He also conducted oral history interviews with local veterns of World War II, previewed films and filmstrips about the period and collected letters from elderly citizens sent to them from their sons stationed overseas.

5	4	3	2	1	NA
To a great extent		Somewhat		To a limited extent	

Figure 11-2   Sample Pages from the Pyramid Project's Needs Assessment
Form

Pyramid Project Gifted and Talented Program
Needs Assessment Form
This brief survey is being conducted by the Pyramid Project to assess public
opinion about the need for programs for gifted and able learners. Your response is very important and we appreciate your willingness to complete this
survey.

_____   _____
Superintendent   Assistant Superintendent

Instructions
You are asked two questions for each of the recommendations about programs for the able learners in your school district.

First, how IMPORTANT is the recommendation stated.

Second, how well do you think the recommendation is PRESENTLY
BEING IMPLEMENTED in your district.

Please read each recommendation and select your response from the six
choices given on the scales below. Write ONE number in each space provided
under the column for IMPORTANCE and ONE number under the column for
PRESENT LEVEL OF IMPLEMENTATION which best expresses your opinion.

Importance	Present Level of Implementation
5— Extremely Important	5— Fully Implemented/Exemplary
4— Very Important	4— Fully Implemented
3— Important	3— Implemented/Minor Adjustment
2— Somewhat Important	2— Implemented/Major Adjustment
1— Not Important	1— Not Implemented
0— No Opinion	0— No Opinion

EXAMPLE:

	Importance	Present Level of Implementation
Assess abilities of all students and use results for programming deci-sions.	5	3

This response indicates that the respondent feels it is extremely important
to assess but feels that the district needs minor adjustment in the way it's
using assessments for program decisions.

Figure 11–2   *(Continued)*

Recommendations for Educating Able Learners

	Importance	Present Level of Implementation
1. Adopt flexible pacing at all levels allowing all students to learn at what ever rate is most natural to them.	_____	_____
2. Give thoughtful attention to special groups, such as minorities. Avoid tests that are dependent on English vocabulary and comprehension and use lists of characteristics valued by the subculture for assessment purposes.	_____	_____
3. Throw a wide net to include more students, keeping entrance requirements for special classes fairly modest and tentative. The goal is to include all students who can benefit from enriched programming rather than to exclude any who are marginal.	_____	_____
4. Recognize the importance of counselors in student testing, ministering to emotional needs, guiding program selection, and counseling students in career and college choices.	_____	_____
5. Offer programs that reach through and beyond the normal school boundaries: across disciplines, grade levels, and levels of intelligence.	_____	_____
6. Encourage independence with projects that culminate in real products and employ the methods of inquiry used by real scholars.	_____	_____
7. Develop specific plans for concurrent dual enrollment programs at all levels—elementary/middle, middle/high school, and high school/college.	_____	_____
8. Recognize that a few students will benefit from the opportunity to leave school and enter college early.	_____	_____

(continued)

Figure 11-2   (*Continued*)

Recommendations for Educating Able Learners (*Continued*)

	Importance	Present Level of Implementation
9. Make use of community resources, including the private sector for internships and one-to-one experiences.	_____	_____
10. Cooperate with museums, arts organizations and civic groups to increase educational options.	_____	_____
11. Encourage students to participate in after/before school programs.	_____	_____
12. Develop teaching strategies appropriate to the learning styles of the able students.	_____	_____
13. Help teachers develop manageable record keeping systems that allow them to monitor student progress without undue loss of instructional time.	_____	_____
14. Provide regular classroom teachers with adequate support services—such as a resource teacher—so that enrichment is available to learners in the regular classroom.	_____	_____
15. Use nearby colleges or universities for staff development.	_____	_____

Source: Reprinted by permission by Gifted Students Institute. Copyright © 1985.

Figure 11-3   Sample Items from the District Self-Assessment Document of Programming for the Gifted and Talented.

	Yes	In Progress	No	N/A

A PLANNING ACTIVITIES

1. A planning committee is composed of parents, teachers, support personnel, ISD representative, administrators, students, and members of the community for the purpose of developing the Gifted/Talented (G/T) program and to provide ongoing direction and leadership for the program.

2. To determine the current needs for programming, an assessment was conducted, in both the school and community, that includes:
   a. Student needs
   b. Existing in- and out-of-school provisions.

3. The planning committee became familiar with G/T education through a variety of sources such as readings, guest speakers, school visitations, and state and intermediate school district documents.

4. The planning committee meets on a regular basis. Activities that are accomplished in the developmental years are:
   a. Developing the district philosophy on gifted education.
   b. Establishing both program and students goals and objectives.
   c. Establishing both short and long-range goals.
   d. Defining programming implementation and a long-range administrative plan.
   e. Designing an evaluation plan of the program and student outcomes.

Source: Reprinted by permission by Michigan Department of Education. Copyright © 1986.

SUMMARY

Anticipating problems that may occur and instituting procedures to avoid problems is the most effective way to maintain programs for the gifted and talented. In order to assure that programs for these students grow and flourish, it is necessary to be acquainted with the types of problems that may occur. Being aware of potential student attitude problems, their causes, and their remedies is a beginning point for this process. Following that up with strategies to build cooperation and acceptance for the program among the staff and parents is a second step to building programming efforts. Gaining administrative cooperation and participation is a third step in this process, which will serve as the underpinning for all additional program planning. Finally, developing a plan for and conducting ongoing comprehensive program evaluation will enable program planners to anticipate problems and appreciate their successes. Incorporating these four factors into program activities will increase the likelihood that programs for gifted and talented students will succeed in their attempts to provide a strong educational experience.

ACTION STEPS

1. Talk to the building administrator about your plans for providing programs for the gifted and talented students. Solicit the principal's support for your plans and find out the ways that she or he can be of assistance.

2. Volunteer to be a part of district-wide committees or panels who are involved in this type of programming and decision making for these students.

3. Talk to Board of Education members and acquaint them with the special needs that gifted and talented students have.

4. Encourage the administrators to hire a coordinator for the district's program. This person can assist you in program development plans and in obtaining resources.

5. Choose a student or two who you feel have attitude problems that block their achievement. Talk with the school counselor about possible explanations for these behaviors and develop a plan with the student(s) for learning more positive attitudes and behaviors.

REFERENCES YOU CAN USE

Daniels, P. (1983). *Teaching the gifted learning disabled child.* Rockville, MD: Aspen Systems Corporation.

Kerr, B. (1985). *Smart girls, gifted women.* Columbus, OH: Ohio Psychology Publication Company.

Perino, S. (1981). *Parenting the gifted: Developing the promise.* New York: R. R. Bowker Company.

Whitmore, J. (1980). *Giftedness, conflict, and underachievement.* Boston: Allyn and Bacon.

Whitmore, J., & Maker, J. (1985). *Intellectual giftedness in disabled persons.* Rockville, MD: Aspen Systems Corporation.

12

Beyond
the Regular Classroom

Some gifted and talented students will not be well served in a regular classroom setting. The abilities of highly gifted students are advanced to the extreme that the regular classroom teacher cannot always make modifications to the extent needed for appropriate programming to occur while still providing adequate educational experiences for the rest of the class. There are other less gifted students who benefit more from being in the regular classroom setting for part of their school time and in an alternative setting for the balance of their time. *The more advanced the students' abilities are, the more likely it is that the regular classroom setting is an inappropriate setting.*

Keeping in mind that students are gifted all day long, it is necessary to consider the full range of programming that is occurring for them during their school days. For some, a regular classroom that is geared to their needs may be an adequate placement; others will profit from pullout programs for part of the day or full-time placements in special schools or advanced classes.

FULL PROGRAMMING
FOR THE GIFTED AND TALENTED

To provide appropriate educational experiences for gifted and talented students, full programming should be in place. That is the condition under which there are programs at each level that adequately correspond to the ability, achievement, and interest levels of the students under consideration. Students can find options within the programming mosaic configurations that meet their needs for flexible pacing, studying topics in depth, and pursuing interests that are different from their classmates' interests. Full programming for the gifted and talented is in place when there is evidence of the following provisions:

1. *Comprehensive and ongoing assessment program.* Assessment information should be gathered for the purposes of program selection, program placements, and program evaluation. Keeping up-to-date files of students' testing information, product evaluations, and interest inventories can provide a valuable source of information for program placements and program development.

2. *Mosaic of programming options.* This includes programs in all the academic areas and the arts across all grade levels. Students advanced in any area of the curriculum should be able to find courses and placements that are appropriate for their levels of ability.

3. *K-12 articulation of curriculum.* There should be a written document that outlines how the provisions for the students interrelate and follow in a planned manner. This document should reflect agreement about what skills are being developed, at what time, and in what ways, so that programming decisions are not made in a haphazard fashion.

4. *Instructional techniques that allow flexible pacing, exploring topics in depth, and the pursuit of individual interests.* The instruction by individual teachers makes a difference in the extent to which gifted and talented students receive appropriate programs. Teachers must be trained in and use such techniques as managing students with differing levels of ability, independent study, higher level thinking skills, and problem-solving methods.

5. *Coordinator in charge of the program.* In order to have full programming efforts it is necessary for someone to have responsibility for their development and maintenance. This person can be a central office administrator, building principal, coordinator, or coordinating council. Regardless of who the person is, he or she should be an advocate for the gifted, understanding of their needs and characteristics, and well versed on programming and curricular configurations.

Without these provisions, it is easy to have programs that are not adequately resourceful for the unique needs of gifted and talented students. When full programming is not in place, it is not unusual to find students who have special programming at one level only to discover there are no programs at the next, or students who are unable to get advanced instruction in their area of talent and must either look to private sources or do without. Certainly, most gifted and talented students in schools today are underserved by their present educational programs. Mounting full programming efforts is time and resource consuming; however, it is the only way to provide educational programs for the gifted and talented that are suited to their needs.

ALTERNATIVE PROGRAM CONFIGURATIONS

Gifted and talented students who are being well served in regular classroom settings are usually also involved in some type of programming outside of the regular classroom structure. Most successful programs for these students employ a number of different configurations in order to offer meaningful classes. When a regular classroom placement is made for these students, they usually are also engaged in one or more pull-out programs in addition to their classroom-based work. For students who are too advanced for regular classroom placements, a full-time program is prescribed in an alternative setting, usually involving students from a number of schools or school districts.

PULL-OUT PROGRAMS

The most frequently used pull-out program configurations fall into three categories: special classes, resource rooms, and the Revolving Door Identification Model (Renzulli, Reis, and Smith, 1981). Each has its own purpose and provides students who are enrolled in it with unique opportunities for growth. These programming options are mounted *in addition to* the regular classroom program. *They do not replace programming provisions in the regular classroom, nor do they negate the need for strong classroom-based programs.*

Special Classes

Special classes are courses that are separate from and in lieu of the regular class or classes in which a student is enrolled. These can be advanced (normally accelerated to some degree), university-based courses (accelerated or enriched), or interest-based classes (typically of the enrichment variety). Students in regular classroom placements can then take advantage of courses in their talent areas, which are either advanced and/or enriched, leading to learning experiences at the appropriate levels.

Advanced Classes.   Since many gifted and talented students learn at rates that exceed that of their classmates, they may be ready to learn content that is beyond what is normally prescribed for their grade level. In these instances, having advanced classes available for the students is one way to respond to the gap between what is offered programatically and the abilities displayed by the students. This is particularly true in the upper elementary grades.

Most advanced classes are in one content area. That is, there will be an advanced mathematics, language arts, music, science, art, or social science course geared to students who learn more rapidly and who have skills that exceed the skills of their age-peers. The classes become a regular part of the students' schedule and are the credit-producing courses in those content areas. For some students, their entire schedule of classes may be composed of advanced classes. For other students, enrollment in one or two may be all that they need.

It is important to note that advance classes should be offered in the arts as well as the more traditionally academic subjects. For students adept in the areas of the arts, classes at their ability levels are equally necessary. Along with such advanced courses as computer programming, pre-algebra, and English literature, such classes as advanced art or honors orchestra and choir should be available as a part of the programming mosaic.

University-based Courses.   Some universities choose to offer courses for gifted and talented students who are interested in advanced or enriched classes. Although most of the programs are for students no younger than middle school or junior high school, some Saturday classes are geared for students as young as preschoolers. These classes usually feature topics that are not covered in the scope and sequence of most schools. In that way, they can attract students who are interested in going beyond the regular class curriculum.

At times, universities will work together with school districts to offer classes at advanced levels that are not part of the school districts' course listings. Advanced laboratory techniques, psychology, and folklore are just a few classes that universities have sponsored for upper elementary and middle school-aged students.

When classes are held on a university campus or by a university professor at a local school, courses may or may not be considered for credit by the university or the local school district. Some school districts do choose to grant credit toward graduation or high school requirements for such courses. Others will sponsor the classes but not consider them to be in lieu of other course work. This decision is usually made by the Board of Education and/or the Office of the Provost at the university.

Interest-based Classes.   Another way to focus advanced courses for the gifted is by capitalizing on their interests. Since these may differ from the interests held by other students, there may be a market for classes in such topics as foreign languages, PASCAL computer language, or the paintings of Picasso. Most interest-based classes are not considered part of the basic curriculum and are, therefore, not eligible for credits. Students who enroll in these classes do so as an elective or in their free time.

The regulations of some school districts will allow people without teaching credentials to teach these classes. When this is the case, community members can be recruited to teach some of the classes that are in specialty areas other than those of faculty members. When this is not the case, teachers may volunteer to design and teach such classes as either a part of their regular assignment or under an extended service contract.

Resource Rooms

The most frequently found configuration of programs for the gifted and talented is to have a resource room program in addition to the regular classroom placement (Cox, Daniel, and Boston, 1985). Students spend most of their week in their homeroom, but are involved with the pull-out program for about two to six hours a week. During their time in the resource room, they work with other students of similar ability, often in small groups or on individual projects.

A typical resource room is staffed by one teacher who meets with four to eight groups of students a week. These students either travel to the site of the program (if it is at another school) or go to another classroom (if the program is within their home school). Most class meetings last for two to three hours, once or twice a week. In some instances, students are in the resource room setting for a full day each week. During that time, they generally work on such skills as independent learning, higher level thinking processes, problem solving, and creative expression. The day usually starts with a whole-group activity followed by small-group projects or independent study. Due to the short time the students are with the resource room teacher, the classes tend to be project-oriented and often require the students to do work outside the class time.

Resource room teachers are busy people. Keeping track of the many students they see in a week is a difficult task, but their jobs do not stop there. One of the most time-consuming duties that resource room teachers have is helping students locate resources. When ninety different independent studies are being conducted at one time, there are a lot of materials being used! Assessing students and planning lessons are two additional responsibilities that are continual. Another major duty is communicating and coordinating with the students' homeroom teachers so that lessons can be compatible and they know what activities are occurring in the resource room. Finally, many resource room teachers travel to more than one building during the course of the week. These *itinerant teachers* find themselves placed in all sorts of room arrangements. Sometimes their major challenge is with the physical plant rather than the students. Teachers with this type of travel schedule spend a great deal of energy just getting to their assignments and setting up the classrooms when they arrive, making this a taxing assignment, indeed.

The biggest danger inherent in this type of program is that home-room teachers may feel that the students' needs are being met through their participation in the resource room program and that further provisions are not needed. *This is not the case!* The students are gifted throughout the week and should be treated accordingly.

A point of contention comes when policies are set regarding whether or not students must make up the work they miss while they are out of class and in the resource room program. Most schools do have policies stating that the program is in lieu of the class work, but this position is not always shared by the staff and breaches do occur. In those instances, participation in the program can actually be punitive to the students as their workload is doubled and they feel the additional stress.

Revolving Door Identification Model

An adaptation of the resource room model has been suggested (Renzulli, Reis, and Smith, 1981) and termed the *Revolving Door Identification Model* (RDIM). This model is predicated on the belief that some students can benefit from programming at certain times, but full-time placement may not be appropriate. In these instances, a program such as this will provide a structure through which students can "revolve" in and out of the resource room, depending on their interests at the time.

Students are eligible for the RDIM when they submit a plan for research, called an Action Information Message (see Figure 12–1), which is deemed acceptable by the resource room teacher or person judging these requests. After acceptance, students enter into the program for the time it takes them to complete their project, at which time they are revolved out of the program until they have another Action Information Message accepted.

This type of program has two advantages. First, it involves students at the point when their interests are piqued. Motivation is internally generated and students tend to be more task oriented than usual. Second, by revolving students in and out, more students can participate in the program and more students can be served. It has been suggested that this type of program may be appropriate for as many as 20 percent of the student population. Thus, the program casts a wide net and catches students when they are quite likely to succeed.

The students' time in a RDIM program tends to be mostly consumed with research projects. These investigations can take many forms and have unlimited outcomes. The teacher in this program spends time in the same way regular resource room teachers do, but may have the additional responsibilities of scheduling students into the program and identifying students who qualify.

Figure 12–1   Example of an Action Information Message

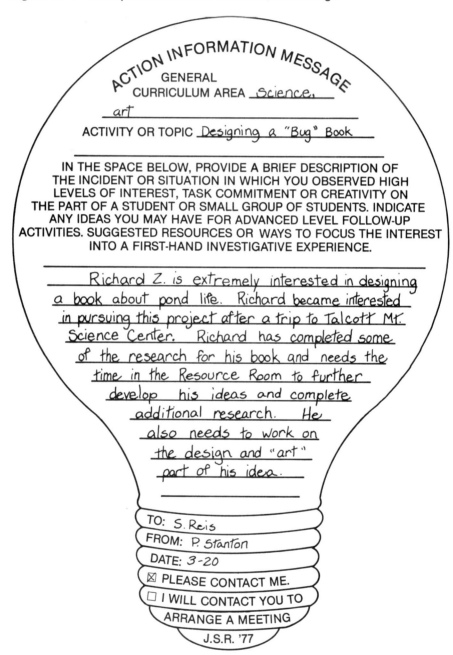

FULL-TIME PROGRAMS

For a number of gifted and talented students, regular classroom placements are inappropriate. Their skills and capabilities are advanced from their age-peers to the extent that full-time placements in alternative programming best suit their needs. Classrooms in which students can learn at their advanced levels with students of similar abilities are necessary and the need for such placements supersede any concern about the effects of segregating students into this type of program. Three different configurations are discussed in this section: magnet schools, schools within schools, and consortia programs.

Magnet Schools

Due to the small percentage of students in any school who qualify for a full-time program, most magnet schools are composed of students from schools throughout a district. The magnet school becomes their home school and they are no longer enrolled at their neighborhood schools. Students are either bused by the district or driven by their parents to the school, depending on the transportation constraints of the district. Some districts alter their bus schedules and magnet school schedule so that students can be transported via the district's bus service.

Magnet schools typically have from one to three classes per grade level, depending on the size of the district and the number of students who qualify for the program, starting as early as kindergarten or the first grade. Generally, these classes are arranged and schedules are determined in the same way as more traditional schools. A range in student abilities still exists in the classrooms, however, and differentiated programming is still necessary.

There are advantages to having magnet schools for both the students and the teachers involved. The students have more opportunity to learn at the rate and depth that they need because the curricula in these placements are generally more advanced than in their home school placements. Additionally, students have the opportunity to meet and work with other students of their same ability level. For gifted students, this is particularly important and has been suggested as reason enough to mount this type of programming effort.

Teachers in magnet schools also enjoy this type of program configuration because the magnet school concept brings a central focus and mission to the school that is often missing in other settings. Although they still experience a range in student abilities, teachers can much more effectively prepare for the students' needs when the students are all potentially accomplished. However, their job is not an easy one, as students who qualify for this type of placement can be very demanding of the teacher and the resources at hand.

Although most magnet schools are academically based, some districts sponsor schools in other areas. For example, many large city school districts are now opening full-time programs that focus on the arts. Students balance their time spent in classes like language arts and mathematics with music, art, or dance classes. There is usually a mix of teachers and artists who have teaching responsibilities for students in the early elementary grades on up.

Schools Within Schools

When there is an insufficient number of students to mount a full-time magnet program for the gifted and talented, some districts choose to employ the school-within-a-school concept. In these cases, regular schools with a small enrollment are chosen and their numbers are increased by placing full-time programs for the gifted in their buildings. In effect, there are two schools within one building at the same time. The programs for the gifted are usually conducted in the same manner as a magnet school with one exception. Since the students are sharing the same building and are in close proximity, efforts are usually made to integrate the students to some degree. This can be accomplished through joint assemblies, same hour lunch periods, or by sharing in special speakers and activities.

The attempts to share the programs can help to diffuse the greatest problem associated with the school-within-a-school program. In many of these programs, the staff and students from the regular programs begin to feel neglected. The designations of the "haves" and the "have nots" can crop up before you know it and can cause a great deal of damage. Sharing of resources, inservice presentations, ideas, and activities can close this gap to some extent.

The small size of most of these programs brings some distinct advantages for students and teachers. The students still have the bonus of being with other students of similar abilities in challenging circumstances. The staff is of a size where team planning and teaching is possible and joint decision making is enhanced.

Consortia Programs

Under some circumstances, school systems find it necessary to join together in order to offer full-time placements for their gifted and talented students. When student numbers are too small or a specialized program is in mind, consortia efforts may enable programs to be mounted. In these cases, each district sends students to the school and contributes to the budget for the program.

The consortia programs have also been used on a part-time basis in order to deliver programs to gifted and talented students. When an individual district cannot justify offering certain advanced coursework, they may solicit cooperation from another adjoining district in order for the classes to exist. Often, these classes are in nonacademic areas or computer science. However, more typical resource room programs have also been sponsored through the joint efforts of cooperating school districts in consortium.

In full-time consortia programs, transporting the students to the site seems to be the biggest problem faced by program organizers. In part-time consortia programs, communication with the home school as well as transportation seems to be the biggest challenge. Regardless, the benefits to the students engaged in consortia programs far outweigh the problems encountered in building and maintaining such programs.

HIGHLY GIFTED STUDENTS

Highly gifted students are those who exhibit capabilities that far exceed their age-peers and make regular classroom placements all but impossible. These students are usually identified on the basis of an IQ score beginning anywhere from 150 to 180 and up—a level higher than one-tenth of one percent of the students, or one student in one thousand. They are as different from average students (IQ of about 100) as are the severely mentally retarded population, and their educational needs are as radically different.

The regular classroom setting is often an inappropriate placement for these students. Their abilities are so far beyond that of their classmates, that it is nearly impossible for an at-grade level teacher to provide adequate programs for them and maintain sound programs for the rest of the class as well. Therefore, alternative placements are needed that are more suited to the students' skill and ability levels.

Characteristics and Needs

The most predominant characteristic of highly gifted students is a high IQ. The same capabilities that result in the high scores on intelligence tests also lead to other behaviors that are different from the norm. Powell and Haden (1984) list three characteristics that separate this group from more moderately gifted students and students of normal ability. These characteristics are: an ability to create structures and frameworks for comprehending the universe, extremely efficient information-processing capability and problem-finding and problem-solving skills, and a high desire to know (see Table 12-1). They note that highly gifted people are integrated thinkers, meaning that they can think both analytically (in a step-by-step fashion) and synthetically (in a skip-think manner).

From the standpoint of social and emotional characteristics, differing

Table 12-1   Comparison of Average, Moderately Gifted, and Extremely
Gifted Persons

Traits	Normal Ability	Moderately Gifted	Extremely Gifted
Intellectual Traits	Need Structure Little desire to know Inefficient information processing	Create own structure Desire to know Efficient information processing	Create structure for culture at extreme High desire to know Extremely efficient information processing
Type of Thinker	Analytical thinkers	Synthetic thinkers	Integrated thinkers
Approximate IQ	90 to 110	130 to 145–49	150+
Adult Academic Achievement	High School graduation	Graduate school standing	Graduate-post-graduate standing
Adult Occupational Attainments	Blue collar worker	Professional and semi-professional	Professional

Source: P. Powell and T. Haden,"The Intellectual and Psychosocial Nature of Extreme Giftedness," *Roeper Review,* 6(3) (1984): 132. Reprinted by permission by *Roeper Review.* Copyright © 1984.

accounts of how the highly gifted appear can be found in the literature and studies regarding this group. Roedell (1984) states that "there is general agreement that highly gifted children are more susceptible to some types of developmental difficulties than are moderately gifted or average children" (p. 127). She lists the areas of vulnerability as: uneven development wherein the students have extremely advanced cognitive skills and more normal social and physical abilities; perfectionism; unrealistic adult expectations; intense sensitivity and internal responsiveness to inner feelings and external circumstances; unclear self-definition; alienation by and from peers; inappropriate educational placements; and conflicts about their roles in life. Not all highly gifted students experience these problems, but they do appear to be more likely to face unusual challenges while growing up.

What are the factors, then, that teachers should be concerned about when dealing with highly gifted students? First, students need to be evaluated and placed on their profiles of ability and not by an IQ score alone. As the gifted population is heterogeneous, so is the highly gifted population. Second, these students need to be in placements that allow them to flourish academically and socially. The highly gifted students, however, often prefer to be in academic settings that are stimulating rather than be with students of their own age. They do not wish to be held back due to the fact that they are too young to drive or date when they are in advanced placements such as high school or college. Next, highly gifted students should have access to counseling services. Since they are so unique and out of synchronization with their age-peers, they can use the resources of a counselor to help them learn to cope with the unusual circumstances and challenges that they will face across their lifetimes. Finally, they need to be taught the skills to survive in their advanced educational placements. When students are accelerated to the extent that some highly gifted students warrant, they may not have developed the basic skills such as note taking, consulting with teachers, and test taking needed for program success.

Programming Options for the Highly Gifted

The guidelines described for placing gifted students in programs also apply to highly gifted students. The types of programs that are needed, however, may be outside of the normal settings or policies that apply to placement decisions. It is almost always inappropriate to place highly advanced students in classrooms with their age-peers. The curriculum, even if enriched or accelerated, is most likely inappropriate and the students are unlikely to have much in common with the other students. Therefore, other placements must be considered.

One of the most common ways to deal with these students is through radical acceleration. Under this option, the student is placed at a level deemed appropriate by the placement committee—two or more grade levels above that in which the age-peers are placed. Often elementary-aged students will be advanced to the junior high or middle school level, whereas older students may be placed in high school or college classes. Since there are so few students who need such extreme measures, each case has to be heard and responded to on an individual basis.

Lewis (1984) discusses the possible pitfalls in planning programs for the highly gifted. She cautions that (1) programs may use inflexible or limited selection procedures that may cause some highly gifted students to be overlooked; (2) acceleration is not a guarantee that children will receive good teaching; (3) finding the best teacher for the child, one who epitomizes the art and science of teaching and who has good knowledge of content, may not be easy; (4) although radical acceleration may meet the academic needs of the child, it must be determined whether it meets the child's affective needs in each separate case; (5) acceleration is not necessarily the appropriate answer across subjects for any one child; and (6) although accelerative methods can be used with success in an area such as math, mentorships should be considered as a method of dealing with widely different content interests (p. 134).

Keeping these potential pitfalls in mind, the programming mosaic for the highly gifted should reflect the many different ways in which a student can be highly gifted. This, along with a willingness to be flexible and student-centered in decision making, will enhance the students' chances of attaining educational experiences that will be appropriate to their abilities and needs. Internships, independent studies, mentorships, and visiting scholar programs are among the many configurations that may be used to respond to students' profiles in these rare cases.

SUMMARY

Regular classroom placements may not be appropriate for some gifted and talented students. Having a number of programming possibilities available to match to students' profiles of ability will insure that the students will be able to assemble programs that meet their needs. Highly gifted students are in the most jeopardy of being inappropriately placed. Their cases need particular attention to be sure that the educational opportunities are adequate to their needs. When developing programs for the gifted, a full range of programming options should be put in place along with a commitment to student-centered decision making and flexibility to make the programs work for the students.

ACTION STEPS

1. Look at the full range of programming options that are available for gifted students. If they do not extend beyond the regular classroom, take steps to have the program reviewed by a group of decision makers.

2. Establish your district's mosaic of programs, remembering that coordination between schools or districts can enhance the capabilities of any one district in serving the students.

3. Review the procedures and programs for dealing with the highly gifted and take steps to make these responsive to the students' unique needs.

REFERENCES YOU CAN USE

American Association for Gifted Children (1980). *Reaching out: Advocacy for the gifted.* New York: Teachers College Press.

Hall, E., & Skinner, N. (1980). *Somewhere to turn: Strategies for parents of the gifted.* New York: Teachers College Press.

Maker, J. (Ed.). (1986). *Defensible programs for the gifted.* Rockville, MD: Aspens Systems Corporation.

Powell, P., & Haden, T. (1984). The intellectual and psychological nature of extreme giftedness. *Roeper Review, 6*(3), 131–133.

Appendix

COUNCIL OF STATE DIRECTORS OF PROGRAMS FOR THE GIFTED

Alabama

Programs for Gifted
Alabama State Department of Education
868 State Office Building
Montgomery, AL 36130-3903

Alaska

Office for Exceptional Children
Department of Education
Goldbelt Place
801 W. 10th St.
Pouch F
Juneau, AK 99811

American Samoa

Consultant
Gifted/Talented Education
Pago Pago, AS 96799

Arizona

Education Programs Specialist
Arizona Department of Education
1535 West Jefferson
Phoenix, AZ 85007

Arkansas

Programs for Gifted/Talented
Special Education Section
Arch Ford Education Building
Little Rock, AR 72201

California

Gifted and Talented Education
721 Capitol Mall
Sacramento, CA 95814

Colorado

Gifted and Talented Student Programs
Colorado Department of Education
First Western Plaza
303 W. Colfax
Denver, CO 80204

Connecticut

Gifted/Talented Programs
State Department of Education
165 Capitol Avenue
Hartford, CT 06145

Delaware

Programs for Gifted and Talented
State Department of Public Instruction
P. O. Box 1402
Townsend Building
Dover, DE 19903

District of Columbia

Gifted and Talented Education Program
Bryan Elementary School
13th and Independence Ave., SE
Washington, DC 20003

Florida

Gifted Programs
DOE/Bureau of Education for Exceptional Children
Knott Building
Tallahassee, FL 32301

Georgia

Programs for the Gifted
Department of Education
Twin Towers East, Suite 1970
Atlanta, GA 30334

Guam

Associate Superintendent for Special Education
Department of Education
P. O. Box DE
Agana, GU 96910

Hawaii

Education Specialist, Gifted and Talented
Office of Instructional Services
189 Lunalilo Homo Road
Honolulu, HI 96825

Idaho

Supervisor of Special Education
State Department of Education
Len B. Jordan Office Building
650 West State
Boise, ID 83720

Illinois

Educational Innovation/Support Section
State Department of Education
100 North First Street
Springfield, IL 62777

Indiana

Gifted/Talented Education
Indiana Department of Education
299 State House
Indianapolis, IN 46204

Iowa

Gifted Education
Department of Public Instruction
Grimes State Office Building
Des Moines, IA 50319

Kansas

Education Program Specialist for Gifted
State Department of Education
120 E. 10th
Topeka, KS 66612

Kentucky

Gifted/Talented Education
Kentucky Department of Education
1831 Capitol Plaza Tower
Frankfort, KY 40601

Louisiana

Gifted and Talented Programs
Louisana Department of Education
P. O. Box 94064
Baton Rouge, LA 70804-9064

Maine

Consultant, Gifted/Talented
State House Station #23
Augusta, ME 04333

Maryland

Learning Improvement Section, Gifted/Talented Programs
State Department of Education
200 W. Baltimore St.
Baltimore, MD 21201

Massachusetts

Office of Gifted and Talented
Massachusetts Department of Education
Bureau of Curriculum Services
1385 Hancock Street
Quincy, MA 02169

Michigan

Programs for Gifted and Talented
Michigan Department of Education
P. O. Box 30008
Lansing, MI 48909

Minnesota

Gifted Education
State Department of Education
641 Capitol Square
St. Paul, MN 55101

Mississippi

State Consultant for Gifted
State Department of Education
P. O. Box 771
Jackson, MS 39205

Missouri

Director, Gifted Education Program
State Department of Elementary and Secondary Education
P. O. Box 480
100 East Capitol
Jefferson City, MO 65102

Montana

Gifted and Talented Programs
Office of Public Instruction
State Capitol
Helena, MT 59601

Nebraska

Program for the Gifted
State Department of Education
P. O. Box 94987
300 Centennial Mall South
Lincoln, NE 68509

Nevada

Special Education Programs/GT
Nevada Department of Education
400 West King St.
Carson City, NV 89710

New Hampshire

Consultant, Gifted Education
New Hampshire Department of Education
State Office Park South
101 Pleasant Street
Concord, NH 03301

New Jersey

Education Program Specialist/GT
Division of General Academic Education
Department of Education
225 West State Street, CN 500
Trenton, NJ 08625-0500

New Mexico

Special Education/GT
Education Building
Santa Fe, NM 87501-2786

New York

State Department of Education
Room 310 EB
Albany, NY 12234

North Carolina

Academically Gifted Programs
Division for Exceptional Children
State Department of Public Instruction
Raleigh, NC 27611

North Dakota

Special Education/GT
Department of Public Instruction
State Capitol
Bismarck, ND 58505

Ohio

Programs for Gifted
Division of Special Education
933 High Street
Worthington, OH 43085

Oklahoma

Gifted/Talented Section
State Department of Education
2500 N. Lincoln Blvd.
Oklahoma City, OK 73105

Oregon

Gifted/Talented Specialist
700 Pringle Parkway SE
Salem, OR 97219

Pennsylvania

Bureau of Special Education/GT
Department of Education
333 Market St.
Harrisburg, PA 17126-0333

Puerto Rico

Consultant, Gifted
Office of External Resources
Department of Education
Hato Rey, PR 99024

Rhode Island

Gifted/Talented Education
Department of Elementary/Secondary Education
22 Hayes Street
Providence, RI 02908

South Carolina

Programs for the Gifted
802 Rutledge Building
1429 Senate St.
Columbia, SC 29201

South Dakota

Programs for the Gifted
Special Education Section
Richard F. Kneip Building
700 N. Illinois
Pierre, SD 57501

Tennessee

Gifted/Talented Programs and Services
132-A Cordell Hull Building
Nashville, TN 37219

Texas

Director of Gifted/Talented Education
Texas Education Agency
1701 Congress Avenue
Austin, TX 78701

Trust Territory

Office of Special Education/GT
Trust Territory Office of Education
Office of the High Commissioner
Saipan, CM 96950

Utah

State Consultant for Gifted
State Office of Education
250 E. 5th, South
Salt Lake City, UT 84111

Vermont

Gifted Consultant
State Department of Education
Montpelier, VT 05602

Virgin Islands

Gifted Consultant
State Director of Special Education
Department of Education
Box 630, Charlotte Amalie
St. Thomas, VI 00801

Virginia

Programs for the Gifted
Division of Special Education
Virginia Department of Education
P. O. Box 60
Richmond, VA 23216

Washington

Programs for the Gifted
Superintendent of Public Instruction
Old Capitol Building FG-11
Olympia, WA 98504

West Virginia

Programs for the Gifted
357 B, Capitol Complex
Charleston, VW 25305

Wisconsin

Gifted Coordinator
School Improvement Office
P. O. Box 7841
125 S. Webster
Madison, WI 53707

Wyoming

Gifted/Talented
Wyoming Department of Education
Hathaway Building
Cheyenne, WY 82002

PROFESSIONAL ORGANIZATIONS CONTRIBUTING TO THE EDUCATION OF THE GIFTED AND TALENTED

American Association for Gifted Children
15 Gramercy Park
New York, NY 10003

Center for Creative Learning
Box 619
Honeoye, NY 14471

Coalition for the Advancement of Gifted Education (CAGE)
c/o Mr. George Fichter, Director
Division of Special Education
933 High Street
Columbus, OH 43085

Council for Exceptional Children/
The Association for Gifted (TAG)
1920 Association Dr.
Reston, VA 22091

Council of State Directors of Programs for the Gifted
c/o Ms. Nancy Luckenbill, President
Gifted and Talented Programs
Office of Public Instruction
State Capitol
Helena. MT 59601

Future Problem Solving
St. Andrews College
Laurinburg, NC 28352

Great Books Foundation
40 E. Huron St.
Chicago, IL 60611

National Association for Gifted Children (NAGC)
5100 N. Edgewood Dr.
St. Paul, MN 55112

National/State Leadership Training Institute for the Gifted and Talented
316 W. Second St., Suite PH-C
Los Angeles, CA 90012

World Council for Gifted and Talented, Inc.
Dorothy Sisk, Executive Secretary
College of Education
University of South Florida
Tampa, FL 33620

PERIODICALS FOR AND ABOUT GIFTED, CREATIVE, AND TALENTED PEOPLE

Creative Kids
P.O. Box 637
Holmes, PA 19043

Exceptional Children
Council for Exceptional Children
1920 Association Dr.
Reston, VA 22091

Gifted Child Monthly
RD #1, Box 128-A
Egg Harbor Road
Sewell, NJ 08080

Gifted Child Quarterly
National Association for Gifted Children
5100 N. Edgewood Dr.
St. Paul, MN 55112

Gifted Child Today
P.O. Box 6448
Mobile, AL 36660

Gifted International
World Council for Gifted and Talented Children
College of Education
University of South Florida
Tampa, FL 33620

Journal of Creative Behavior
Creative Education Foundation
State University College
1300 Elmwood Ave.
Buffalo, NY 14222

Journal for the Education of the Gifted
The Association for the Gifted
1920 Association Dr.
Reston, VA 22091

Roeper Review
2190 North Woodward
Bloomfield Hills, MI 48013

Teaching Exceptional Children
Council for Exceptional Children
1920 Association Dr.
Reston, VA 22091

References

Albrecht, K. (1979). *Stress and the manager.* Englewood Cliffs, NJ: Prentice Hall.

Anastasi, A. (1976). *Psychological testing* (4th ed.). New York: Macmillan.

Atwood, B. (1974). *Building independent learning skills.* Palo Alto, CA: Learning Handbooks.

Avallone, M. (1978). *5-minute mysteries.* New York: Scholastic Books.

Baldwin, A. (1977). *Baldwin identification matrix inservice kit for the identification of gifted and talented students.* Buffalo, NY: D.O.K. Publishers.

Baldwin, A. (1981). Effect of process oriented instruction on thought processes in gifted students. *Exceptional Children, 47*(5), 326–330.

Blackburn, J., and Powell, W. (1976). *One day at a time all at once: The creative teacher's guide to individualized instruction without anarchy.* Santa Monica, CA: Scott, Foresman.

Bloom, B. (Ed.). (1985). *Developing talent in young people.* New York: Ballantine Books.

Bloom, B. (1956). *Taxonomy of educational objectives: The classification of educational goals. Handbook I: Cognitive domain.* New York: Longman, Greens & Co.

Borland, J. (1978). Teacher identification of the gifted: A new look. *Journal for the Education of the Gifted, 2*(1), 22–32.

Boud, D. (Ed.). (1981). *Developing student autonomy in learning.* New York: Nicholas Publishing Co.

Brink, C. (1935). *Caddie Woodlawn.* New York: Macmillan.

Bruner, J. (1960). *The process of education.* Cambridge, MA: Harvard University Press.

Callahan, C. (1985). *Evaluation of programs for the gifted and talented.*

1985 Digest. Reston, VA: ERIC Clearinghouse on Handicapped and Gifted Children.

Canady, R., & McCullen, J. (1985). Elementary scheduling practices designed to support programs for gifted students. *Roeper Review, 7*(3), 142–145.

Carter, K., & Hamilton, W. (1985). Formative evaluation of gifted programs: A process and model. *Gifted Child Quarterly, 29*(1), 5–11.

Charles, C. (1976). *Individualizing instruction.* St. Louis, MO: C. V. Mosby Company.

Charles, C. (1983). *Elementary classroom management.* New York: Longman.

Christopherson, S. (1981). Developmental placement in the regular school program. *G/C/T,* 19 (September/October), 40–41.

Clark, B. (1983). *Growing up gifted* (2nd ed.). Columbus, OH: Merrill Publishing Co.

Clark, B. (1986). *Optimizing learning: The integrative education model in the classroom.* Columbus, OH: Merrill Publishing Co.

Clenening, C., & Davies, R. (1983). *Challenging the gifted: Curriculum enrichment and acceleration models.* New York: R. R. Bowker Company.

Clifford, G., Heger, R., & Sebree, S. (1974). *The world of the gifted.* Toledo, OH: Toledo Public Schools.

Colon, P., & Treffinger, D. (1980). Providing for the gifted in the regular classroom—Am I really MAD? *Roeper Review, 3*(2), 18–21.

Council for Exceptional Children (1978). *The nation's commitment to gifted and talented children and youth: Summary of findings from a 1977 survey of states and territories.* Reston, VA: Author.

Council of State Directors of Programs for the Gifted (1986). *The state of the state's gifted and talented education.* Augusta, ME: Author.

Cox, J. (1982). Continuous progress and nongraded schools. *G/C/T,* 25 (November/December), 15–21.

Cox, J., Daniel, N., & Boston, B. (1985). *Educating able learners: Programs and promising practices.* Austin: University of Texas Press.

Cronbach, L. (1970). *Essentials of psychological testing* (3rd ed.). New York: Harper & Row.

Davis, G., & Rimm, S. (1985). *Education of the gifted and talented.* Englewood Cliffs, NJ: Prentice-Hall.

DeBono, E. (1986). *CoRT thinking teacher's notes.* New York: Pergamon Press.

Dunn, R., & Dunn, K. (1972). *Practical approaches to individualizing instruction: Contracts and other effective teaching strategies.* West Nyack, NY: Parker Publishing Company.

Dunn, R., & Dunn, K. (1975). *Educator's self-teaching guide to individualizing instructional programs.* West Nyack, NY: Parker Publishing Company.

Dunn, R., & Griggs, S. (1985). Teaching and counseling gifted students with their learning styles preferences: Two case studies. *G/C/T,* 41 (November/December), 40–43.

Ebmeier, H., Dyche, B., Taylor, P., & Hall, M. (1985). An empirical comparison of two program models for elementary gifted education. *Gifted Child Quarterly, 29*(1), 15–19.

Edmonds, R. (1979). Effective schools for the urban poor. *Educational Leadership* (October), 15–24.

Elman, L., & Elman, D. (1983). Mainstreaming the gifted: An approach that works. *G/C/T,* 26 (January/February), 45–46.

Epstein, C. (1979). *The gifted and talented: Programs that work.* Arlington, VA.: National School Public Relations Association.

Feldhusen, H. (1981). Teaching gifted, creative, and talented students in an individualized classroom. *Gifted Child Quarterly, 25*(3), 108–111.

Feldhusen, J., Baska, L., & Womble, S. (1981). Using standard scores to synthesize data in identifying the gifted. *Journal for the Education of the Gifted, 4*(3), 177–186.

Fizzell, R. (1980). Individualizing for the gifted student—And others too. *Roeper Review, 3*(1), 31–33.

Gagne, F. (1985). Giftedness and talent: Reexamining a reexamination of the definitions. *Gifted Child Quarterly, 29*(3), 103–112.

Gallagher, J. (1985). *Teaching the gifted child* (3rd ed.). Boston: Allyn and Bacon.

Gardner, H. (1983). *Frames of mind.* New York: Basic Books.

Gear, G. (1978). Effects of training on teachers' accuracy in the identification of gifted children. *Gifted Child Quarterly, 22*(1), 90–97.

Goertzel, V., & Goertzel, M. (1962). *Cradles of eminence.* Boston: Little Brown.

Guilford, J. (1956). The structure of intellect. *Psychological Bulletin, 53,* 267–293.

Guilford, J. (1967). *The nature of human intelligence.* New York: McGraw-Hill Book Company.

Gwynne, F. (1970). *The king who reigned.* New York: Young Readers Press.

Gwynne, F. (1976). *A chocolate moose for dinner.* New York: Windmill Books & E. P. Dutton & Co.

Hatch, T., & Gardner, H. (1986). From testing intelligence to assessing competences: A pluralistic view of intellect. *Roeper Review, 8*(3), 147–150.

Hershey, M. (1980). Individual educational planning for gifted students: A report from Kansas. *Journal for the Education of the Gifted, 3*(1), 207–213.

Hershey, M. (1981). The least restrictive environment for gifted and talented students. *Roeper Review, 4*(2), 27–28.

Immerzeel, G., & Thomas, M. (1982). *Ideas from the Arithmetic Teacher.* Reston, VA: The National Council of Teachers of Mathematics.

Jacobs, J. (1971). Effectiveness of teacher and parent identification of gifted children as a function of school level. *Psychology in the Schools, 8,* 140–142.

Kaplan, S. (1974). *Providing programs for the gifted and talented: A handbook.* Ventura, CA: Office of the Ventura County Superintendent of Schools.

Kaplan, S., Kaplan, J., Madsen, S., & Taylor, B. (1973). *Change for children.* Pacific Palisades, CA: Goodyear Publishing Company.

Kohlberg, L. (1966). Moral education in the schools: A developmental view. *The School Review, 74,* 1–29.

Krathwohl, D., Bloom, B., & Masia, B. (1964). *Taxonomy of educational objectives: The classification of educational goals. Handbook II: Affective Domain.* New York: David McKay Company.

Krulik, S., & Rudnick, J. (1980). *Problem solving: A handbook for teachers.* Boston: Allyn and Bacon.

Levy, P. (1981). The story of Marie, David, Richard, Jane, and John: Teaching gifted children in the regular classroom. *Teaching Exceptional Children, 13*(4), 136–142.

Lewis, C., & Kanes, L. (1979). Gifted IEPS: Impact of expectations and perspectives. *Journal for the Education of the Gifted, 2*(2), 61–69.

Lewis, G. (1984). Alternatives to acceleration for the highly gifted child. *Roeper Review, 6*(3), 133–136.

Lipman, M., Sharp, A., & Oscanyan, F. (1984). *Philosophical inquiry.* New York: University Press of America.

Maddox, C. (1983). Early school entry for the gifted: New evidence and concerns. *Roeper Review, 5*(4), 15–17.

Maker, J. (1982). *Curriculum development for the gifted.* Rockville, MD: Aspen Systems Corporation.

Maker, J. (1982). *Teaching models in education of the gifted.* Rockville, MD: Aspen Systems Corporation.

Marland, S. (1972). *Education of the gifted and talented.* Report to the Congress of the United States by the U.S. Commissioner of Education. Washington, D.C.: U.S. Government Printing Office.

Mulhern, J. (1978). The gifted child in the regular classroom. *Roeper Review, 1*(1), 3-6.

Naisbitt, J. (1982). *Megatrends: Ten new directions transforming our lives.* New York: Warner Books.

Ness, B., & Latessa, E. (1979). Gifted children and self-teaching techniques. *Directive Teacher, 2,* 10-12.

O'Daffer, P. (1985). Problem solving tips for teachers. *Arithmetic Teacher, 32*(6), 62-63.

Parke, B. (1981). Identification of gifted and talented students. *Journal of Career Education, 7*(4), 311-317.

Parke, B. (1983). Use of self-instructional materials with gifted primary-aged students. *Gifted Child Quarterly, 27*(1), 29-34.

Parke, B. (1985). Methods of developing creativity. In R. Swassing (Ed.), *Teaching gifted children and adolescents.* Columbus, OH: Merrill Publishing Company.

Parke, B., & Buescher, T. (1982). Evaluating programs for the gifted through student self-documentation. *Roeper Review, 5,* 15-17.

Parnes, S. (1977). Guiding creative action. *Gifted Child Quarterly, 21*(4), 460-472.

Parnes, S., Noller, R., & Biondi, A. (1977). *Guide to creative action.* New York: Charles Scribner's Sons.

Passow, H. (1981). The four curricula of the gifted and talented: Toward a total learning environment. *G/C/T,* 20 (November/December), 2-7.

Paulus, P. (1984). Acceleration: More than grade skipping. *Roeper Review, 7*(2), 98-100.

Pegnato, C., & Birch, J. (1959). Locating gifted children in junior high schools: A comparison of methods. *Exceptional Children, 25,* 300-304.

Powell, P., & Haden, T. (1984). The intellectual and psychosocial nature of extreme giftedness. *Roeper Review, 6*(3), 131-133.

Renzulli, J. (1977). *The enrichment triad model: A guide for developing defensible programs for the gifted and talented.* Mansfield Center, CN: Creative Learning Press.

Renzulli, J. (1978). What makes giftedness? Reexamining the definition. *Phi Delta Kappan, 60*(3), 180-184, 261.

Renzulli, J., Reis, S., & Smith, L. (1981). *The revolving door identification model.* Mansfield Center, CN: Creative Learning Press.

Renzulli, J., & Smith, L. (1979). *A guidebook for developing individualized educational programs for gifted and talented students.* Mansfield Center, CT: Creative Learning Press.

Renzulli, J., & Smith, L. (1980). A practical model for designing individual educational programs (IEPs) for gifted and talented students. *G/C/T,* 11 (January/February), 3–8.

Renzulli, J., Smith, L., White, A., Callahan, C., & Hartman, R. (1976). *Scales of rating the behavioral characteristics of superior students.* Mansfield Center, CN: Creative Learning Press.

Rimm, S. (1976). *GIFT: Group inventory for finding creative talent.* Watertown, WI: Educational Assessment Service.

Rimm, S., Davis, G., & Bien, Y. (1982). Identifying creativity: A characteristics approach. *Gifted Child Quarterly, 26*(4), 165–171.

Roberson, T. (1984). Curriculum design for the gifted: Determining curriculum content for the gifted. *Roeper Review, 6*(3), 137–139.

Roedell, W. (1984). Vulnerabilities of highly gifted children. *Roeper Review, 6*(3), 127–131.

Shore, B. (1981). Gifted children's feelings about school and themselves in open and open-area classes. *Journal for Education of the Gifted, 4*(2), 112–121.

Simon, S. (1979). *Animal fact/animal fable.* New York: Crown Publishers.

Singleton, W., & Nelson, M. (1980). Alternative forms of objectives for the gifted and talented learner in school. *G/C/T,* 15 (November/December), 49–51.

Slotnick, H., Reichelt, C., & Gardner, R. (1985). Gifted students meet the institutionalized elderly: Learning about aging and the aged in a rural nursing home. *Journal for the Education of the Gifted, 9*(1), 45–58.

Smith, L. (no date). *Are we cheating kids? Continuous progress/individualized education K-6.* Englewood, CO: Educational Consulting Associates.

Stanley, J., Keating, D., & Fox, L. (Eds.). (1974). *Mathematical talent: Discovery, description, and development.* Baltimore, MD: Johns Hopkins University Press.

Sternberg, R. (1981). A componential theory of intellectual giftedness. *Gifted Child Quarterly, 25*(2), 86–93.

Sternberg, R. (Ed.). (1982). *Handbook of human intelligence.* Cambridge: Cambridge University Press.

Sternberg, R. (1986). Identifying the gifted through IQ: Why a little bit of knowledge is a dangerous thing. *Roeper Review, 8*(3), 143–147.

Stories with holes. (1987). Hightstown, NJ: NL Associates.

Suchman, J. (1975). A model for the analysis of inquiry. In W. Barbe and J. Renzulli (Eds.), *Psychology and education of the gifted* (2nd ed.). New York: Irvington Publishers.

Taba, H. (1962). *Curriculum development: Theory and practice.* New York: Harcourt, Brace, & World.

Taylor, C. (1968). The multiple talent approach. *Instructor, 77*(27), 142, 144, 146.

Terman, L. (1925). *Genetic studies of genius* (Vol. 1). Stanford, CA: Stanford University Press.

Treffinger, D. (1975). Teaching for self-directed learning: A priority for the gifted and talented. *Gifted Child Quarterly, 19*(1), 46–59.

Treffinger, D. (1986). *Thinking skills and problem solving.* Honeoye, NY: Center for Creative Learning.

Treffinger, D., & Barton, B. (1979). Fostering independent learning. *G/C/T,* 7 (March/April), 3–6, 54.

Tuttle, F., & Becker, L. (1980). *Program design and development for gifted and talented students.* Washington, D.C.: National Education Association.

VanTassel-Baska, J., & Strykowski, B. (1986). *An identification resource guide on the gifted & talented.* Evanston, IL: Northwestern University Center for Talent Development.

Viorst, J. (1971). *The tenth good thing about Barney.* New York: Antheum.

Ward, L. (1973). *The silver pony.* Boston: Houghton Mifflin Company.

Ward, P., & Williams, E. (1976). *Learning packets: New approach to individualized instruction.* West Nyack, NY: Parker Publishing Company.

Whitmore, J. (1980). *Giftedness, conflict, and underachievement.* Boston: Allyn and Bacon.

Whitmore, J. (1985). *Underachieving gifted students, 1985 Digest.* Reston, VA: ERIC Clearinghouse on Handicapped and Gifted Children.

Wilder, L. (1932). *Little house in the big woods.* New York: Harper & Row.

Williams, F. (1970). *Classroom ideas for encouraging thinking and feeling* (2nd ed.). Buffalo, NY: D.O.K. Publishers.

Witty, P. (1953). How to identify the gifted. *Childhood Education,* 312–316.

Yamamoto, K. (1965). Effects of restriction of range and test unreliability on correlation between measures of intelligence and creative thinking. *British Journal of Educational Psychology, 35,* 300–305.

Zadra, D., & Moawad, B. (1986). *Mistakes are great.* Mankato, MN: Creative Education.

Index

Ability (*see* General ability; Profiles of
    ability)
Achievement tests, 29
Action information message, 119
Activity, 67
Administrative participation, 218
Administrator's role, 220–221
Advanced materials, 89
Advanced classes, 234–235
Advanced seminars, 118–119
Anticipation of problems (*see* Trouble-
    shooting)
Arrogance, 211–212
Arts, case study, 202–206
Assessment, 23–37, 233
    information gathering, 28–33
    model, 24–28
    sample plans, 33–37
    steps, 26–28

Balance in program, 61–62
Behavior checklists, 31
Bloom's Taxonomy of Objectives
    for the Cognitive Domain,
    144–148
Brain/mind research, 148
Brainstorming, 132

Case studies, 178–206, 223
    arts, 202–206
    language arts, 185–193
    mathematics, 178–185
    science, 193–197
    social studies, 198–202
Case study approach to placement, 39
Characteristics of gifted and talented,
    18–23
    affective, 20–21

cognitive, 19–20
    learning characteristics, 42–43
Clark's Integrative Education Model,
    148–151
Cluster groups, 52–53, 119
Commercial programs, 106–108
Community internships, 105
Compacting (*see* Curriculum com-
    pacting)
Competitions, 120–121, 221
Comprehension, 19
    depth of, 19, 42
Computer-assisted instruction (*see*
    Programmed instruction)
Concentration, 19–20
Concerns of educators, 12–14
Conferences, 72–74
Consortia programs, 240–241
Content of curriculum, 130–131
Continuous progress curriculum,
    89–90
Contracts, 70–72, 100, 10ℒ
Convergent questions, 98–99
Cooperative ventures, 216
Coordinator of programs, 221, 233
Correspondence courses, 87
Council of State Directors of Pro-
    grams for the Gifted, listing,
    247–256
Creativity, 51, 133, 160–162, 169–172
    characteristis of students, 21–22
Criterion-referenced tests, 29, 223
Cross-level grouping, 92
Curiosity, 20
Curriculum:
    compacting, 84–85, 86
    decision making, 65
    definition of, 129

Curriculum (*cont.*)
  differentiation, 129–142
    content, 130–131
    modifications, 138
    process/method, 131–133
    products of learning, 133–134
    sample plans, 138–141
    student outcomes, 141
  models, 143–147
    Affective Taxonomy, 156–160
    Bloom's Taxonomy, 144–148
    CoRT Thinking Model, 151–153
    Creative Problem Solving Model,
      160–162
    Enrichment Triad Model,
      163–166
    Inquiry Development Model,
      166–169
    Integrative Education Model,
      148–151
    Model for Content Modifications,
      153–156
    Model for Encouraging Creative
      Learning, 169–172
    Model for Implementing
      Cognitive-Affective Behav-
      iors, 172–175
  modifications, 134–138
  versus program, 129
  sample plans, 138–141

Debono's CoRT Thinking Model,
    151–153
Decision making, 65, 67, 68–70
Depth of learning, 97–111
  program options, 98–108
  students' responsibilities, 110
  teacher's responsibilities, 108–109
Differentiating instruction, 153
Divergent questions, 98–99

Early admission, 91–92
Educators, dealing with others,
    214–217
Enrichment, 163–166
Enrichment Triad Model, 163–166

Environment for learning, 61, 64–79
  managing learning, 70–76
  self-directed learning, 68–70
  student-centered, 65–67
  students' responsibilities, 77–78
  teacher's responsibilities, 76–77
Evaluation (*see* Program evaluation)

Fast-paced classes, 91
Flexible pacing, 83–93, 121, 233
  classroom, 84–89
  school-wide, 89–93
Flow charting, 182, 183
Full programming, 232–245
Full-time programs, 239–241
Future Problem Solving, 120, 131

Gagne's Differentiated Model of Gift-
    edness and Talent, 9–10, 11
Gallagher's Model for Content Modifi-
    cations, 153–156
Gardner's Theory of Multiple Intelli-
    gences, 9
General ability, assessing for, 33, 35
Generalizing, ability, 19
Gifted as a label, 6
Giftedness, definitions of, 7–11
Girls, 23, 213–214
Grade skipping, 55–56
Grouping patterns, 51–57 (*see also*
    Skill grouping)
  cluster groups, 52–53
  cross-level, 92
  grade skipping, 55–56
  interest groups, 53
  multiaged classes, 55
  skill groups, 53–55
  telescoping, 56–57
Guest lecture series, 113–114, 115
Guiding the gifted, 5

Handicapped students, 22–23
Highly gifted students, 241–244

Identification of gifted students,
    17–41
  assessment, 23–37

characteristics, 18–23
placement decisions, 38–39
profiles of ability, 37–38
Independent learning skills, 166
Independent studies, 99–102
Individual interests, 20, 43, 112–125,
203
program options, 113–121
students' responsibilities, 123–124
teacher's responsibilities, 123
Individuality, 4, 14
Individualization, 57–60
advantages, 59–60
defined, 57–58
IEPs, 60
Individualized Educational Plan
(IEP), 60, 67
Information gathering for assess-
ment, 28–33
Inquiry questions, 107
Instruction models, 14
Integration, 103
Intensity, 21
Interest-based classes, 235–236
Interest centers, 116–117
Interest groups, 53, 114–116
Interests (see Individual interests)
Internships (see Community intern-
ships)
Interviews, 223
Inventories, 29

Journals/diaries, 223
Junior Great Books Program, 106–
107, 122, 131, 186, 218

Krathwohl's Taxonomy of Objectives
for the Affective Domain,
156–160

Language arts, case study, 185–193
Leadership ability, 21
Learning centers, 103–104
Learning characteristics of gifted stu-
dents, 42–43
Learning packets, 87–89
Lesson plans, samples of, 138–141
Long-term problems, 120

Magnet schools, 239–240
Management contracts (see Con-
tracts)
Management sheets, 74–76, 188
Managing learning, 70–76
Mathematics, case study, 178–185
Mathematics program, assessing for,
35, 36
Matrix approach, 39
Mazes, 181
Memory, 19
Mentors, 114, 117–118
Moralistic, 21
Multiaged groupings, 92–93
Multiaged classes, 55
Multifactored assessment, 25
Multiple-year plan for curriculum de-
velopment, 134, 135
Multiple intelligences, 9
Multiple programming approach,
43–44
Musical talent, 37, 122
Myths about the gifted, 3–7

National programs, 119–121
Needs of students, 45–46
Nominations to programs, 31
Norm-referenced tests, 29–30, 223

Objectives for students, 47–49
Observations, 223
Odyssey of the Mind, 120, 135
Options in programs, 44–51

Pace of learning, 20, 42, 83–96
flexible pacing, 83–93
program options, 84–93
students' responsibilities, 94–95
teacher's responsibilities, 94
Parents and their roles, 217–218
Parnes' Creative Problem-Solving
Model, 160
Perfectionism, 21
Performance level, 6
Performance review, 137
Periodicals, listing, 257–258

Philosophy for Children Program, 106–107, 186
Placement decisions, 38–39
Planning form, 100, 102
Planning the programs, 42–63, 215
creativity, 51
differentiating the program, 43–44
grouping patterns, 51–57
IEPs, 60
individualization, 57–60
learning characteristics, 42–43
selecting options, 44–51
Policy decisions, 220
Principal's role, 219–220
Process/method of instruction, 131–133
Product folders, 76
Product scales, 223
Products of learning, 133–134 (see also Student products)
Professional development opportunities, 220
Professional organizations, listing, 256–257
Profiles of ability, 23–24, 37–38
Program planning (see Planning the program)
Program balance, 61–62
Program evaluation, 221–229
Program mosaics, 60–62, 93–94, 108, 121–123, 233
Program patterns, 12–13
Programmed instruction, 85, 87–89
Pull-out programs, 234–238
Pyramid Project, 49–50

Questioning techniques, 98–99
Questionnaires, 223

Reading program, assessing for, 35, 36
Recognition of student work, 221
Renzulli's Enrichment Triad Model, 119
Renzulli's Revolving Door Model, 119
Renzulli's Three-Ring Conception of Giftedness, 8–9
Resource rooms, 236–237

Resourcefulness, 21
Resources/materials, 136
Revolving Door Identification Model, 237–238
Richardson Study Survey, 13
Rights of students, 47–48

Schools within schools, 240
Science, case study, 193–197
Science Olympiad, 121
Scope and sequence of skills, 215, 233
Seating patterns, 65–66
Self-directed learning, 68–70
Self-instructional programs, 85, 87–89
Seminars (see Advanced seminars)
Sense of humor, 21
Sensitivity, 20–21
Simulations, 106, 136
Skill cards, 90
Skill development centers, 103
Skill groups, 53–55, 102–103
Social studies, case study, 198–202
Sociograms, 223
Special classes, 234–236
Split-grade arrangement, 55
Spontaneous problems, 120
Staffing, 215–216, 219, 220
Standard score approach, 39
Strengths, 5–6, 26, 37
Student-centered learning environment, 14, 65–67
Student interest inventory, 115
Student products, 31–33
Study form, 100–101
Suchman's Inquiry Development Model, 166–169
Surveys, 223

Talent pool, 26, 37
Teaching style, 136
Telescoping, 56–57
Tests, 29–30, 45
Thinking as a skill, 151
high level, 144–148
Tracking system, 90
Treffinger's Model for Encouraging Creative Learning, 169–172
Triangulation, 29

Troubleshooting, 209–231
  administrative participation,
    218–221
  dealing with parents and others,
    214–218
  program evaluation, 221–229
  students with problems, 209–214

Uncooperativeness, 212–213
Underachievement, 209–211
United States Department of Educa-
    tion, 7–8, 25

University-based courses, 235

Values, 158
Volunteers, 105, 114, 116, 117–118,
    136

Weaknesses, 5–6, 26, 37
Well-being of students, 13–14
Williams' Model for Implementing
    Cognitive-Affective Behav-
    iors, 172–175
Word puzzles, 181–182